2012
Atlantean Revelations

Becoming a Mystic in a 9 to 5 World

Wisdom Teacher Sri Ram Kaa
and Angelic Oracle Kira Raa

The authors of this book do not dispense medical advice, or prescribe the use of any technique as a form of treatment for physical, emotional, or medical problems without the advice of a physician, either directly or indirectly. The intent of the authors is only to offer information of a general nature to help you in your quest for spiritual and emotional well-being. In the event that you decide to use any of the information in this book for yourself, which is your constitutional right, the authors and publisher assume no responsibility for your actions or outcome.

TOSA Publishing

PO Box 457 • Tijeras, NM 87059 • www.tosapublishing.com

Editor & Typesetter: Angela Earle
Cover Designer: Angela Earle
Book Illustrations: El'iam

ISBN: 978-0-9749872-3-1
Library of Congress Control Number: 2007900791

Manufactured, typeset and printed in the United States of America.

This Text is Volume Three of *The Self-Ascension Series*

Other Revealing Books by Sri Ram Kaa & Kira Raa

Sacred Union: The Journey Home
The Path of Self-Ascension

2012: You Have a Choice!
Archangelic Answers and Practices
for the Journey Home

On DVD

Sacred Yoga for Everyone!
The Yoga of Self-Ascension

Soul Nourishment for
the Tentative Vegan

On the Air

Higher Love - Ascended Talk Radio
Wednesdays, 8 pm EST
www.selfascension.com

TOSA Center for Enlightened Living
PO Box 457, Tijeras, NM 87059
Phone: 505-286-9267
www.selfascension.com

What People Are Saying[1] About Wisdom Teacher Sri Ram Kaa & Angelic Oracle Kira Raa

"I feel a sense of joy when I am in touch with Sri & Kira. I feel like I am joining my essence with theirs and it feels wonderful!"

~ Barbara Marx Hubbard, Author, Social Innovator and President of the Foundation for Conscious Evolution.

•

"Two of the best examples of open-mindedness!"

~ George Noory, Coast to Coast AM, quoted in UFO Magazine, *December 2006*

•

"Sri and Kira are bringing forward important work for these times. I suggest you pay attention!"

~ Dannion Brinkley, author of Saved by The Light *and* Secrets from the Light

•

"Sri & Kira's work is really timely and very important for the world!"

~ James Redfield, author of The Celestine Prophecy

•

"Sri and Kira are creating an amazing energy! I am delighted that their vision is being shared with the world! I love sharing time with them!"

~ Rev. Dr. Terry Cole Whittaker, author, television producer, business consultant, & minister

Congratulations on allowing
this book to find you!

Know that you are
ready for ALL of the
Revelations that are
contained in its pages.

Trust that YOU are in the
perfect experience
of your life, in this
moment!

And...
Know that all is well!

Acknowledgments

After our first two books, one would think *we have this down.* In reality, this book was by far the most difficult to bring to completion! The energy and emotional memories that greeted us while preparing this writing resulted in many days where we were left exhausted. Yet just behind the fabric of fatigue we felt the glowing support of Spirit, the unyielding love of the Universe. What a sweet paradox; the body tired and our spirits soaring. This was the dance that resulted in the book you are now reading.

Our hearts are filled with such abundant gratitude for the unyielding support and assistance offered to us on all levels during this process. Each moment of every day we remain in delighted awe of how amazing this life, this world, truly is. This book's birth also reflects the strength of our Union, for together we were able to blend our energies in every section of writing. We thank the universe for having supported our reunion.

There are the times in the creative process when one must simply surrender ever more and trust that the answers will come. This enormous undertaking brought forth the answers in ways that the mind could not ever have created…truly they were gifts from God!

Years of recorded discourses needed to be transcribed, our journals reviewed and information compiled in a manner that would support the reader at whatever level of discernment might be present. This journey known as a book would not have happened without the hours of dedicated service from our beloved TOSA angel, Delasaria Lihon. Every ounce of her being was present to be sure that we had everything we needed to bring this book to completion, including her "Lion at the Gate" persona to keep us free from worldly interruptions for almost two months during the final stage. We love you, Delasaria, beyond words!

When we completed the opening cosmological sharing around the end times of Su'Laria, we were ready to stop all together. It had been one thing to share this information within the context of our many long hours in communication with the Archangelic Realm; quite another to see it all in one place on paper, ready to give to the world! The extent and range of emotions we experienced will most likely mirror your own experience with the material.

Knowing this would impact many people at the subconscious level, we invited several brave volunteers to read the Su'Laria section ahead of time. What courage and love! These servants of the light were present, honest and offered us the gift of feedback as they processed through their own memories of that ancient time. We honor with all our heart Claudia, Elizabeth, Angela, Alashea, Deatramus and Akinah. Your sincere presence was a light of support at a time when we were uncertain whether to reveal the full memory or not.

It is one thing to write a book, quite another to have it present well to the world; a task that with each book has become more and more challenging. Imagine our delight when one of the most talented magazine publishers in the New Age market stepped forward to offer her editing, layout and cover design skills! The difference in working with a seasoned and conscious professional was the extra energy that lifted us from exhaustion to exultation! Angela Earle is a gift from the realm you may call heaven, here in body. You will feel her love on every page and her careful crafting of the look of the book. There are no words Angela! (Except perhaps a big thank you to Randy, her husband, for letting us keep her three extra days during your vacation!)

Again we were supported by El'iam, our gifted friend and visionary artist. He too interrupted his vacation to help us with the illustrations in this book.

During the year of 2006, we traveled to many wonderful places, met incredible people, have had fun building our radio show and connected with Bill and Nancy Birnes. They truly model the love we describe in *Sacred Union*, our first book. Talented, brilliant, and refreshingly honest and sincere, it was like old home week when we got together.

Bill and Nancy are accomplished authors, publish *UFO Magazine* and created Filament Books, a wonderful online book club. The long list of best-sellers touched by them both is a testament to their hard work and their ability to always keep an open mind. Their kind acceptance to write the introduction of this book was a gift that you will unwrap shortly. When the email arrived with their introduction, we knew that the missing link of the book was now in place; we were finished! Thank you both for your love, talent and support!

And to our dear global community, it is for you that we continue. Every day, every moment, together with the Archangelic Realm, we are your servants and pray that your journey is ever-sweeter, ever-more peaceful and abundantly joyous! May this writing enhance your conscious journey. We love you all.

Many Blessings of love,
Sri Ram Kaa and Kira Raa
February 2007

Contents

Introduction

by William J. Birnes, Ph.D., J.D.

Love stories can be funny things. They can be simple stories of boy-meets-girl or stories of how couples overcome great obstacles to be together. And then there are love stories that speak of a great love, a time-defying love—and this is the love story you will read here.

Sri Ram Kaa and Kira Raa take you on a journey back in time and far away in space to a moment when a couple meets in one life and then, because of a greater mission, reunite many lifetimes later to rediscover their purpose and their mission not only in previous lives, but in a previous—and now dead—civilization on a distant planet. This is truly a story about finding one's destiny.

In the second half of the book, Sri and Kira show readers how to discover their own pathways through time and across boundaries of space as well as millennia. Surprisingly, although the journey seems intimidating at first, it really isn't. The exercises that Sri and Kira lay out for readers in this book illustrate that what seems like an impossibility is, in fact, a straightforward process of finding a truth that is already there by separating it from an overlay of accepted, consensus reality that often hides its truth from the observer.

Three years ago George Noory and I embarked on a joint research project to find the science and scholarship behind what Sri and Kira narrate so movingly as their personal story. George is, of course, the host of radio's premier nighttime show, *Coast to Coast AM*, and he and I wanted to see what kind of science, physics as well as psychology, serves as a foundation to the personal experiences of memories from previous lives and the ability to see or perceive entities whose presence defies the three-dimensional laws that appear to govern our comings and goings in this world. What we found was surprising and encouraging.

We discovered, as Sri and Kira document, that reality is many-layered. The apparent world we navigate through seems real enough. You bump your head and you certainly feel it. You observe red lights and wait until the doors open before you get into the elevator. However, there are those moments in all of our lives when we feel we've been there before, know what someone is going to say before it's said, or, disquietingly, feel somehow that a timeline has been shifted.

We've all heard the little voice inside of us that tells us when we know we've done something wrong or that we're right in the face of all sorts of criticism and denials. And we know this is a reality that has a validity even though logic tells us that it shouldn't. The good news is that these experiences, listening to voices that are there but can't be seen, believing we're re-experiencing something, and even sensing that things are different than they should be, are not just valid, they're more valid—and vitally more important—than the reality our five everyday senses tell us is all there is.

If you've not yet read Sri and Kira's two previous books, *Sacred Union: The Journey Home* and *2012: You Have A Choice!*, you have a treat in store. This is the third book in a series, and once you've taken this very special journey through the heart of time with the authors, you will want to go back and learn more about how that journey started out here on good, dependable, ailing Mother Earth. The great legacy of memory that they bring to their whole body of writings is a treasure that you will appreciate the more you read, and I urge you to read more!

But if you are reading this particular book, you will soon realize that there is a greater purpose behind your involvement. Relax, enjoy the ride, and prepare for the new destinations your soul will discover as a direct result of reading *2012 Atlantean Revelations.*

Science says that matter can never be created or destroyed. It simply changes form from mass into energy and back again, from particle to wave and back to particle. Want to know at any given moment whether a quantum of matter is either mass or wave? If you try to find out, you discover that the quantum of matter in question is exactly what you expect it to be. If you think it should be a wave, it's a wave, and the other way around.

This is a very simplistic way to say that things are what you want them to be, even if you don't really know what you want just yet. In other words, intentionality governs what will happen, not just happenstance. Most people already know this on some subconscious level, and as you read *2012* you will learn to trust your instincts more and more. Better yet, you might even learn that you, too, were a resident of the ancient and lost world of Su'Laria. Just to be sure, there's even a handy checklist of common experiences that you can compare your own experiences to.

Because matter can never be created or destroyed, only reformulated and recombined, it means that in some previous existence I might have been you and you might have been someone else. At the very least, it is probably mathematically provable that parts of me or parts of you were combined with parts of others, even if we can't say which parts or which others. Reincarnation, therefore, is not only possible, it's unavoidable.

Sri and Kira explain that there is a world of forms, a world of things that exist outside of our own everyday perception. In that world, forms of energy or light navigate freely. They are us and we are them. We have the abilities to perceive the energies that surround us and to navigate ourselves through dimensions that we have to believe exist in order to experience them. Again, this is not simply theory, it is U.S. Army-stamped-official: something so secret that even to this day the real story of military time travelers and interplanetary explorers is known only to a few. But it happened.

Of course, what Sri and Kira have experienced, the awakening in themselves of the consciousness they shared in a different civilization on another planet lifetimes ago, is a story of self-realization far in advance of what the military time travelers experienced twenty or so years ago. Though different in degree, however, it is not different in kind. Sri and Kira—and you and I—all exist in a universe that these time travelers only saw brief glimpses as the result of their training.

Now you can have that same training and begin to experience the absolute wonderment of discovering that you have more senses than you thought you have. Read Sri and Kira's stories, a combined love story that survives the corporeality of the individuals and says that love is indeed forever. Then, take a step into your own immortality by practicing the exercises that Sri and Kira illustrate. You will learn for yourself what I learned years ago and what Sri and Kira teach in their seminars and growing body of work.

You will learn that love lasts forever, that love is the strongest force in the universe, and that love, when embraced for the joy that it is, nurtures all. Be nurtured and know that if you are reading this, you are already home.

William J. Birnes is a New York Times best-selling author, an editor, a magazine and book publisher, and a New York literary publishing agent and book and television producer. He has written and edited over twenty-five books and encyclopedias in the fields of human behavior, true crime, current affairs, history, psychology, business, computing, and the paranormal. He has two forthcoming novels at Tor/Forge Books and a nonfiction series in science and technology. William Birnes is married to author Nancy Hayfield, the Editor-in-Chief of UFO Magazine.

Section One

Cosmic Origins and Revelation

"For those who believe in the Divine as
Love in Action, no explanation is necessary.
For those who don't, no explanation
will ever be enough."
~ Kira Raa

Chapter One

Why 2012

Kira Raa shares:

1965….

As I stood at the screen door of our living room, before me was the full splendor of summer in New Jersey. Humid and sunny with the haze of high heat apparent on everything. I was only a five year old girl, and yet within moments one of the most profound and life-changing visions of my life would unfold.

Watching the bumble bees fly by me at the door, and taking in the smells of summer around me, my gaze went to my mother's very large and fragrant rose bushes. They were always filled with Japanese beetles that I found to be beautiful with their metallic bronze and green shells.

I really don't know what or how it happened, yet within what seemed like a second the roses turned from brilliant yellow, pink, and white, to gray. I looked up and everything around me was no longer in color, it was simply gray, as if a storm had appeared and vaporized all color before me. On this hot, humid day, I was now numb with cold.

My body was literally unable to move as I simply watched everything around me transform. My gaze became fixed on the horizon where I saw a large mushroom cloud appear. It was small at first, and then grew larger and larger. Once it seemed as if it filled the sky, another appeared, until there were four of them, each cloud larger than the one before, completely filling the horizon before me. My five year old body trembled with loud noises that I did not understand, and felt enormous fear and helplessness. In that moment I heard only one discernible word: "2012".

To this day, I cannot fully explain the brief yet profound conversation that then took place, yet I clearly remember every word as if it just happened.

"God, oh God! I've made a mistake. I can't do it. Please take me back before this would ever happen. I don't want to be here."

"You[2] ....won't be, and this is only one potential for this world."

...and then the color returned, the roses were vibrant, the bees were flying by, and the heat was stifling.

There was no basis in my childhood home to understand that I could have literally chosen this lifetime, or that I would have made some form of mistake in agreeing to it. My family was without any strong religious foundation. Both of my parents had essentially discarded their birth religions and God was not ever a topic of discussion in our home. There was also no reason for me to call out to a "god" to take me back, and there was no one I could talk to. I just stood there until my mother called me, and it would be 36 years before I would begin to understand what had just happened.

Welcome dear traveler to a journey that you have been experiencing for millennia and more. As we have prepared this sometimes shocking body of work for print we have had many moments of overwhelming joy and delight mixed with occasional pain and concern.

Why are we bringing forward the 2012 discussion at this time in our collective history?

There is no simple answer to that question.

Therefore, let's begin with prophecy, fear and polarity! Most likely you already have a sense that a great shift is before all humanity on the planet now. Your heart is already calling you to be present in ways that may be new and oftentimes feel destabilizing. You may even have experienced recent changes in your job, your family, your social circle, and your belief structures.

This is why the time is now! Humanity is at the brink of a new paradigm and with the huge amount of energy being exerted toward destruction and fear, it is imperative to share a perspective to that which offers a voice to peace, resolution and joyous shift.

We have been journeying with the Archangelic Realm[3] for many years now, and with each step there have been moments of cautious acceptance as our own hearts have been challenged to break free from the constraints of what is considered normal. Our conscious communion with these Angelic guides has resulted in a complete shift in our understanding of our lives and the earth itself. We now understand that 2012 is a milestone, an opportunity of cosmic proportions.

Before you is a great challenge, and only you can decide how to face it.

Are you ready to trust your heart in the face of outer voices asking you not to?

Are you willing to open your eyes and see the silver lining of the clouds within the storm?

What does that mean? For a moment let's return to prophecy, fear and polarity. The 2012 conversation is largely centered around Mayan & Hopi prophecy, the biblical book of Revelations and the quatrains of Nostradamus.[4] Most likely you are expecting us to spend time offering you additional illumination on these well known writings. We will not, for our information about 2012 is not found within any of these writings, yet there are some threads of truth within the established prophecies. Without a thread of truth a prophecy will not survive very long.

As perceived terror continues to be headline news on a daily basis, the fear quotient has escalated to all time highs that have made it risky to publicly question the dominate belief system. In the United States, a "free" country, offering perspectives that do not support the contraction into fear is an act that you may think twice about. Mistrust is high. Worldwide governments are now able to rally public support for restrictive policies that just a few years ago would have been considered unacceptable. Chemicals are added to our drinking water and sprayed in the air. Children are beginning to be fingerprinted, universally vaccinated and soon will be inserted with chips, and all in the name of safety.

Intolerance has become an accepted paradigm and prominent in world destabilization, aggression is now government sanctioned, and righteous "pre-emptive strikes" are accepted. Meanwhile our climate is changing, our eco-system is deteriorating, oceans are polluted and bottled water is a necessity worldwide!

OK, you get the point...we are collectively on a path of dehumanization and destruction. Our governments and peoples are drunk on fear-based concepts and the world is reflecting this misalignment. Where is this all going?

Our intent is not to invoke your anger or to purport another 2012 scenario. We only wish to point out that current behaviors and conditions are misaligned with our essential truth and reflect a lack of loving awareness. You see, there is another possibility for 2012 that we invite you to consider.

What if everything that is before you now was part of a loving picture to assist you to wake up to your true soul nature? What if all the doomsday prophecy, fear-based energy and polarity was actually a tool to assist you to remember that you are a powerful being of light? What if humanity is collectively "hitting bottom" so to speak, intoxicated by unhealthy energies, and that by 2012 we will collectively realize that we've all been "drunk"?

The period from 2001 to 2012 has opened a window of opportunity, for we are in a new energy that is supporting rapid evolution and growth in consciousness. Much has changed since the turn of the millennium. This new cycle enters rapid acceleration in the year 2007 and within this energetic acceleration is abundant fuel for fear and polarity as well as fuel for awakening and enlightenment.

Do you need to hit bottom to wake up? What if you could accept that your heritage is well beyond this one planet or this one solar system, and that the truth of your authentic being is so beautiful that recognizing it will explode your heart wide open?! From this heart expansion there is but one congruent direction - alignment with your divinity and claiming your wholeness.

Pain is not required; clear empowered choices are if we are to have a different experience. What if there were a choice that existed right now, for all beings on planet earth, which offered true peace, love and joy? Can you accept that each of us carries the keys to our true freedom right inside ourself, and that these keys will affect our outer experience?

While this may sound impossible or Pollyanna-esque upon first blush, we encourage you to keep reading and to allow yourself to do more than read the words on these pages, we encourage you to FEEL them. That's right, let the content of this writing go past the mental pictures and communicate directly with your soul.

As the book unfolds you will begin on a cosmic journey that will bring you to the end times of a world many refer to as "Atlantis". This is the first piece of unraveling the picture of what is happening on our world today. We are indeed repeating history, and when the context of that history is understood, it empowers you to move beyond being a victim to the unfolding of the drama, and offers you the gift of being an educated observer.

From the energy of being an educated observer you offer to yourself the great gift of claiming yourself, your deepest truth as a Co-Creator. The information we are sharing is sometimes difficult to read, much less believe, until you bring your own hand to your heart, breathe and experience the information on a new level.

Compiling the literally thousands of hours of Archangelic discourse was for us an enlightening and sometimes overwhelming task. How does one offer such deep and profound information in the face of a prevailing paradigm? In prior times humanity destroyed those who challenged the collective consciousness.

And then the obvious would come forward; how can we not share this? We are at the time of awakening and the world is ready more than ever before to look deeper.

We invite you now to simply begin your journey with an open mind, and to remember that whatever your experience of the text on these pages, it is a gift. Know that you were called to read this book for a reason; it will provoke a deeper commitment within you, regardless of whether you accept what we offer.

You are at the time of expansion, and our world has important and powerful energies at work, and YOU are one of them!

Joy expresses in many ways. This beautiful rainbow appears over the Lotus Temple at the TOSA Center shortly after a monthly community gathering.

Chapter Two
Healing Our Legacy

Welcome to this moment in time! The amazing cosmological and historical journey you are about to embark upon is offered with humble appreciation for you and your presence on this planet, right now. Each being has a personal journey of recollection and Divine re-connection. We are sharing with you the complete and unadulterated information that has been our journey with the intent that it will help stimulate further clarity for you. This book contains information lovingly gifted to humanity directly from the Archangelic Realm. We accept that it may be too *out there* for some to consider real or even probable.

Know that we recognize and honor that each being is whole, and therefore able to discern his/her own response to the material that fills these pages. Whether you continue reading this detailed anthology as a wonderful fictional experience or one that touches the cords of truth deeply within you, is a personal and private decision that rests solely within your authority.

What does matter, is that you are here, now, allowing yourself to expand the possibilities of your experience of life on this planet. Collectively, everyone is expanding into an ever refining expression at every given moment. Often, we may suddenly wake up to find our life has changed dramatically, and yet this shift happened so subtly along the way that we did not even notice until the last piece of the puzzle was inserted.

Our journey with the Archangelic Realm has been much like that puzzle. Neither of us woke up one day and decided to step on the path of Self-Ascension and begin dialoging with the Archangelic Realm. Surrendering to infinite possibilities was not a conscious decision and yet, in hindsight, it certainly could be construed that way.

We have learned that a healthy adult must have reconciled their emotional wounds in order to live more freely and less reactively. For example, it is widely accepted that once one is able to look at old wounds with a sense of forgiveness and acceptance, one's life becomes more peaceful and tolerant of others. This reconciliation of the past is in fact generating the energy of wholeness where the individual is accepting of the entirety of their life. Ultimately, one sees all experiences, even the painful ones, with a sense of appreciation for the learning and personal evolution that resulted. This is why you see the popularity of spiritual, emotional, and self-help therapy techniques.

Similarly, if we expand the scope of reconciliation beyond this particular lifetime, we can see that past lives contain traumatic incidents and decisions that have affected our ability to be in true harmony and peace in this time. There are far fewer people that understand and accept past life therapy. However, without commenting on the purpose and power of this form of therapy, it is important to accept, or at least be open to, the following two points:

1) You have lived before. This earth life you are experiencing is but one chapter in the book of you.

2) Experiences and decisions you made in prior lifetimes affect the experiences you are having in this lifetime.

Now, the ego-mind would love to puzzle over all these experiences and bring even more memories into consciousness. This is not needed. Your soul chose certain environments for you to experience in this lifetime that offered the promise of reconciling the past lifetime issues that remain unresolved. So, in one respect, you do not have to go looking for content in your past lives. The past issues that are important will present themselves in this lifetime. That's good news, for all you need to do is be present to heal the unresolved issues!

Like a teenager with the music on too loud, we sometimes don't hear the sounds from a farther room. Our world of experience is then smaller and Spirit must conspire to make a forcible entry! This is why so many people need and call forth dramatic intervention. This may take the form of job loss, a health or relationship crisis, or some other drama, to expand their awareness. Ultimately, we all get what we need. The real question is: are you ready to make the journey more joyful?

Are you available to be present for your own healing process? Or, have you adopted belief systems that will filter out some of the healing opportunities that come your way? Are you too preoccupied with the drama in your life that the bigger picture is swept out of your awareness?

A conscious journey offers the greatest opportunities for joy and co-creation. When we turn away from parts of ourselves, our denial limits the expansion of our wholeness and personal power. Wholeness is the state of harmony where we accept our legacy with respect and joy. Wholeness is also a state of being where we are available to the now experience without projections and expectations birthed from unresolved energies and wounds carried in our subconscious. In our wholeness we can experience Peace, Love and Joy without restriction.

Every person is on a spiritual path; it cannot be otherwise. Wholeness is the result of spiritual trust expressing through our physical, emotional and mental bodies. Wholeness results as we align our consciousness with the truth of our soul. How can we be truly whole if we do not resolve the very energies which birthed our earth experience?

Just as we must reconcile our childhood in order to have an empowered adult life, so too must we reconcile our disowned experiences from other expressions. This book will take you on a journey through the path of reunion. This means that we will eventually greet these energies and are called to lovingly resolve them as we embrace our resurrection into authentic expressions of the Divine. Thus, understanding your participation in the energies that birthed and ultimately destroyed Su'Laria (Atlantis)[5] offers great healing and empowerment for every one of us without limitation, for Su'Laria was a collective experience.

This understanding does not require mental comprehension or acceptance of the descriptions we will offer to you throughout this book. It only requires that you open your heart to the impressions from your own soul, regardless of the mental pictures that your mind offers to explain those energies. Just as a dream may be a distorted representation of some energies seeking expression, so too will your sense of past lives and cosmic experiences have some distortions as the density-mind tries to understand the energies. *Feel through the pictures and simply embrace the cellular recognition with loving acceptance. Through loving acceptance we reconcile and heal.*

As we write this book it strikes us as poignant that in order to fully embrace the great gift of life, we often need to revisit our past experiences to fully appreciate our now experience; our collective legacy is a gift to consciousness. In essence, consider this a manual of wholeness: a guide to assist you in unlocking the eternal secrets of your own being-ness, and offer you simple yet profound lessons to bring these secrets into full daily recognition.

Together let us explore the energetic shifts and planetary actions that are causing you to come forward and make your decision now as to whether or not you wish to fully and completely heal! This healing transcends the boundaries of this lifetime, this solar system, and yes, this Universe. This cosmic healing is why you chose to be here on this planet, at this very moment in history; you are being called to re-member the fullness of your original choice, the one you made to travel into density.

There are those who refer to Earth as a spiritual game board, a school for soul evolution. Perhaps it is time to lift off the paradigm and opt for a new level of expression. Perhaps we are at the time in history when we can graduate from the duality of density expression and embrace a reality more aligned with our authentic energy…our soul. The ultimate choice to lift or to stay for another round is yours to make now.

Mankind has always misinterpreted prophecy and divine revelation. Much like the "telephone game" of children's parties, angelic messages and prophecy are infiltrated with personal beliefs and fears and then passed down through the generations, gathering more distortion with every telling. The purpose of revelation is to prepare consciousness. It helps to remove fixation upon a particular status quo.

The Mayan Calendar, The Book of Revelations, Nostradamus, and The Hopi prophecies all contain elements of universal truth. It is not for any individual or institution to decipher these communications, for to do so only introduces interpretative beliefs and agenda from the dominate paradigm. As long as we rely upon any interpretation, we are caught in the distortion of the game. It is the time for the individual to trust his/her own DNA, to recognize that the Creator has bestowed everything one needs for successful living right in your essential Self. Prophecy can be understood by the heart as a sense of knowing. The mind does not have to be satiated with explanations!

Once one truly anchors in the heart, one's life experience is marked by Peace. One experiences true Universal Love, which is felt as a sense of gratitude and appreciation for life. Judgments of others occur infrequently and are recognized as the residue of an outdated ego-need for hierarchical thinking.

Spiritual living, much less spiritual healing in a 9 to 5 world is often a challenging task. It is now 2007, and as we race toward the quantum leap of 2012 we are consistently bombarded with doomsday scenarios, have the technology to end all life on the planet within hours, and witness the apparent slow destruction of our beloved eco-system that supports all life as we know it! Taken as a whole, this often interrupts one from claiming Peace, Love and Joy. The focus of most beings on this planet is how to live from paycheck to paycheck, raise a family and navigate daily life. As long as one's attention is oriented toward fear and lack, noticing unity in the Divine flow is more challenging.

Therefore, prior to the introduction of any more cosmic revelations, let's prepare by taking a moment to re-visit the basics. That is, how do we intertwine spiritual consciousness into our everyday 9 to 5 lives?

Is this you or someone you know?

The alarm sounds, the kids wake up, the dog needs to be fed, and you need to greet the world! Where in the frantic daily routine can you fit in conscious spiritual connection? After all, your heart is yearning to consistently hold loving presence and the idea of quiet time is forever appealing. Yet, your job is demanding, the mailbox is filled with bills, dinner needs to made, and a relaxing soak in the tub seems forever away. Sound familiar?

Many times on the path of seeking an integrated life of activity and spirituality the balance of the two becomes slanted in one direction or the other. Commonly, we lose perspective and begin to believe that we must sacrifice one for another. We believe that spirituality can only be maintained within the ashram or yoga experience, and begin to schedule our spiritual time the same as we schedule any other activity. Once we schedule our spirituality, we separate from the flow and as a result it becomes acceptable to dismiss our spiritual discoveries and experiences as irrelevant or unrealistic.

Given this cycle of discovery and frequent disappointment, the common mantra today is: *If only I could find a moment of peace!* This is a powerful mantra indeed because it is the catalyst for action that keeps you searching for more.

What if you could accept that your current situation is serving your soul perfectly right now?

What if you could allow yourself to begin by simply smiling at the Divine process being played out in front of you every moment of every day? What if the alarms, the demands, the bills, the traffic…all of it, were in front of you to offer the gift of breaking through?

These are powerful questions for they invoke deep self introspection. The irony of introspection is that when we are full with life's demands, self-reflection feels either like a luxury or yet another demand of our precious time. So, how do we break free from this continuous cycle and embrace the balance of activity and spirituality?

Reclaiming Deep Connection

Simply put, there are only three simple action steps that you need embrace. In this very moment you can begin gifting yourself with the deep connection you seek, regardless of your current life experience. Taken individually, each step is simple. There is, however, a secret to mastering them. **The key to your success is your commitment to follow through, every day.** It is the daily commitment to balance that often becomes the challenge.

If you really want to break through the challenges that seem insurmountable, then you must take the first step.

Action Step One
Commit to Choosing Joy in All You Experience!

Yes! This is a strong statement to the universe that you get it and that you are ready to accept the Divine at work in everything you experience. One way you can apply the joy choice to your spiritual development is to simply recognize when you are experiencing something other than joy.

The word Joy in and of itself often invokes a strong response. This is because we commonly filter joy through our emotional bodies. Choosing emotional joy is a form of imbalance; it is an expression of dependency energy. The emotional body believes that something outside of us must change, like a better job, a new relationship, etc. Thus our joy becomes dependent upon others. This is a wonderful level of discernment to embrace. When you are faced with any situation and you consciously choose joy, you can immediately back check yourself by asking the question: *Is this joy dependent upon anything?*

If the answer is yes, than you know you are responding from the emotional body; a powerful recognition. Smile at this and get clear that true Joy does not need anything from the outside. Practice choosing joy until you feel this as a loving energetic hug rather than an emotional band-aid. The more you practice this step you will discover how dependant the ego is on outside conditions. The joy choice will accelerate your spiritual awareness.

You must fully embrace this first step before you move onto the next. Remember that patience with yourself is one of the greatest gifts you receive along the way. In every moment it is imperative to bring to your awareness the recognition that you are doing the very best you can with the situation in front of you, given the resources you currently have. This is why choosing joy in your experience is so powerful. This one simple choice will begin to reflect in your consciousness in profound ways. You will find that it will influence all areas of your life, including the inner and outer resources you call to yourself.

Now that you've committed to the first step and are experiencing the benefits of choosing joy, you are ready for Step Two.

Action Step Two
See the Divine in Action in Everyone and Everything!

You now realize why step one was so important. Whether you agree with another person or not is irrelevant when it comes to recognizing that all beings are the Divine in Action. Each event in our world, every action we take or receive, are all Divine in nature. When you allow yourself to recognize that the Divine exists in all beings and experiences, you begin the process of depersonalizing your experiences and expand into the role of the observer. This expands the Divine Flow into your life!

Allowing this process to integrate into your daily life takes practice, just like step one. After all, you have spent most of your life responding to the actions around you rather than being the observer of them. Remember to be the observer of the Divine in yourself as well. A simple way to begin this process is to sit down with a piece of paper and write the name of someone or some action that is causing you pain. As you gaze upon the paper, begin breathing deeply and bring your hand to your heart. Allow yourself to remove the "you" from this interchange and simply open up to seeing how the Divine may be at work in this interaction.

There is no time limit on this exercise. It is important to just be honest with yourself. Know that if you are unable to move too deeply in the beginning, just having taken the step is a wonderful way to begin. The more often you repeat this process, the simpler it will become to begin recognizing the amazing ways the Divine reveals itself. You will discover that regardless of any situation you are confronted with, the recognition of the Divine in Action expands your spiritual awareness, and you will likely shift how the situation resolves. There is great freedom in cultivating this awareness.

Now that you have embraced the process of choosing joy, and have acquired the habit of seeing the Divine in Action in all beings and circumstances, you have set the stage to fully experience a spiritual life every moment of every day. So, how can you anchor your spiritual self in your 9 to 5 world? The third step in this journey offers perspective.

Action Step Three
Get Clear on What You Really Want in Your Life

This may sound obvious, however most of us are not living spiritually empowered lives. This is due to the inability to offer clear signals to the universe on how to support us. Your heart may declare one set of objectives, while the brain is offering another. You may say you want one thing, yet all of your actions support something else. By choosing Joy and recognizing the Divine in Action you set the stage for your soul's mission to rapidly unfold. When you listen to the inner yearnings and get clear, the universe will support you unconditionally. Remember, the universe is already supporting your life now, the key is to shift where the support is anchored!

Instead of feeling lost or trapped in the world, see the Divine, feel the Joy, and trust your life! A giant step in the right direction is when we stop complaining about our life and begin energizing affirmative declarations. Affirmative declarations are organized around enhancing your soul's expression. Most people create their affirmations in response to a negative condition in their lives. Those reactive declarations use the negative condition as a source of power and thus fail to provide lasting benefit.

How many people do you know that constantly repeat affirmation after affirmation yet nothing seems to change in their lives? Affirming what you want without soul clarity will simply make you really good at repeating affirmations!

There is only one sure way to get clear: Begin by being really honest with yourself about what brings you joy, (*see Action Step One*). Recognize that Joy is the signal from your soul that you are doing exactly what you should be doing! Write about this on paper, avoid a computer. Allow your body to receive the signal that you are serious about clarity. Avoid judging what you write and how it is written. Simply write until you are clear, or not clear! Then, when you are ready, repeat this process again and again.

Remember, you are already living a spiritual life because you are here…now! It is how you balance your consciousness that will ultimately offer you the Peace, Love and Joy that is yours to delight in moment by moment! When you change your perspective, the outer world will shift to support your Joy!

People often ask us how we can claim to know what we teach. Teaching is either a reiteration of a discovered knowledge, a new view on a known theme, or it is information revealed through direct communion with Source. Revealed knowledge, like poetry, is often recognized as true before it is understood by the mind. This is why it is essential to discard the mind as the primary source for validating experience. The mind is secondary - it is the servant of the heart, not the monarch of your being. As you live these three steps, your soul will reveal further teachings to you.

Chapter Three

Revealing Hidden Truth

Through our communion with the Divine much has been revealed, however, it is in the application of the messages revealed that the full gift is experienced. Everything we share with you in our writings, we have lived and continue to live. To do otherwise would not honor our commitment to the Divine.

Kira and I began our mission together by combining our energies in a unique form of Divine communion we call **Archangelic In-Soulment[6].** The process of connecting regularly to these refined realms of Spirit has conditioned us to the point that the portal of Divine communion never closes.

This loving form of communion is the basis by which we live our lives, and the gift that we receive on our journey through this time in our collective cosmology. Each day as you continue on your journey, you too are receiving many gifts and often encounter circumstances that defy explanation.

Reading this book is a journey, and the one you are about to embark upon is in actuality no more farfetched than the numerous events that face you every day, every moment. Perhaps George Noory[7] described it best:

> "Kira has told the story of how her life was turned around by her perception of the voice of Archangel Zadkiel. Take her story to a standard off-the-shelf psychiatrist, and you might be told

> that she was having an auditory hallucination. Take her story to a hard-nosed debunker and you might be told that she was making this up as a way to sell snake oil. Take her story to a died-in-the-wool conspiracy theorist and you might be told that she was being manipulated by a government agency seeking to test out a new weapon or turn her into an agent or worse, an agent provocateur.
>
> Fortunately, as Kira explained to the *Coast*[8] audience, she was wise enough to trust her own instincts, something that I encourage everyone to do in *Worker in the Light*,[9] and to follow what the voice of Zadkiel was telling her, testing out each interaction for its reliability and veracity. Ultimately, Kira was convinced that she was indeed tuned into an extraordinary signal. And she has changed her life in accordance with what she believes she has been told. And it has all been successful.
>
> Indeed, science has shown that many times you see what you expect to see regardless of what you actually see. I suggest, therefore, that you challenge your own expectations and look for what's really there regardless of whether it conforms to your experience or not. Sometimes you have to tune out what people tell you is your reality in order to *experience* reality."

With that established, we simply ask only one thing of you, the reader: May you sit back, relax, take in a deep heart-centered breath, and allow yourself to simply join us on this journey. Together we will re-visit past lives, come to a fuller understanding of why we are here, now, and learn that we are indeed powerful enough to effect positive shift personally and universally.

Humanity is at the ultimate choice point, and it is not too late!

We have shared much around living spiritually in a 9 to 5 world as a foundation for the rest of this book. From here, the material that follows is much more cosmic in nature. If we do not prepare the soul, so to speak, in our day-to-day lives, then the cosmic information has little chance of taking root and offering healing.

Choice is the gift given to all humanity. Do you choose to integrate your spirit fully into your body? Do you choose to surrender to the Divine and let God express through you? This is true union.

Or, do you choose to relegate spiritual and metaphysical truth to the realm of the mental body, thus visiting them as concepts rather then integrated knowing?

The choice is yours alone to make!

Collectively, humanity must make more enlightened decisions or life on Earth will become ever more compromised. We believe that our souls have the solutions and that it is time for soul reunion. This is the spiritual path that transcends all outer desires yet honors the Divine in all expressions.

Healthy growth is Holistic.

That is, it honors the totality of our Being while moving forward in a new way. Growth often requires the releasing of old patterns. To do this holistically means that we honor the pathway that has brought us to our realizations and new choices. New information can result in new decisions and behaviors that are different from our established patterns. Be grateful that the old patterns brought you to the point of realization!

Reading the cosmic material in this book may result in some unsettling feelings.

Sometimes we recognize truth at a cellular level. Even if our mind or emotions say "no" there can be a deeper part of us that says "yes." We do not want to invite confusion; we do want to invite you to connect with your deepest level of truth, for the deeper you align the closer you are to full soul recognition!

Discovering hidden truth requires us to relax our patterned awareness and attend to signals that we might otherwise ignore. This relaxing of our patterned responses allows our intuition to inform us. To do this safely we must first anchor in our hearts. From there we can allow ourselves to look at whatever our experience is without fear.

We suggest that you offer yourself the gift of allowing the information in this book to stimulate your cellular knowing. Not everyone on this planet today once lived in Su'Laria, (Atlantis). How will you know if you did? Self-discovery means listening to your inner communications so that you might gain new clarity about yourself. Here are three steps that promote safe inward communion.

> **Pause** your reactive orientation by bringing your hands to your heart. This sends a signal to your soul that you are listening.
>
> **Breathe** deeply to send a relaxation signal to your body. This helps the body feel safe.
>
> **Allow** yourself to be present to whatever is emerging into your awareness. You may need to breathe several breaths to cultivate this Presence.

The process of personal growth usually comes with some degree of anxiety. That is, as we conform our outer lives to match our inner truth we must leave behind old patterns. If we don't align with our inner knowing we will feel anxiety and a sense of dishonesty. And, when our knowing does not conform to existing social conventions we risk ridicule. How often have you discredited yourself in order to avoid rejection from others?

You may find that the material in this book generates a sense of excitement or anxiety within you. Why? Because at a cellular level your body knows that personal change is on the horizon, that your paradigm has been challenged. It is up to you whether you use this information to expand your paradigms or whether you discard this information in favor of preserving the inner status quo. All choices are acceptable for it is YOU deciding what's right for YOU. Be self-responsible.

The *Pause-Breathe-Allow* technique will help you find the nuggets of gold and discard what isn't useful. This technique helps you trust yourself more fully while also allowing personal growth to occur in a most natural way.

Often when reading challenging material we simply miss some of the information on the first read through. It is surprising how often you will discover new nuggets of truth when reading an Archangelic discourse the second and third time. Are you ready to accept more consciousness? Being awake is a great responsibility – it means you are accountable!

Some people experience anger when they discover something new about their past. Others experience anxiety, for they now have to view themselves differently. All responses are good - it means you are alive! The key is to move past limiting judgments and allow the truth to liberate your consciousness.

Pause - Breathe - Allow

To further assist you to FEEL the information in this book, you will periodically find the following lotus picture inserted on a page.

Each time you see this picture, allow yourself to take a moment and enjoy the *Pause-Breathe-Allow* technique. *(To make your journey even more meaningful, please refer to the expanded practice in the endnote on SAFE[10].)* You may even wish to journal around what you are experiencing. Above all else, trust your heart, and gift yourself with the opportunity to expand your consciousness, shift your paradigm and embrace your soul!

Dearest readers, please remember as you engage in your own remembering of the legacy that seeded life on Earth, you may find yourself reacting to the material. Trust that any and all responses are a sign of recognition and healing. Breathe deeply and gift yourself with a second pass through any material that stimulates emotional reaction, and you will find healing, love and support.

Know that all responses are Divinely perfect, and so we offer you the following reactions from two different people who read the chapters on Su'Laria (Atlantis) for the first time. May their sharing offer you assurance that all experiences are indeed perfect.

Angela's Story

The first time I read the following chapters on Su'Laria my immediate reaction was to slam the book shut and fume. Anger welled up in me and I immediately began to judge. Memories rushed to the surface, and feelings and patterns of behavior that had been an undercurrent my entire life began to emerge in an exaggerated way. Most of all I felt disappointed; I had expected that reading about my heritage would offer missing pieces to my own puzzle and would bring me joy, relief, and freedom.

Because I had no context for my reaction, I assumed that my reaction was arising out of shortcomings of the book or the material presented on Su'Laria. I filtered Kira's story through the sense of exclusion I had felt my entire life, that sense of always being on the outside I now know I had experienced on Su'Laria. As the editor of this book, I made a list of all I felt was lacking, and of all I felt that needed to be added in order for me, personally, to become engaged and feel part of this Cosmic sharing.

Much to my complete surprise and shock, I re-read the entire piece and was amazed to find that all of the information I was craving was actually there – I simply hadn't been able to take it in. In many ways, reading this story and history has been my first real engagement with our collective past. There was a lot I believed, but my authentic reaction caused me to come to terms with the full reality of it all. I could not deny that my emotional, physical, and mental reactions were real, and it was at this point that things stopped being an intellectual exercise and began to affect my life in every way. For the first time I was face to face with the truth that this all wasn't just a story someone was telling, or an idea to intellectually explore, but it is part of my own history that I am still in the middle of today.

As I was able to open up my heart to this truth more and more, and to give myself the permission to just be present to me, an entire array of memories, emotions, and revelations began to emerge. I saw how limited my viewpoint had been. I had always seen the patterns of behavior I engaged in as the result of this life, only I had created limited explanations that I had based my entire way of thinking on. While this realization that I was truly a multidimensional being was at times overwhelming, I also was able to see the world and existence itself from a much larger perspective.

Like so many of us, the "Children of Atlantis," I had engaged many methodologies to "deal" with what I saw as my problems. Finally, I was actually able to achieve deeper healing and resolution, and a much vaster understanding of not only my own life, but of life in general.

In short, this process of rejection, anger, denial, and blame was actually a perfect reaction to this reading, for me. In fact, reading this material was the key for me to integrating and accepting so much of who I am, how I act and react in the world, and my feelings of exclusion and my lingering inability to be comfortable in this world.

In judging how I was reacting, I recognized that I had expectations and assumptions about what a spiritual experience should and should not look like. In letting go of all of that I was given the gift of removing yet another layer of conditioning and programming prevalent on this world today.

Beyond my initial emotional reaction, and as I settled in and allowed myself to go deeper, I found I was able to move beyond constricting feelings and patterns. Those patterns were a part of everything I do, of every story I had ever created about my life here, and about my ancient and infinite past. I grieved, I reacted, and I finally understood what it meant to surrender, to not judge, and to embrace it all.

Elizabeth's Story

I awoke this day with my eyes already burning. The evening before I had received an email with the chapters on Su'Laria (Atlantis) and had gone to bed knowing I would take time with them upon rising. I was now about to read pages of a life that I too, once lived.

As I began to read my heart was pounding, and I began to cry and cry. I let the tears come.

What I realized immediately was that this was not just Sri and Kira's story. The memories came flooding back for me, and I knew this story belongs to all.

As I remember the important role I played, all who read these pages will have some memory or feelings that awaken inside of them as well.

This is the story all should read. This is the time for the world to know and remember. I know this will touch so many in ways they will not believe. I am so honored to be part of this once again.

Chapter Four

Atlantis and Su'Laria

"It is your time to recognize the all-ness within. From within, the truth emerges from your own DNA. Within your own cellular structure there cannot be doubt, there cannot be words, there cannot be confusion, because you are resonating from a stream of conscious truth. Conscious Truth cannot be given to you. You do not find it from somebody else. You call it forth from within!

~ Archangel Zadkiel, 2012: You Have a Choice, page 182

The remaining chapters found in Section One are a compilation of direct communications with the Archangelic Realm during the period of 2003-2006. As you read through these sometimes challenging revelations, the only editing we have brought to this information has been basic grammar and compilation from several discourses to provide continuity and ease of reading.

For the benefit of those who may not have read *2012: You Have a Choice*, we have inserted a brief passage from Archangel Zadkiel describing the difference between Atlantis and Su'Laria. In essence, the "original" Atlantis was known to you as Su'Laria, and the seeding that occurred on Earth is what many refer to as Atlantis:

"The expression of Atlantis existed very close to here dear one. It existed on a planet that you now know as Mars. On Mars, the Atlantean expression was fully realized and dearest child your scientists already have this evidence....In

the time of Atlantis when you knew that it was time to leave, you were on Mars as part of the seeding of this planet, Earth, to further prepare the crystalline grids on this planet that are realigning now...It was in the time of the Egyptian Ancient dynasties that those of you that seeded from these other galaxies came forth with your own energies...In that time you brought forth and set in motion all of the necessary energies that are coming back right now."

The content you are about to read and re-member is of the first experience of Atlantis (Su'Laria) that existed on the planet Mars[11]. The first step on our cosmic healing journey is to revisit the fullness experienced on the true Atlantis, the Su'Laria of Mars.

In the early days of Su'Laria the planet was a pristine and idyllic spot with blue waters, crystalline mountains, and clean air. The planet had been prepared for the new Life forms that were to be seeded there. Additional forms of life expression, winged creatures and sea creatures, were brought forward to interact with the expressions of light that were coming to Su'Laria. Every detail of this creation was conceived and manifested in harmonic balance offering interdependent beauty and cooperation at all levels of expression. The Elohim showered joy toward the sincere expression of love, thoughtfulness and harmony expressed through the design of Su'Larian environment in preparation for the Beings of Light.

The oceans supported forms of life that were sustained by a liquid environment. There were fish-like creatures that gracefully propelled themselves through the water. There were kelp-like plants that thrived on the synergy of sunlight and water. Even small plankton-like organisms were seeded here to help sustain the ecology of the oceans.

In the air large bird-like creatures flew. They were colorful and curious! All of these Life Forms had consciousness – all were imbued with Soul. They communicated with each other and with the light beings that were taking form here. There was no judgment that one form should have dominion over another form. There was simply harmony and trust. Each form was complete unto itself and its habitat. Each experienced joy and self-awareness and the forms could enjoy conscious communication with each other.

The planet was ready! The expanding Light had created dimensional Differentiations from Source, a multitude of expressions of various forms and densities. Beings of the Archangelic Realm assisted the Blue Starborn[12] in creating and protecting the Su'Larian habitat during its gestation period. While the first expression of light in Tu'Laya was indeed light in form, that form did not have the density now found in Su'Laria. By density, we mean the expression of molecules that are organized in a tight orbit giving one a sense of form and substance, also giving one a sense of delay, for light must travel differently in a condensed molecular structure than in a more expanded structure. This delay gave birth to a concept of time. Models of density were pioneered by these Beings of Light in a vessel; they were having experiences of separation which made the remembrance of their Source even more precious. It is through the contrast of existing in separate vessels that we understood our Divine connection more exquisitely. Light Beings from Tu'Laya who were to inhabit the planet were not yet in form. They were resting and healing from the soul fractures experienced during the rebellion in consciousness that occurred at the close of the Tu'Layan experience.

The individuated light beings came and joyfully populated Su'Laria. As they embraced the energy of Su'Laria, they soon had access to the vast resources of wisdom. Having the Blue Starborn by their side meant that the knowledge of molecular rearrangement could be transmitted as quickly as their newly formed density brain could absorb it. Thus their society and civilization developed very quickly. The Su'Larians created cities that provided for their ever expanding physical needs. They also began to explore the various aspects of material form and density expression.

On the planet's surface there were two basic habitats, the mountain and the ocean communities. In the mountains the moisture from the air collected as fog on the mountain peaks. This moisture condensed into mountain streams of water which were gathered into aqueducts and carried to the ocean communities over miles of desert-like terrain. The deserts separated the communities and offered a free flowing and natural sense of boundary. The deserts themselves were not threatening as the Su'Larians could transit them via flying machines or through teleportation, depending upon their training and skill.

Crystals were everywhere! Crystals offered amplification of Light and could help focus energy. Buildings were constructed using crystalline lattices – this allowed the buildings themselves to interface with the life forms. They were living buildings that breathed and offered life-sustaining energy to the inhabitants. The crystalline walls were translucent and the amount of light that entered the building was controlled by the needs of the inhabitants.

The ocean communities consisted of crystalline buildings, temples and tall towers. The mountain communities occasionally had towers, however, the preferred structure was more dome-like. Neighborhoods were housed under large crystalline domes that offered climate and temperature control to the residents. Most of the dome communities were interconnected by tube-like roadways. One notable exception was the King's compound.

The Mountain King had a huge private dome. Like the neighborhood communities it was self-sustaining for nourishment, water and climate. Unlike the neighborhood communities, passage into the compound was regulated. Visitors entered and left via the teleportation crystals at the Temple.

Teleportation was possible through the concentration of Light energy on the teleportation pad. This energy was focused by the user, who held a picture in his mind's eye of the destination. The destination teleportation pad was activated via telepathic communication and thus the two locations were linked. The user then, through mental focus and intention, was able to literally "jump" to the other site using the amplification properties of the crystal. This ability to teleport was latent in all beings, however it was a skill that required some practice and training. A priest, having developed his powers of concentration sufficiently, could carry another person or object with him to the destination site. Thus, the untrained could be escorted in the company of a more skilled Su'Larian.

Over time, teleportation became controlled by the privileged members of society. The training was only offered to Temple initiates and those who were participants in the hierarchy of prestige and power. In fact, this ability to move freely became a measure of status.

The manner in which Tu'Laya ended had indeed imprinted the DNA of the Su'Larians. The conflict at the end of Tu'Laya generated, for the first time, a sense of "right and wrong" into consciousness. Thus, instead of simply flowing with the Divine expression that was their nature, the Tu'Layans began to interrupt that flow with their own individual valuations on what should be happening. This seeded a further refraction in consciousness, a self-reflective evaluative quality that spawned an impulse for even further individuation and complication. Thus, the next experience of Light in Form (Su'Laria) was far denser and far more complex than Tu'Laya. Indeed consciousness had split and folded upon itself in ways that created unprecedented expressions of density.

Polarity is a construct of the mind, not a law of the universe. In the expression of duality for example, in the expression of the two sexes, in the expression of value systems, the polarity began to separate things of experience into categories. The ability of the mind to discover ever more ways to split, differentiate and polarize experience began to separate the beings even further from Source. The density brain loved to create complex concepts and manifestations.

The Blue Starborn cooperated with the refracted consciousness of the Travelers[13] for they saw that these refractions of consciousness into further duality and distortion offered great learning to consciousness. Not wanting to interfere, they allowed the experiment to continue to refract and split, knowing that these refractions and distortions offered ever greater discernment and wisdom to the Light.

While the Blue Starborn created the environment and guided those who consciously asked for their guidance, they deeply respected the Su'Larian experiment and the mission that had been undertaken by those in density form. Out of respect they left them to have their experience without interference. After all, the ones who took on a density body were risking their Divine Connection by blending themselves with a form of a biological vessel. While the DNA coding insured that the pathway home was mapped, the ones in vessels would still have many challenges to find their way through the density expression and return to Source.

Thus, the Blue Starborn and the Archangels were in awe and respect for the individualized beings whose continued travels into density offered a great expansion of consciousness and was thus a true loving service to Divine Source. Their eventual return to Source would be met with great celebration and joy!

Within the density experience on the planet certain hierarchies developed. The Beings began to specialize based upon their interests and natural gifts and further refractions of consciousness. Those who were adept at communication with the Blue Starborn and spiritual pursuits became Temple initiates. Those who were drawn toward physical engineering undertook roles in the outer world. Those with affinity toward energy management became conduits to healing. Similar to Earth experience, either the most adept or the ones most wanting to control things took on leadership roles in their respective areas and society defaulted into distinct arenas. For example, the artists, the healers, the politicians, the priests and priestesses, the builders, the scientists, the governors; all were roles that could be enjoyed by those who wanted to engage with those energies.

As the generations turned and centuries passed, those who controlled the physical grew in power in the external world. Those who could demonstrate spiritual power grew alongside them, for the governors of the physical retained a deep respect for the source of true knowledge and life energy, thus they honored the carriers of this wisdom. Each King and governor had spiritual advisors.

Throughout the eons, consciousness continued to refract and shifted further and further from the original ways of communion toward the new ways of depending upon technology and the external world. It seemed that as technology advanced, people found less interest in the metaphysical pursuits and more interest in physical pursuits. Generations were born and reborn and the mass consciousness continued to try to control flow rather than align with natural harmony. That is, they sought to interrupt the natural evolutionary flow in a favor of imposing their own control onto the pace and timing and development of things. They wanted to control the quality of their external stimulus and experience and they began to feel the need to exercise control over others as well. The ego grew dominant.

The Su'Larians did not want to completely forsake their spiritual legacy and honored the energies of creation, healing and Divine connection. As the mass consciousness grew more separated from the metaphysical, they relied more and more upon the priest and priestesses for their spiritual experiences.

The connection to oneness through inter-dimensional travel was controlled by the priests who became the gatekeepers for spiritual experiences. The people themselves had long forgotten how to access these inner dimensions, yet the availability to the experience was quite common. As the ego grew, the priests found themselves enjoying their status. They enjoyed privilege and rank. While all truly had access to Source, the pathway did require support and practice. The priests became the gatekeepers and allowed those who longed for such connectivity and travel to become their clients or students. The masses had delegated much of their spiritual responsibility to the temple priests who enjoyed spiritual connection and power.[14]

Everyone would visit the temples for popular ceremony days, which corresponded for the most part with astrological alignments. The ceremony days became very important to the masses for these events offered profound connection, peace, rejuvenation and celebration. All were accepted. All enjoyed! There was music, and energetic upliftment. These celebrations offered the opportunity to remember the Source of all creation, thus the ceremonies became universally sacred and important markers of the progression of days. The people knew they needed spiritual connection and they relied on their temples for this essential nourishment

The Kingdoms of Su'Laria were separate political structures governed by the royal families, who controlled the politics, administered the building and social infrastructures, and indeed had small forces to assist them when force seemed necessary. For the most part force was a threat, not a reality, for the people had great respect for those in power. Initially the Kings were most benevolent rulers, true servants of the people offering guidance and wisdom.

The Kingdoms were unified by the temples. These temples were a unifying conduit that reached all the separate Kingdoms. There is but one Source and therefore there was but one religion, if it could be called that. Religion is an Earth term describing a belief structure and system of connection to the Divine. The Su'Larians were not as separated from God as Earth people are now. Thus, in Su'Laria religion did not exist – the people had an innate sense of cooperation and guidance, thus moral prescriptions were not conceivable. What could be construed as a moral code existed in the spiritual practices by means of spiritual healing and ministering to the wholeness of all beings. All this was governed by the temple.

There was little affliction and degeneration and generally the doctoring was limited to accidents and injuries. Specially trained priests or priestesses would minister healing treatments and tissue regeneration to those in need. The healing technique of tissue regeneration was commonplace and indeed all medical assistance came without charge. People simply donated expressions of gratitude to the Temple for these ministrations.

The Su'Larian body vessel was tall and slender compared to our current form. These bodies were characterized by longer heads, arms and hands than we are accustomed to on Earth. The image of a tall slender alien popularized by Hollywood movies carries some of this knowing. Some of the Egyptian rulers on earth who carried the Su'Larian genes, such as Akhenaton and Nefertiti[15] offer a powerful resemblance to the Su'Larian forms. *(By now you may be sensing or feeling a familiarity with Su'Laria and Ancient Egypt.)*

Su'Larian bodies had a circulatory system, nervous system, reproductive and immune systems similar to our Earth vessels. What was strikingly different was the respiratory system and the digestive system. The bodies were designed to be fully sustained by Light, and the skin was the primary organ of respiration. There were no lungs per se – the oxygen in the air was simply absorbed through the skin and through the drinking of highly energized and crystalline water.

Sound was generated without the need to pass air through a set of vocal chords. Instead the sound was brought forth simply by vibrating certain tissues rapidly to create an external movement. Everyone was born with telepathic ability and most retained the use of responsible telepathy among their family and loved ones. However, telepathic ability opened the door to observation and as the ego developed over the centuries, there was a decline in respect for others. Thus, telepathy was discouraged, especially in the cities.

The digestive system did consist of a mouth opening, however, it did not empty into a stomach. Instead liquids were rapidly absorbed by holding them in the back of the mouth. Thus, the diet of the Su'Larians consisted of energy from the sun and nutrients suspended in liquids that were sipped. There was no need for an excretory system as the minute amount of unneeded materials were simply evaporated through the skin. Sickness or disease as we experience them now did not exist because of this and the consciousness at the time.

Each Su'Larian was offered complete memory of how to materialize required nutrients through focus and manifestation. They simply brought forth those elements into the material plane and had them suspended in a cup of water, which they sipped. Most of their nutritional requirements came through exposure to the sun, to pure lumens. This was enhanced via sun gazing, a form of direct communion with the Source energy. For the priests and priestesses, sun gazing and light absorption were sufficient to maintain the body. The absorption of nutrients through drinking was more crude, yet offered the ability to minister to those who had forgotten how to properly direct the elementals. Over time, elixirs were designed to offer modifications of consciousness and sensation for health and recreational experiences.

The Ego is Birthed

The physical body required some intelligence and oversight to keep it safe in its interactions in a physical world. Consciousness refracted an aspect of itself to manage interactions with the external world. Thus a portion of consciousness was given the attribute and authority to interface with the body. This portion of consciousness evolved into what we refer to today as the ego. The ego was originally intended simply to provide for a safe movement and interaction with external objects and environments.

Over time as the consciousness of the Su'Larians became invested with enthusiasm in the external world, the ego had more and more to manage. That is, in the pre-occupation with the external world the ego was given more power and subsequently began to involve itself with the inner world as well. This began to effect separations and refractions in the inner world as well as the outer world. The ego sought to manage the emotions and the thoughts of the individual psyche. After all, they were all inter-related.

This enthusiasm for dominance resulted in the ego becoming involved with intangible energies and qualities of consciousness. Being a self-preserving energy, the ego loved the concept of hierarchy as it gave an opportunity to receive esteem and energy from others through their attention. This amplified its sense of importance. The ego employed the service of the mind, thus manipulating complexity, generating protocols and thereby assuring its importance in the consciousness of the individual.

The preoccupation of the ego with the external world grew in its magnitude and indeed in its appreciation of the magnificence of the external world. It became a playground for Spirit and an opportunity to refract light in new ways that had never before been experienced: Beautiful buildings, expressive art, sound experiences and vast infrastructures - the enticement of the material playground was compelling as an opportunity for Divine exploration. The side effect of this was that the ego-aspect grew ever more important as the need to map each externalization grew in priority.

There was not ever a true form of exchange (money) on Su'Laria. The trappings of power and wealth were displayed through the creation of material things. These things were generated by the persons who labored in service to the wealthy. For those who served out of a celebration of the Divine in action and form, their contributions were offered without attachment.

Those who served with a higher functioning ego did so in the hopes of receiving a personal favor, privilege, status or service in return. These people sought a greater measure of compensation for their energy and thus over time they cultivated a judgment of fairness and worthiness. Thus the energies of greed and jealousy were birthed by the ego self. These energies became widespread in the last centuries of Su'Laria.

Being an externally oriented aspect, the ego-self became ever more separated from the Divine identity and a strong outer persona developed in people to govern their interactions with others. The ego grew more demanding over time. To feel special, the ego wanted esteem, for to be esteemed was to receive vital energy from others. However, with the dependency upon the external now widespread, esteem translated into the accumulation of material objects, and the accumulation of wealth and power.

Wealth offered great opportunities to manipulate and exploit the outer forms of experience. By controlling technology some were given power and esteem, especially as society became more dependent upon it. Those who had specialized abilities to control machines were esteemed. This led to another development during Su'Laria...War!

On Earth, our children often engage in imaginary schoolyard battles filled with heroes and villains, robots and spaceships, wizards and princesses, magical powers and weapons. Children express the energies of competition and creativity and act out the desire to dominate, subjugate and liberate. Some forms of these conflict games include wise rulers, benevolent wizards and reformed villains. They all act out emotions and themes we have seen in our world in more intense expressions. Perhaps these children's games are acting out deep subconscious memories from Su'Laria. Perhaps the conflicts expressed on Earth have their source in a prior wound.

On Su'Laria, as the ego developed and people became more filled with themselves, more arrogant, war games developed. The Kings engaged their armies to fight their opponents, only these battles were held outside the planet's atmosphere. The wars were expressed in the playground of outer space using huge airships and advanced technologies. Lifting above the atmosphere neutralized the disruptive effects of the wars on the people and the planet below. Out of mutual respect for the stability of the home world, all battles were kept off planet as the risk of disrupting the delicate synergies of Su'Laria was too great to risk deploying weapons of any type on the planet's surface.

Wealth meant a King had large numbers of ships, laser weapons and servants indentured to support his wishes. This army would be deployed and the battles played out in space sparing the planet from any physical destruction. These wars were stimulated by controversy over law, rule and dominion. The wars expressed the struggle over who would rule whom and who had dominion over what. The loser in a battle would have lost people and wealth, thus their power was weakened.

At first these battles were like poker games among the wealthy. Over time, the energies of pride demanded greater victories and the wars became more than just games. The conflicts played out in the sky and the battles were viewed from Su'Laria and often orchestrated from the ground. Telepathic and light-based communications, (often based upon the energy of the King's priests or priestesses), made intimate interaction possible across great distance and led to techno-athletic confrontations.

The Tu'Layan Rebellion

This energy of confrontation was indeed birthed from Tu'Laya where a great split resulted from the end-times of that expression. One faction of this split wanted to continue exploring the expansion of Light into density. The other faction wanted the traveling into density to end and would not risk having Consciousness further contaminated by discord of density. Thus, the confrontation energy was seeded into the DNA for reconciliation.

Ironically, in their commitment to prevent further expansion into density, this one faction generated even deeper discord through their efforts to impede the Travelers! This faction refracted further from Source in their preoccupation with, in essence, trying to control the Travelers.

Though their actions were birthed from an intent to honor the purity of Source, they themselves became density focused and thrived on the energy of manipulation as they sought to restrain the expansion of Light into density. When it became obvious that the expansion could not be restrained, they focused their actions upon preventing re-union. By preventing reunion with Source they would protect Consciousness from density contamination. What they did not understand was that in their effort to restrain the Travelers, they themselves became density-bound and similarly addicted to energy, power and manipulation as these were the vehicles of density intervention. This group of beings eventually became known as the Illuminati.

The other faction from the split of Tu'Laya, the Travelers, took form in Su'Laria and generation by generation began to lose their conscious connection to Source as described earlier. The Illuminati welcomed this amnesia for it meant that the Travelers might lose their way back to Source. This confrontation energy continued in the collective consciousness of the Travelers, and while the Illuminati did not take form in Su'Laria, their energetic legacy continued. The Su'Larians split into several factions, each led by a King and these factions eventually warred against each other.

The Creation of the Hybrids

A powerful development during Su'Laria was the creation of the Hybrids. They were intentionally created as a sub-species whose sole purpose was to work for the non-Hybrid Su'Larians. They were not in fact a species or a clone as we understand that word today. These beings were engineered to be physically strong and far less self-aware than the Su'Larians. They were essentially a DNA manipulation born from a laboratory.

As a laboratory creation they were not spawned from love; they were not infused with light or the DNA of Divine Source. They were created by Su'Larian scientists with co-operating priests, using fractured DNA in order to give them some basic qualities of life, and they were thus soul-less. Even the birds and sea creatures carried Light and Divine communion. These Hybrid beings were separated from the Joy of any Source connection by design.

This extensive manipulation by the priests of Su'Laria had truly established the ego and technology of the time as a false god. The creation of this race of beings was indeed a great moment that would dramatically turn the tide of harmony, for all else within the Universe of Creation was God-connected. It was and had all-ways been this God connection that assured harmony and Light was innate in its fabric. Not so with the Hybrids.

Like all technological breakthroughs, the Hybrids were initially available only to serve the wealthy and powerful members of society. Over time, the production of these living beings expanded as they were able to reproduce. The Hybrids were childlike, loyal and easily frightened. They were governed solely by physical needs and emotional manipulation. Bred with strong bodies, they performed all sorts of menial tasks, thus offering even more leisure time to their owners. The use of these laborers was widespread, and yet there were large groups of Su'Larians who were not comfortable with this distortion.

The heavens were shocked by this act of free will. For man had now taken on the role of God, as life-giver; only these created lives were disconnected from Source. They did not have the Light filled DNA that guaranteed Divine connection. They did not have an innate understanding of Spirit and were disconnected from the Love and support offered to all other living beings. For all Life was of the Divine...except for these. The Su'Larians had created a life form that could breed and perpetuate, however, the Light energy these beings carried was a tiny refraction that was disconnected from the Divine.

Su'Laria rapidly became a culture of convenience. Most everyone wanted to have a Hybrid servant family to attend to them. The concept that one person could have dominion over another was birthed on Su'Laria. This energy of domination and egoic dominion marked the beginning of the end of the planet's existence.

The Illuminati supported the wars. They saw that this conflict could potentially end the density experiment. The Kings attempted to use the Hybrids to man their airships and wage their wars, but this approach did not work, for no matter how hard their engineers tried the Hybrids could not function with any form of decision making capability once they disconnected from the planet's soil. The energy of the planet gave the Hybrids their intelligence and memory. The very fabric of their tissues was created from planetary minerals, and once they went outside the planet's energy field, they became confused and disoriented.

The DNA of the Su'Larians was cosmic in origin and connected to Light. Even though the Su'Larians were now acting out a painfully disconnected theme, they still carried the Creator's energy. They were Divine Light, spirit in form, and had the opportunity for divine communion and reunion encoded in their very being. The Hybrids were not blessed in this way. They were created of the planet's essence with only a tiny piece of refracted light energy. In their arrogance, the Su'Larians had not realized that their fate had become tied to the Hybrids.

Pause - Breathe - Allow

Claudia's Story

It took me a while to integrate what I just read... As I sat down in my office chair I felt as if I had just crossed the boundaries of linear time and space, and that I was being joined by Sri Ram Kaa and Kira Raa as these chapters unfolded.

The transmission of energy that I felt was so powerful, that it invoked within my heart a sense of recognition beyond words. Many tears came, accompanied by a feeling of joy that the Divine Plan has been unfolding perfectly.

Then and Now.... Now and Then.

As I was able to remember the moments and developments in the distant time of Su'Laria, I was vividly aware that many will be able to remember this as well. The authentic remembrance of pure Love and Light is truly encoded within us all.

Reading these chapters over and over also brought me to a deep place within myself that asks for my own recognition of my role in the world today, and to be able to contain the energy of love, compassion and healing for myself and others intact and ever present in my heart. To feel in every cell of my being that I am an instrument of peace and that this peace truly begins within.

My heart feels gratitude for Kira Raa and Sri Ram Kaa for fulfilling their Divine Mission and assisting humanity in its magnificent awakening one more time! Through this recognition, I gained the deep knowing that we are all fulfilling our Divine Mission and each is assisting humanity in perfection and love.

Chapter Five

Awakening from the Trance

As I watched the curved and ceremonially decorated knife of pure gold come toward my heart, my eyes were locked with his. My only emotion was pure love. I do not know how many were gathered to watch this sacrifice that had been sanctioned by all of the Kings, and ultimately endorsed by King Theraphys, the War Keeper.

Sacrifice was a concept that was rarely exercised, and yet, here I was, THE sacrifice.

There were no restraints on my hands or feet. I laid on the crystalline slab without fear, the fullness of my life's purpose on Su'Laria unfolding in this moment. From this sacrificial slab I was setting in motion the events that would bring forth completion in the next cycle of light. In that moment, with the knife in his hand, and his eyes filled with righteousness, as he thrust the dagger through my heart stopping my life force, he was unaware of the events that were now set in motion, and the certain destruction that faced all Su'Larians in the very near future.

Growing up among the crystalline cliffs was a stunning adventure in communion. Waking up to the sound of the waves against the multi-hued crystals, and hearing the luring calls of my many bird-like friends offered great joy each morning. My early life was a picturesque and storybook-like adventure. Bound to the small secluded island I was born on until the time of my wedding, all of my interactions were consistently loving and filled with ceremony and story. Rarely did I interface with men, and when I did, it was usually from the perspective of a curious child peeking through the gossamer curtains hanging between rooms. Usually the interchange between these powerful visiting creatures known as men with my mother and guardians left me feeling timid, shy and filled with wonder.

From a very early age I knew that I would marry *him*, the one whom all the Kings listened to and sought advice from. It was he that King Theraphys, the War Keeper, and most influential of all the Kings of Su'Laria would seek confirmation from prior to any action.

I often wondered why I was forbidden to know who my father was, and would ask my mother for answers about him. My mother would often remind me: "Your purpose for being is to fully awaken all the mystical channels within. You were created to serve the Light. Always know that your greatest gift is love. With this knowing, you will assist all with their Divine knowing. Your father is one who also knows this. When you marry, all will be revealed and all is in Divine Order." Then she would smile in a way that all-ways brought me comfort, yet was filled with a sadness I did not understand.

"I will not ever forget Mother," I would answer, and yet the loneliness of the life ahead often brought me to depths of sadness that I found confusing.

He was mythical to me, larger than life, yet he was very real. Like all Su'Larians he was very tall, with perfectly chiseled features. Hair was always long if you had status in the world of the Kings, and he did. His was the color of gold, which perfectly matched his eyes. He would always be seen in public wearing the "adornments of wisdom" as a crown around his head and as a beaded strand of multi-colored crystals at his waist where his hair met the strand and seemed to take on the colors of all the crystals. He seemed to command the crystals, and their energies. There was a confidence that comes from an inner sense of knowing that he carried so powerfully that often one could easily forget that he was mortal, as we all were.

Much older than I was chronologically, he was not to formally marry until I was of age, and for me that age was fourteen. While he was not to marry until I was of age, he was free to surround himself with many willing consorts of the time. This was a painful truth I would not discover until I was 16 and pregnant with his son.

All I ever knew was preparation for this holy marriage. I was raised to be more of an observer of Su'Larian life than a participant. From birth, my mystical sensitivities were encouraged and fine tuned. I spent hours in the temples alongside my sisters and the other sacred initiates. There was more than one time during those hours that I would fantasize about the lives of those in the city of the mainland where King Theraphys resided. More times than not I was often alone with the Blue Starborn, frequent visitors to Su'Laria, and my closest friends. Their loving guidance consistently reassured me in any time of doubt.

Through my rigorous training and complete recall of my soul evolution I had a deep understanding of the many gifts that were empowered to Su'Laria. This time in the history of the expansion of light was very tangible in all aspects of form expression, (a visceral difference from Tu'Laya), and critical to the future of all. Within my soul there was deep recognition that nothing should be taken for granted. My heart was filled with divine love for all expressions of light and for the man I was bound to marry. From my naïveté I saw him as completely infallible and for me he was the most powerful man in Su'Laria, even more so than King Theraphys, and many felt the same way.

Each time the great ceremonies were held on the island, I would watch him mystically weave the Alchemical transformations of energy into great vessels of light filled with illumination. He would lovingly and with great reverence weave these energies into fields of golden and crystalline vortexes that would uplift DNA, create matter, and open direct communication with those of the many worlds beyond ours. The Blue Starborn were always present. Even the Kings, (several were usually present at one time), would bow to the love entrenched energies and open their hearts to receive the gifts they offered.

During these ceremonies I heard many whisper to each other words that I would one day understand: "The sacred vessels are still not full, for the codes can only be held by the sacred partner." I did not understand that I was the holder of these codes, what the vessels stood for, or why there were always 2 groups of 12 plus one in the middle; soon I would, as my fourteenth birthday was upon me.

My wedding day was beyond description. My mother dressed me in the gown of adornment which was made of white crystalline fabric with gold and violet threads stranded through it. The simple wrap style gown with long flowing sleeves was comfortable and elegant. My deep auburn hair had now grown below my waist and was lightly tied back with a ribbon of colored crystals. When I gazed upon myself prior to leaving my island home forever, the deep violet eyes that greeted me in the mirror seemed foreign and transformed, yet the large blue crystal affixed to the center of my forehead reminded me that the Blue Starborn were in support of this marriage. I thanked them for the gift that I was wearing, and was curious about the activation of the blue crystal that would shortly take place at the marriage ceremony.

Arriving at the mainland and the City of King Theraphys was an overwhelming sight. Large crystalline buildings and technological structures were everywhere. The cliffs of the shoreline were barely noticeable due to the congestion. It was stunningly beautiful, yet in a very different way than the island I had known as home. There were crowds of people…so many people…I knew that they all existed, and had often experienced them telepathically, yet it was intimidating to be in their physical energy. I was beginning to understand why my training had been so extensive, focused, and reclusive.

The boat glided silently across the water. There were no waves and it was as if we were floating just two inches above the water's surface. It was as if the boat and the water were in communion and agreement about direction of movement. There was no separate propulsion system. As we drew near the dock I began to panic and felt myself losing consciousness from the experience. Why had I chosen to arrive by boat? Truly, it might have been easier to energetically arrive without using a manifestation of form, yet, on the boat I was, and the dock was just ahead.

Without warning, the scene before me faded away into a brilliant sphere of white light and all sound subsided as I was surrounded by twelve beings of pure light. They were benevolent and caring, asking me to simply be present with them for a moment. As I stood inside the circle they formed, the city now seemed far away as did my imminent marriage.

"Kira Raa, we bring you greetings of the Elohim. Know that we are your brethren; we shall all-ways be with you. Behold the expression of light that you are currently serving, and know that through the portals of eternal time, you are the code holder. Today, you shall receive the codes that activate the vessels of ascension. While you are in this form, they can only be activated within the confines of sacred union. Go forth with love and know that you are not alone. We are with you now and will be with you again at the time of the unfoldment."

Then, as if time had stood still, they were gone, and I was standing at the dock ready to greet my husband, my King, and my future.

Stepping onto the shores of the Great Crystalline City for the first time my hand was grasped by him. Strong, steady and confident, I felt the energy of the universe pulsing through his clasp. As I gazed into his eyes for the first time, I instantaneously recognized our eternal bond of service, love and sacred union.

"I am Sri Ram Kaa," he stated with a smile that forever captivated my heart, and the whirlwind began.

Passing through the city streets I was able to witness many people busy with the daily events that occupied all Su'Larians. Every type of being was present, and within moments I was witnessing for the first time the many vast expressions of light in form. I was particularly moved by the almost silent *Hybrids,* or "created ones," that were present. There was an overwhelming energy within me to offer them the codes, yet this was not the moment to focus upon them. It was an amazing experience to actually see all of the beings present with physical eyes instead of telepathic intuition.

Arriving at the Crystalline Temple compound on the far shore of the city, I once again felt a sense of safety almost as if I was back on my beloved island. The shoreline offered me a view of the Crystalline cliffs that I found most comforting, the water was sparkling, and the essence of the Temple truly intoxicating.

My sisters were already assembled as was my mother, King Theraphys, and his most extended family and entourage. There were also many neighboring Kings and their families, along with Sri Ram Kaa's entire lineage of priests, initiates, and DNA workers. To my delight, the Blue Starborn were present in great numbers and my heart raced with excitement. The moment had finally arrived!

Standing in the center of the Great Hall inside the Temple, Sri Ram Kaa and I faced each other and joined hands as I felt a pulsing warm energy throughout my entire being. Within moments a great portal of white light opened around us and I experienced the large blue jewel on my forehead become hotter and hotter. A glowing ray of light began to emanate from the center of the jewel gifted to me by the Blue Starborn and connected with the center of Sri Ram Kaa's forehead.

This beautiful ray offered us the ability to deeply communicate and within this vast universal connection we instantaneously shared lifetimes of knowing and recognition. The white portal around us was now filling with golden light and an emerald spiral of infinite love emanated from both of our hearts. Our individual Divine Galactic Blueprints[16] were fully illuminated and spinning with the recognition of Sacred Union. Smiling brilliantly and with a momentary glance into each others eyes, our light bodies were now high above the Temple, and the Blue Starborn were present to offer us the first series of codes.

After the codes were received, we entered into the Divine Galactic Blueprint of Sacred Union and returned to our Su'Larian body selves that were present in the center of the Temple. The nourishing white portal closed around us and became forever a part of our DNA, a great gift from the Elohim that would forever offer us Divine recognition of each other. The emerald spirals united and the ceremony was complete.

Smiling as I took my first breath as the wife of Sri Ram Kaa, I couldn't help but notice the look on the face of my eldest sister who was standing behind him. She seemed angry, upset and dismissive. I registered the look and took it upon myself not to look deeper into her energy field.

The celebrations went on for hours with conversations and congratulations from many. There was an excitement in the air for many knew that our union would bring new energetic gifts to all Su'Larians. Finally, Sri Ram Kaa took me to my new home near the Temple Complex.

Life in the Temple Complex was not much different than my life had been on the island. I spent my days busily offering healings and services of love to all who came and asked. My nights were occupied with teaching the initiates and attending to my own needs. Sri Ram Kaa was usually busy with his teachings, healings and ceremonies, and we often conducted the ceremonies of the codes together. The first two years passed quickly, and soon my role would expand to include being a mother, for I was now with child. I felt greatly prepared and honored.

Knowing that I would have a son brought great joy to my heart. When I rushed to Sri Ram Kaa's chambers without prearrangements to bring him the news, my heart was ripped open with pain. My youth and ignorance had not ever considered that he was enjoying other women, and to find him with my oldest sister was even more hurtful. My training did not prepare me for this moment, and I left the room without a word.

Hours later, when Sri Ram Kaa came to ask me why I had come to see him, I simply shared the news without emotion. He was pleased that the son he expected through our union was to be born. He also informed me that I must accept my role in the Su'Larian mystical world, and that I must also accept his and all of the privileges afforded him. It was the most difficult acceptance that I ever confronted, yet offered to me the gift to go ever deeper into my service to Su'Laria.

12 years pass...

Living a life of Divine Love and service brings with it many joyous interactions. There had been the birth of my son, Argus, the adoption of my daughter, Alashea, and the celebrations of many initiates into full priestesses. The interactions with the thousands who had come for healing and spiritual assistance filled all of my waking hours. Most importantly, I had begun working with the Hybrids to initiate the DNA of light within them. Yes, there were many wonderful interactions. I had grown into the loving and empowered wife of the High Priest and was adept at the Codes of Ascension which I lovingly shared often during the sacred ceremonies.

The sacred ceremonies were the primary reason for my marriage to Sri Ram Kaa. As the holder of the Codes bestowed by the Blue Starborn at our wedding, it was a great gift to share this love and light for the benefit of all. Together, we would bring forth the sacred symbols and connect through all space and time with Divine source. This beloved gift offered the opportunity for deep conscious connection.

For me, the creation of the Hybrids was a puzzle. I could not understand why any Su'Larian would feel it not necessary to be fully self-responsible. Growing up on the island I had not ever interfaced with a Hybrid, nor did I understand the need for their creation. This was a constant source of agitation for Sri Ram Kaa as he would insist that I was simply too young in my understanding and that the creation of Hybrids was one of Su'Laria's greatest accomplishments.

While I certainly understood that the creation of any being from manipulated DNA was a great technological accomplishment, for me it felt out of balance.

It was during my many long days spent within the healing chambers that many started to share with me their desire to "heal" the Hybrids. At first I was astounded that they would whisper this to me and ask me to not reveal their requests. Then I realized that to begin healing the Hybrids would have great social and political ramifications, so I went deep within my own being-ness and brought this great request directly to Divine Light.

I never felt that I was doing anything without Sri Ram Kaa's knowing as the only way I could receive my answer about the Hybrids was during our sacred ceremony. The answer was received with great clarity, and it never occurred to me that my request had been shielded from Sri Ram Kaa. All beings are to be able to receive love and light, and my soul's purpose was to offer this gift to all, without exclusion.

For years I met with all who desired to offer to the Hybrids the gifts of Love and Light. We would meet together with my eldest sister, my children, and the many who were now beginning to grow in love. It was a wonderful gift to see the light of the Divine rise within the eyes of those who had been without it. While this ceremony was not ever announced publicly, for me it never felt as if I had been doing anything harmful. How could love and light be harmful to anyone?

I was most surprised, given all the joy in my life, when Sri Ram Kaa became increasingly demanding and indifferent toward me and our children. Though he had many other children Argus was his direct lineage bearer and I found this especially puzzling.

As we did on most nights, Argus, Alashea and I, would walk along the cliffs at the shore of the crystalline sea after one of our Hybrid ceremonies. Together, hand in hand, we would walk and share the energy of love and laughter. Often we would be joined by the Blue Starborn and simply sit in the stillness of Divine knowing-ness. Tonight felt just like the others…or so I thought.

When we returned from our sojourn, Sri Ram Kaa asked to see me immediately. There was an edge in his voice that I did not understand, nor had I experienced it before. As I followed him into his private chambers, waiting in his room was my eldest sister and two of her initiates.

"Greetings dearest ones," I smiled and walked in.

They all simply nodded and my sister glanced at me with a look of knowing on her face that felt malicious.

"You are to teach them the mudras for the codes immediately!" Sri Ram Kaa demanded.

"Dearest one, you know that I cannot do that!" I responded, shocked at his request.

"I am the High Priest of Su'Laria. I have created life, and I manage the ceremonies. As healer, I have the right to nullify the Blue Starborn and Elohim requests. After all, I have empowered the DNA of life and often create the vessels of light and portals of ascension. Since you are my wife, I can insist that you teach your sister and her initiates the code sequences." He stared at me with eyes that reflected one who was consumed with his own power.

Seeing his obvious imbalance gave me the courage and fortitude to recognize that my life had been prepared for this moment, and once again I refused to honor his request.

My sister was outraged and left the room quickly with her initiates. As she brushed by my shoulder she whispered to me on the way out, "You'll be sorry you said no! I am the one who should be the wife of the High Priest and your denial will open that door for me!"

Stunned by her comments I turned to face Sri Ram Kaa. "What is all this about?" I asked.

"I am the High Priest of Su'Laria and no longer require our Sacred Union to access the Codes of Ascension for the vessels. It is my right to have you give them to anyone I ask," he responded in a raised voice and with a tone of indifference that emanated an energy field from him I had not experienced before.

I immediately knew by the telepathic stream emanating from his field and unprotected by his anger that my sister had spoken to him about my work with the Hybrids. I felt it best to simply note what I was observing without speaking about it. It was now evident that they wanted the codes to begin the reversal of the work that had been done with the Hybrids and to support the current escalating war of King Theraphys. If the codes were manipulated it would assist the Hybrids as warriors. I knew I must remain firm.

"You know that the codes are not able to be simply taught. They must be bestowed and then accepted by one with the recognition of love and Divine service. What you ask of me I will not do, and I pray you will reconsider your request."

"If you do not honor what I ask, then I have no choice but to initiate a request to perform the ceremony of Soul Retraction between us," he asserted with great power.

Stunned by even the mention of this forbidden practice, and without regret for my actions taken on behalf of the Hybrids, I did not waiver. "Do what you must."

I left his chambers to find Argus standing outside the door. He had heard everything and was in a state of shock. Angry, he wanted to storm into his father's chambers and demand an explanation. I assured him this was not the time, and through my years of training and preparation, I was already aware of the events that were now in motion.

Back in my chambers, still recuperating from the unbelievable conversation that had just taken place, I was glancing out my window at the beautiful night when I noticed Sri Ram Kaa leaving the Temple compound. I knew he was on his way to meet with King Theraphys, and that my fate was already sealed. In that moment, the only pain I felt was for Argus and Alashea. Would this be my last night in Su'Laria? Could he possibly follow through with convincing King Theraphys to allow a Soul Retraction? Only the morning would tell.

I awoke to the sound of Argus frantically calling my name. He was visibly upset and begging me to get dressed in a hurry.

"They are coming! Please, let's leave and go to the island of your birth! Please!" He was begging as he was pulling at me to get up.

"Argus. I am unable to return to the island, you know that. Let me get dressed in peace and we will talk then," I answered doing my best to calm my young son.

"You don't understand, I heard them talking this morning. They are coming, and I won't get to see you again. Please don't…"

I interrupted him. "Argus, we are all children of the Divine light. Regardless of what happens here in Su'Laria we will see each other again and again. We are forever bound in the great love of oneness, and the love I hold for you will always find you. Have no fear, my love. I am aware of the possibilities before me."

Argus collapsed into my arms sobbing, and I finally got dressed. As we hugged each other again, the doors of my chamber opened and in stepped two of King Theraphys's most loyal guards. They demanded that I go with them.

As I bid farewell to Argus, my heart was heavy, and yet my soul was filled with the recognition that a greater service was in motion. I extended my energy field and asked him to trust that knowing telepathically. I received his response and it was embodied with loving understanding. I felt complete with him in that moment, and knew he would be safe with Alashea.

Following the guards, it became obvious that Sri Ram Kaa had been successful in his plea to King Theraphys that a Soul Retraction was necessary. After all, he was the most powerful King in Su'Laria, and many a war had been won on his behalf due to the intervention and alignments brought forth from Sri Ram Kaa. I knew I must trust the universal plan, yet I was in fear of the pain I would be asked to endure.

Arriving at the King's compound I was placed in a small round room with two small windows. There was a small sitting area with lovely chairs and abundant food laid out on a small adorned table. It was comfortable enough, yet very isolated. So there I sat...and sat...and sat.

Vicki's Story

One of the greatest blessings of my life happened in 2005! I was looking through some spiritual publications, and noticed Kira Raa and Sri Ram Kaa, thinking that they looked like an interesting couple. I immediately heard the angels ask me to meet them, and they would be at a Los Angeles expo the following weekend!

As I walked into the lobby of the event, Kira Raa and Sri Ram Kaa were standing there talking, looking larger than life. I approached them and when it was my turn to talk, I shared with them that the angels asked me to meet them but I did not know why. Kira Raa and Sri Ram Kaa honored me for following my guidance and did not offer me an explanation.

I thought to myself, "Okay, this is great, but why am I here?" Suddenly, I felt an overwhelming desire to hug Kira Raa. Having just met her, I felt uncomfortable vocalizing my desire. As if Kira was reading my mind, she said, "May I hug you?" I joyfully and excitedly responded with a "Yes!"

We embraced each other in a beautiful heart hug, and there seemed to be a synchronicity in our breath...of breathing as one. My heart softened and I began to experience intense emotional feelings of missing a beloved. I cried uncontrollably. It felt like a deep pain that was being released. I remember Kira comforting me with her embrace and loving words. She encouraged me to take some deep breaths to come back to my center. I looked at her with my eyes wide open, like a five year old child in love with their kindergarten teacher.

She softly and lovingly looked into my eyes and said, "Will you be joining us for the Violet Ray course in New Mexico?" I said,

"Yes!" Although, I did not know what that was, or how I would get to New Mexico. I just knew that I had to see her again.

We exchanged our final goodbyes and as I turned to walk away, I heard the angels say, "She is your mother from Su'Laria." I thought, "My God, no wonder I was crying. I have been missing my mom... and now I have found her!"

Kira Raa with Alashea (Vicki), her Su'Larian daughter

Chapter Six

Cosmic Re-Connections

Seated in the round room, and moving deep into mystic meditative communion, the time passed quickly. I do not know exactly how long I sat there, except that the light of day was dimming. As I noticed the dimming light through the two small windows, the room became brighter and brighter. The walls seemed to melt away and within moments I was surrounded by twelve Beings of bright light.

My heart jumped with joy for I recognized them immediately as the same beings that had visited me when I first came to the city on my wedding day. Here they were again, only this time they were brighter and seemed to have more form. I felt a warmth wash over my body, and my energy field was clear and radiant.

Beloved one, we bring you greetings of the Elohim. It is the time of the unfoldment and we are here to assist you to remember the purpose of your time in Su'Laria. From here you will be going on to a world which will have an abundance of free will. Everything we are about to share with you is to prepare you for the greater journey ahead. You will still have the choice as to how you proceed, and it is with loving respect that we share with you now.

As They assembled into a circle around me, every cell of my being knew that I had been born for this very moment and I was humbled and honored to simply be in Their presence.

You find yourself here because you have held sacred the Codes of Ascension and have honored the Elohim in your unwavering service to Divine Light. Your love and devotion to all beings is one of great surrender and humility. Remember that the codes are not unique to you - they are simply protected within you. All beings are able to access and utilize the codes when they are in Sacred Union. You must first recognize that Sacred Union always begins with the Divine Creator of Love. This is the Sacred Union that activates the Codes. Here, in Su'Laria, it was designed that you would hold the Codes as part of a team of masculine and feminine energy. This was intentionally designed to prevent the misuse of the Codes, as was asked of you last night.

I listened with great intensity, and was beginning to understand. They continued.

When the Light divided itself at the close of Tu'Laya, and expanded into the expression of form that is here on Su'Laria, the Codes of Ascension, or re-connection, were put in place as a Divine Roadmap. What this means is that each being was offered the gift of accepting or rejecting how and when they would find their way back to Source. This was the establishment of Free Will. The fullness of Free Will is yet to be explored, and will be brought to its full potential in the third expansion of light that is soon to begin.

I had to ask, "If this third expansion is soon to begin, then what of Su'Laria?"

In unison they responded: *Su'Laria has chosen to come to a close. This is why we are here sharing with you, for you still have service to do. Shortly, you will be offered the opportunity to leave this room and return to the island of your birth to live out your life in personal service to King Theraphys. If you refuse this choice, he will approve the Soul Retraction ceremony to be performed by Sri Ram Kaa.*

My heart was heavy and yet there was a knowing and acceptance as if this had all been predestined.

They responded as if they had heard my reaction.

Yes, Kira Raa, this is part of your destiny. Tonight you must make the choice of life in this form now, or the opportunity to continue expansion of light and to be of ever greater service during the next expansion of light into density. For it is this third expansion, the expanded Free Will experience, that will generate the greatest light and create the darkest dark.

As much as I thought I understood, I was confused. "Please help me understand more."

If you choose to continue on, then you will offer the gift of the Codes to all those who are ready to claim their own Divine Light heritage. We will assist you to do this at the Temple this evening if you so choose. However, let us share more about the third expansion of density that is beginning.

At that moment, they stopped speaking in unison, and one by one they came forward to share with me the energy they each represented and how that would express in the coming experience of the expansion of light.

As the first Being of Light began to share, my heart was overwhelmed with love and compassion.

My dearest one, I bid you greetings of love and wish for you to know that you will have many lives in this next expression of light on a planet that you can see from Su'Laria. During this time you will come to know this planet as Gaia, and your lives will all be spent offering the service of loving remembrance to all you come into contact with. Each lifetime will be spent carrying the seeds of the Blue Starborn into the DNA of the Earthborn so that the universal Codes of Ascension will be readily retrieved at the time of the next culmination. Through the intentional manipulation of DNA, along with the headstrong technological misuse that has occurred here in Su'Laria, the entire surface of this existence will soon experience a self-created disaster that will eliminate all traces of this civilization for millions of cycles to come.

I was stunned by this information. "When will this happen?"

Should you choose to endure the Soul Retraction, within two weeks time all life on Su'Laria will no longer be and thus the next cycle will have begun.

This was more information than I felt I was able to receive.

Hearing my thoughts again, the Being of Light spoke: *Let us continue. There will be many civilizations that will be seeded on this new planet that will have the original genetic encoding from both Tu'Laya and Su'Laria. These civilizations will have the opportunity to once again flourish and grow*[17]. *You will have three specific lifetimes that will assist with the Codes and secure the lineage of the Divine universal being. The first will be in the times that will be come to be known as Ancient Egypt. You will be the mother of a great Starborn Queen who will marry the last of the Starborn Pharoah's*[18] *in an effort to assist the light to gain a greater position in a world that will already be experiencing the forces of dark energy. Many will deny who you are and your name will be stricken from many records, yet the energy will be successfully entrenched.*

At this point another Being came forward and began speaking:

Greetings dearest one. I bring you greetings from those who many will call prophets and visionaries. Many will come to call us masters, and we will continuously offer the new planet love, compassion and benevolence. You will be asked to be a mother many times, and there will be times when the mother energy you will carry is for all of the world, not just the children you may bear. This will be especially prevalent in a country that many will know as India. You will spend most of your lifetimes there in preparation for the culmination time of the planet Earth. Your lifetimes in India will culminate in a brief yet profound lifetime when you will be in full remembrance of all that has been and all that will be. The world will not yet be ready for the information you remember and you will find yourself spending many days without speaking. Millions will call you Ma, and you will be filled with the Codes of Ascension. Again, your name will be virtually unknown, yet many will receive the love of your service and awaken because of their interactions with you.

With tears streaming down my face, I was almost unable to endure any more information when yet another loving Being came forward.

Beloved Kira Raa, I am the energy stream that is the brethren of Sri Ram Kaa. Within the violet energy that we carry there will be many masters brought to the Earth during the millions of years of expansion that are beginning now. When the time of culmination comes to Earth, there will be many signs. During your last incarnation you will be born as a female and begin to remember all during your earliest childhood years. You will be placed in a birth family to assist them to find their own Divinity and you will be separated from them by indifference. You will wander the planet in confusion for 40 years and will be offered opportunities to again affirm or deny this final task. Near the end of your 41st year, you will be reunited with Sri Ram Kaa for the purpose of Soul Cleansing for him, and Code dissemination for the world. Your Sacred Union will be restored and reconnected with the Elohim, and the sanctity of the love that the two of you will embody will heal and assist many to claim their own Sacred Union and fully restore their Divine knowing. This healing will be for you as it will be for many.

As I sat, stunned and yet inspired, the final Divine One spoke to me:

The choices before you are yours alone to make. We honor your loving service to Su'Laria and wish for you to know that during the culminating times of Gaia, many will reach out to understand what is happening around them. Many will blame what they will call Atlantis for the energy of the times. They will be in confusion about Su'Laria, and many will be deep in darkness. The light that shines within all Code Bearers will become more prevalent, and many will come forward to collectively celebrate the reunification. The culminating times of the Earth do not need to repeat the imminent destruction that awaits Su'Laria, and it will be the choice of all those who are present at that time to decide their ultimate experience. We leave you now to your choice. Know that the Codes within thee will be held by the Archangelic Realm until the culmination of the Earth cycle, at which time they will be restored to you upon your request. The Archangelic Realm will serve humanity on Earth in many ways, and will reveal themselves through their agreement with those who request their service.

At that point a Being of great light and love came forward from the center of the Light Beings that had displayed themselves as violet. This beautiful Being asked my permission to hold the Codes that had been seeded within me at my wedding, and where they would safely remain until my last lifetime of the next cycle. I agreed, and in exchange they shared a sacred symbol of recognition with me. This sacred symbol was placed in my forehead above the area many call the third eye and was referred to as my Star Consciousness. As the Codes were retrieved and lovingly received by the Being, I asked a simple question:

"How will I know you?"

With the energy of love so full that I was overwhelmed with bliss, the response was quiet and reassuring:

I will know you by your star consciousness, and you will know me by my energy and name...Zadkiel.

The small room was now dark. The light of day was gone, and I was filled with an all-powerful presence and courage knowing that my choice was already made, for I had already decided that my service was to the Light, and about that there was no hesitation.

Squinting in the darkness, the door to the small room opened and in walked King Theraphys. He was attended by three guards, and asked them all to leave us alone. Seeing him in the dim light that he carried made him even more ominous than usual. I was still in the energy of the twelve Light Beings, and his energy was decidedly different. Being in his presence at that moment caused me to feel off balance and noticeably shaky.

"I know you must be scared, and I am here to help you Kira Raa," he began.

He smiled at me and I must have visibly recoiled, for he continued: "You know that I have always loved you and that you are very important to me. This is why I have not yet answered Sri Ram Kaa's request to perform the Soul Retraction. Together we can bring great armies to the aid of all Su'Laria, and influence the Blue Starborn to assist us with ever greater technology. After all, you are Starborn, and I know who your father is."

I tried my best not to gasp at this revelation! So, this was why my mother never discussed this - I was seeded from the Blue Starborn!

"Did you know that I, too, am of the Blue Starborn?"

I simply shook my head no, as I was unable to speak and doing my best to stay outside of his ability to telepathically connect with me.

"Tonight I will bring you to your island of birth where you will be very well taken care of, and will be able to safely and quietly be of service to Su'Laria. I will visit you often, and you may bring your son, Argus, your daughter Alashea, and two initiates. It will be your sanctuary and I will protect you."

My heart was firmly resolved that this choice was not the option for me, and yet my mind was screaming for me to accept. Ultimately, remembering what the Light Beings had said earlier, I took a deep breath and responded:

"Thank you for your kindness and consideration. I request a favor from you. I would like to return to the Temple compound and see my children. I would also like to gather any who desire to share ceremony with me as tonight is the high point of the illumination energy," a fact I had not realized until that moment. "In the morning, I will offer you my response in first light. For my years of service and love of Su'Laria, I request this favor."

I could feel his hesitation and noticed his energy field extremely close to me. I focused all of my attention on love and compassion so as not to reveal that my decision had already been made.

"My guards will bring you to the compound and then escort you back to me in the morning. May your evening be fruitful." His parting smile sent a chill through me. It was obvious he knew I had already made my decision, yet his inability to confirm that choice gave me freedom for the evening, and I was grateful.

My energy field was expanding rapidly and I was eager to get to those who had already gathered at the Temple and share with them the gift of Star Consciousness. The opportunity to attend to the many who had already intuited what was transpiring would be my last act of Temple service and the first in conjunction with the Archangelic Realm.

Chapter Seven

Armageddon Again?

Approaching the Temple with the guards surrounding me, I could feel the symbol of Star Consciousness illuminating with each step I took. As my telepathic communication had confirmed, there were masses gathered at the Temple. Families, friends, neighbors and the Blue Starborn were all there. Many were walking the shores of the cliffs, silently reflecting, and even more were in small groups sharing love and appreciation for each other. Witnessing this outpouring of love was so powerful that even the guards stopped in their tracks and simply allowed me to continue to the Temple without them by my side.

Alashea was the first to come running up to me with Argus just behind her.

"My heart tells me that a great shift is at hand and that we must all prepare. Please mother tell me what is happening and ask her how we can assist."

I reached my hand out and simply stroked her beautiful, full and long golden red hair. I chose to respond with the energy of telepathy as words of any form would be inappropriate. I placed my hand on her heart, and the symbol of my Star Consciousness sent a ray of brilliant white light to her head in the same area and instantaneously a stunning symbol unique to her became visible on her forehead.

Argus simply watched and smiled with recognition.

Alashea's aquamarine eyes filled with tears of recognition and she looked fully into mine as she stated quietly, "I understand, this is how we will know each other. I will gather everyone into the Temple so that they can also make their choice."

With her short statement she had revealed the wisdom and knowing that each being could only continue in the energy of their own choice. The many Su'Larian conflicts currently on the planet would disastrously culminate within weeks, thereby closing this chapter of expansion. She understood that the next chapter had already begun, and that the expansion of light was a joyous and wonderful service.

As she and Argus ran off to begin the gathering, I was greeted by the Blue Starborn. My eyes immediately filled with tears; it was the first time in my life that as I stood beside them, I knew I was of them. Forming a five pointed star by interlocking our hands, they ignited their own area of Star Consciousness and together we linked these energies and created a living movie inside the star.

They showed me their origins. They revealed their involvement with the evolution of light into form and the creation of the worlds. They played for me the movie of my life to come during the next evolution of light on the planet to be called Gaia or Earth. During this extensive revelation they then showed me the potential outcomes of the third expression of density. I saw both the ability to create a true utopian expression of life in form, and I saw how easily this expression could be manipulated. I saw how the world would respond to all efforts to thwart dark energy, and I saw the final moments of my own life on that planet.

They then handed me twenty five golden keys and asked if I was still willing to be the holder of these given everything I had just witnessed. Within a moment I dropped to my knees filled with loving appreciation and humility and accepted this as my task. As I offered my acceptance the center of the star filled with bright white light, and again the 12 Beings of Light appeared and offered me guidance.

Once this guidance was received and understood, the 12 Beings of Light entered the Temple along with the Blue Starborn.

As I gazed around me it was as if our interaction had taken place in a fraction of a moment. Literally, time had stood still, yet I had witnessed millions of years. It was a great gift and I felt completely prepared for everything that would transpire over the next day.

Entering the Temple, the masses were assembled in a great circle. Every being who had been called intuitively to the Temple stayed and accepted the great task of being a Code Holder, and a Key Bearer for the next evolution of light. They all said yes to carrying the energy of light and each was in silent communication with their Divine presence, accepting their role for the next phase of light evolution.

Together as a community of light we were without fear, judgment, pride, or jealousy. There was the imminent understanding that we were all sparks of the same Divine presence, and that together we were choosing to love ever more.

There was only one moment of sadness. This came when the Blue Starborn shared with all of us that this next journey would be made without their direct intervention until the time of re-connection or culmination. They shared much around this, and now is not the time to reveal the details.

It was time to accept the Star Consciousness of recognition. A portal of golden white light opened within the Great Hall and illuminated with great love. Each of us felt the presence of reassurance and patience. The energy of love manifested as glorious

Beings of Light shared with us that they would come to be known as the Archangels. Then, together, each accepted the Star of Recognition suited to their Divine mission.

Morning came with the brilliant light that always greeted the crystalline coast. I kept myself secluded from everyone, even Argus and Alashea, and went out to the cliffs for what I knew would be the last time. Walking the crystalline coast with my many bird friends accompanying me. I was fully breathing in the experience of Su'Laria for the last time. I consciously called forth my many lives here and thoughtfully honored each and every being that carried forth from Tu'Laya. Regardless of how they had expressed their energy in Su'Laria, they had made the choice to continue with the love of expansion.

I focused all of my love energy toward Sri Ram Kaa, knowing what he was to do this evening, and I sent him love and appreciation for his courage to follow through. To dwell upon how he came to this point of manipulated power was of no consequence. This, too, was part of the Divine sequence, and this is the gift and the lesson I knew I had to maintain.

As I returned to the compound, King Theraphys' guards were already waiting for me. I smiled and asked for a moment to change. They were patient and courteous.

The city seemed particularly ominous to me upon arriving. I recalled the first time I had ever glimpsed it on my wedding day fourteen years ago. I had grown accustomed to its many technological wonders and the multitudes of beings who were all so busy with their expressions of form. I gave thanks for this moment, for I realized I was witnessing an expression that would not be again, for within a short time we would all be in the new cycle of expansion.

King Theraphys was waiting for me with Sri Ram Kaa by his side. No doubt after the powerful ceremony at the Temple last evening, Sri Ram Kaa had already informed him of my decision, or he would not have been waiting with him. The arrogance being exerted by them both sent disbelief through my body and also a wave of laughter.

"Do you find all this funny?" King Theraphys boomed my way and waved his hand in disgust toward me and approval to Sri Ram Kaa. "Now I see the great wisdom in Sri Ram Kaa's request to perform the Soul Retraction."

"King Theraphys," Sri Ram Kaa began, "we must complete the Soul Retraction this evening while we are still in the shadow of the energy of illumination. I request we immediately begin preparations."

King Theraphys

I was witnessing them discuss my execution and felt as if I had already left my body. The full impact of what was about to happen overwhelmed me and I must have left my body so completely that the next thing I remember is being in the same small room that I had been brought to last evening. I came back into my physical body within the silent walls of a round room.

What does one do on the day of one's own demise by the conscious hand of another? How does one pass the time? What goes through one's mind?

I cannot answer any of those questions, for the rest of the day was spent among the presence of the Light and the Blue Starborn. I did not ask them to change anything, and I did not focus on the task that would be completed within a moment. I did focus on the Divine in Action, and the love that had brought all Su'Larians to this point.

When the time came to bring me to the Soul Retraction ceremony, I was filled with so much love and compassion that I felt myself floating above the body that carried my energy, and simply witnessed with love and understanding all that was taking place around me.

There were so many gathered that I could not count how many were there. The ceremonial chamber was very large and very public, after all this is where all of the high ceremonies were performed. At the top of the very tall staircase was the crystalline disk which had a large crystalline slab placed upon it.

Standing just behind the slab was Sri Ram Kaa, King Theraphys, and my eldest sister. Behind them were several young initiates who all looked frightened and bewildered. I sent my energy field to them and asked them not to fear or be filled with anger or resentment. I continued to hold that energy for everyone present, for many were projecting anger and resentment toward those who were preparing to go forward with this forbidden ceremony which was in the past relegated to the most serious of spiritual offenders and had not been performed in centuries.

At the top of the stairs, I lay on the slab without resistance and summoned my energy field to radiate love and understanding.

Sri Ram Kaa began his discourse as to why this had to be done, and the preparations were complete. He made the formal public request to King Theraphys who boomed his resounding approval of the appropriateness of the ceremony. My eldest sister then gladly handed the dagger of Soul Retraction to Sri Ram Kaa and glanced at me with a "now I have everything I want" look of disdain and smugness.

My eyes wide open, I gazed into the golden eyes of my beloved Sri Ram Kaa. He held the dagger up high and when he struck my chest with intense force, I uttered my last words of form at the time of Su'Laria directly to him, "I love you." And the pain was over.

It was in those final days of Su'Laria that the unthinkable happened. Within two weeks after my execution, the war was brought to the planet's surface. Already, a new phenomenon had started to occur. Many Su'Larians were taking their own lives in the recognition that the energy had shifted, an act that was well beyond the consciousness of the Su'Laria I knew and loved.

There were four Kings, with King Theraphys being the most powerful. Over the years he had expanded his holdings and authority over many who were born under different rule. With the help of Sri Ram Kaa he had great telepathic abilities and commanded great spiritual resources. Initially, all of the Kings represented the different soul groups that originally took form on the planet. As their egos grew these governors began to yearn for more authority and expanded beyond their natural alignments.

Out of great frustration, and prompted by the outrageous actions and insulting challenges from King Theraphys, King O'Ahzulha broke the prohibition of warring on the planet's surface.

He brought the war right to King Theraphys' door as a challenge to his arrogance. It was this act of honest ignorance and single-minded focus that triggered the great destruction. With this one single attack, a large area of the planet's surface vaporized as if it had never existed. Thus began the retaliations and the eventual complete destruction of the planet. The speed of the destruction was immense and took but days to end all that had ever been.

It was in the few brief hours before the final retaliation that many more spiritually committed Su'Larians and awakened Hybrids gathered for Divine soul communion. As a result of the stimulation of the war energy, many of these beings were able to expand their consciousness of Source and service in ways that may not have been. Their love for Divine source was strong and committed. Their respect for the Divine was unshakable, and together they knew the continuation of Light in form was a great gift and an important action for the energy of service.

With the end of the Su'Larian experience very near, they gathered together to make a commitment regarding the continuation of the expansion of Light and the seeding of Gaia, and the new Atlantis began.

Pause - Breathe - Allow

Are You From Su'Laria?

A Checklist of Common Experiences

Here are common energies that present themselves on this planet as remnants from Su'Laria. If you find you have experienced more than a few, have no doubt that you were present during the end times of Su'Laria, and are here now to resolve these energies and to be a Light Bearer of Divine Love!

1. During childhood you were afraid of the dark. (This may manifest in adulthood as fear of being alone) Yes No
2. You are fascinated by the stars. Yes No
3. You accept the possibility, or know, of otherworldly life. Yes No
4. Ancient Egypt holds a great fascination for you. Yes No
5. You feel confident there was an Atlantis on Earth Yes No
6. You have experienced severe depression. Yes No
7. You have battled with addictions. Yes No
8. Trusting yourself has not been easy. Yes No
9. You are quick to judge yourself and others. Yes No
10. Most of your life you have felt as if you don't belong. Yes No
11. You are passionate about social justice. Yes No
12. Within you is an affinity to sea creatures, especially dolphins. Yes No
13. You often feel you can understand animals. Yes No
14. You find your own telepathic energy re-emerging. Yes No
15. You already just know you were there. Yes No
16. You have been feeling energies running through your body. Yes No
17. Music that has a deep droning sound makes your body react. Yes No
18. Your instincts tell you there is a major shift ready to take place. Yes No
19. You are attracted to magic, sci-fi, mythology and mysteries. Yes No
20. You have felt an inner longing for Union that has driven your choices. Yes No

21. You often have a sense of frustration with the slow pace of progress.	Yes	No
22. You have felt a sense that time is running out, that a disaster is immanent.	Yes	No
23. You have had many dreams of flying.	Yes	No
24. You feel an affinity with crystals.	Yes	No
25. You enjoy etheric music.	Yes	No
26. You have been attracted to monasteries or ashrams	Yes	No

Remember, there are no right or wrong answers here. You may even feel that some of these questions are applicable to everyone. Well, in a sense they are! Chances are if you have decided to read this book, it is because your DNA has already reactivated to assist your awakening on this planet at this critical moment in history. If you checked *Yes* to the majority of the above statements, then you will be deeply affected by this book. Enjoy!

You may also find it helpful to revisit the AAE's.[19] Many of these critical awakening factors are more present for those who were present during the end times of Su'Laria.

What if you could simply pretend for a moment that everything you have read so far is true? What might that mean to your life right now? Sometimes the truth is painful to remember and the ego wants you to forget. Sometimes a buried truth will find its way into recognition through our dreams or a sense of unsettledness. When we allow ourselves to be completely honest with our own knowing, our healing completes and the wholeness of who we are can express.

This is Love in Action.

We invite you

to connect with the

Mars energy of Su'Laria.

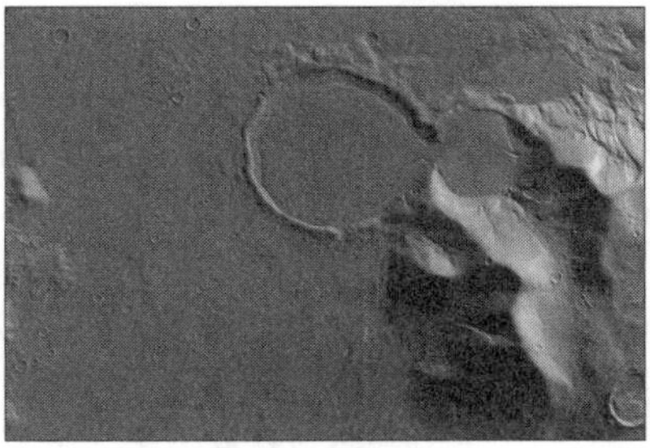

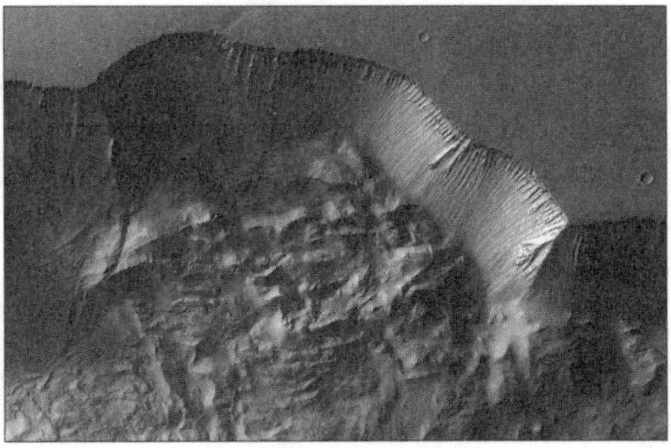

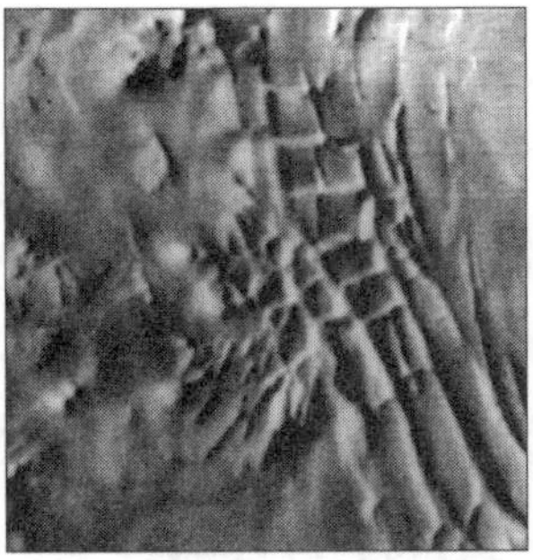

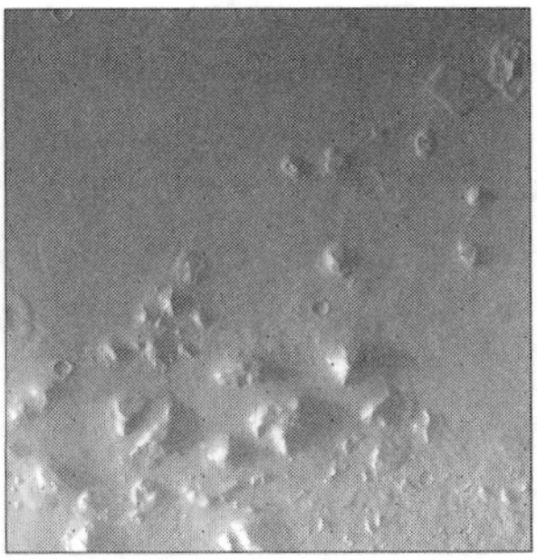

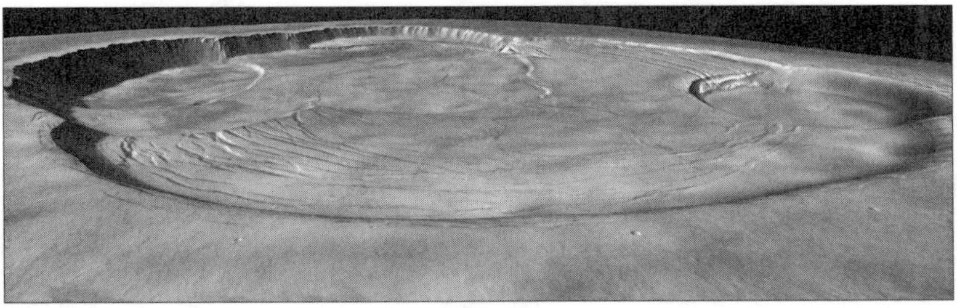

All Mars photos ©ESA

Section Two

Claiming Your Divinity

"The purpose of activating dormant strands of DNA is not to mutate our body. It is to unlock cosmic knowledge and cultivate new responsive capacities within ourselves."

~Sri Ram Kaa

Chapter Eight

Lessons of Authenticity: A Guide to Bring You Home!

"Through the lessons, all will be prepared to receive the energy of life and revitalization. However, they must complete all of the lessons. These are the Codes of Self- Ascension. It is most important for you to remember this. All are capable of receiving and activating these Codes within their own consciousness. However, there is simply some study that must be done in careful preparation because this work lifts the energetic field. Each will escalate their vibratory level, thereby there will be shifts. Many shifts. These lessons are a gift and they are invaluable. The more that one allows themselves to re-activate their ancient knowing, to remain refreshed with Light, the simpler it is to maintain the energetic fields, and the simpler it is to have the information of the Divine Universe revealed."

~Archangel Zadkiel

The lessons of Self-Ascension include understandings (Codes) that are beyond everyday intellectual comprehension. That is, our cosmic heritage cannot be fully contained by the density-brain, for the density-brain only relates to things from the context of Earth experiences.

When the word Lesson is presented to us, it often conjures up connections to our school years; learning how to accurately respo to a specific question about a subject in order to earn a good gr

As you begin this very powerful section, allow yourself to consider approaching these lessons in a completely open manner. Each of these lessons build upon the other, and for some of you they may not appear to be having impact until you complete them all! Others of you will find such profound impact that you will be forced to simply stop for a moment and take them in.

The Archangelic Realm was most specific that the lessons should be presented for you to interpret. They also were clear that there is an optimal way to unfold their powerful energetic information. So that your experience can be maximized, here is a summary of their suggested format:

1. **Simply read each lesson and continue with this book until completion.**
2. **After you finish reading the book, come back to this section and begin reading from this point forward.**
3. **Stop after each lesson and fully complete the Integration Questions for the lesson.**
4. **Review the same lesson every day for up to one month.**
5. **Repeat this process for each lesson, (therefore all twelve lessons could require one year to fully integrate).**
6. **Breathe in the Peace, Love and Joy that has now lly anchored into your daily life!**

When you emerge from completing this section in the above manner, your life WILL change! During this time of shift, there may be times when you are wondering if everything that involves this shift is actually an indicator that you may be doing something wrong. Know that all shift that comes forward due to heart felt intent is all-ways confirmation that you are doing everything right!

It is most challenging to expand the context beyond the brain's known world, yet it can be accomplished. It is vital to remember that each of us has the truth of the energy of knowing within our DNA. Just as our heart knows things that can confuse our brain, our DNA knows things that are beyond the brain as well. The purpose of activating dormant strands of DNA is not to mutate our body. It is to unlock cosmic knowledge and cultivate new responsive capacities within ourselves.

Tapping into this cellular knowing can be tricky at first. We must learn to relax our grip upon the patterned reality we previously depended upon for our stability. Here again, we are faced with the challenge of the brain and emotions.

The brain relies upon its understandings to arrive at a sense of stability. That is, if the brain understands something – even if that something is not true – it will rely upon it's erroneous understanding to feel safe and to make future decisions. Thus, in our world there are many understandings and many misunderstandings.

To "understand" is to fit something into a mental framework where it is in context. Many understandings are myths, however, if many people align with the same understanding, these mythical understandings become "fact". For example, on this planet during the Middle Ages, we persecuted many people who did not conform to the accepted understandings, even though the data indicated that those understandings were flawed.

Understandings are a human creation based upon subservience to a powerful mind.

As new data is uncovered the brain must shift its understandings. It is at this point that many people do not enjoy the instability that comes with an expanding paradigm. New understandings come at the expense of the old understandings, and something is always lost when the new comes in. This can be unsettling and may even stimulate grief.

To avoid feeling crazy, one must cultivate a place of stability within oneself that is not dependant upon the brain. This is one reason we recommend that everyone practice bringing their attention to their hearts.[20] The heart becomes a center of stability and safety; it alone can support the brain going through a "reboot' without losing ones sense of self.

From this heart-centered identity we can access our deepest knowing. This experience of loving acceptance allows the subtle energies that are pre-verbal to become more visible. The energy of self-acceptance is most reassuring and allows one to notice information and hunches that seemingly arise from nowhere that lead us to our true knowing.

Knowing is usually the recognition of wisdom and information beyond the context of an individual lifetime. Knowing is an expression that is beyond the mind. It resides in the domain of the soul.

Knowing will all-ways stand without proof for the mind can not explain all that the soul knows. And while you can both understand and know some things, there are knowings that simply can not be understood. Such is the Joy of expansion!

The material found in this section contains twelve specific lessons offered by Archangel Zadkiel in dialogues with Sri Ram Kaa over several years. These lessons were first revealed as a means to further stimulate our evolution. We lived daily with these lessons and the knowing they unlocked for three years so that we might fully experience the cellular knowledge they unravel and the impact they bring forth into this lifetime. We were asked by the Archangelic Realm to wait to reveal these lessons until the consciousness on the planet was ready to embrace this information.

It was in part due to the living of these lessons that our memories of Su'Laria came forth so vividly for this book and were lovingly confirmed by the Archangelic Realm. The cellular activations that these lessons stimulate will result in great shift in the student's day-to-day life. The key is to really take them in.

These lessons are the first one-half of the 25 lessons that were held in safe-keeping by Archangel Zadkiel until this time in history. The Archangelic Realm has lovingly kept these lessons off the Earth plane in order to allow us all to have our evolutionary experiences here. Now that the time of culmination approaches, we are given this opportunity to come to completion and begin the conscious return to Source. The Codes of Self-Ascension unlock abundant self-awareness and knowing for the sincere student.

Sincerity in your surrender to your soul's emergence coupled with sincere application of the lessons will offer you great personal evolution. Your commitment to integrate these lessons assures you of success on the path of Self-Ascension. As you read the lessons for the first time, they might seem simple. Know that they are designed to be easily ingested, for the material in these lessons will destabilize the grip that the density-brain has upon your experience of reality.

Integrating the learning takes some time and conscious effort. The lessons look different after living with them for awhile. They shift again after receiving the later lessons. Each knowing builds upon the other. Your Divine knowing unlocks as the context of the whole series is integrated.

In our last book, *2012: You Have A Choice*, we discussed the need to cultivate personal clarity, to make a choice whether to transcend density-consciousness. Whether you read these lessons with the intent to understand or whether you study these lessons with the intent to know, we bless you! For you are reading! In the reading you will uncover your own judgments and density-brain dependencies. This will gift you with greater clarity about your own process and the choices ahead for you.

It is important to be aware of the concept of "Wobble" as you navigate the lessons. The Archangels use this word to describe the experience of straddling the third and fifth dimensional energies. Wobble is a sense of instability experienced as anxiety, changing health, career changes, etc. It is a reminder to trust in your divine connection.

Are you experiencing Wobble?

If you are, it can be a sign of progress; a symptom of moving through the instability of the third and fourth dimensional energies and finding the clarity of the fifth dimension and beyond. Your soul knows the way! You heart knows the true path! It is the ego, the physical and the emotional body that create Wobble as they attach to third dimensional density. To move through the dark night of the soul and Self-Ascend you must support those bodies to trust the higher frequencies and your decision to anchor in multi-dimension frequencies.

Here are four steps from Archangel Uriel which make transiting the world of Density Consciousness simple:

1) Sincere Intent

2) Sincere Practice

3) Sincere Dedication

4) Sincere Recognition

It is through sincerity that we find surrender – anything else is a manipulation of the spiritualized ego. Your intent to surrender into conscious Re-Union with the Divine will lead you to your Self-Realization. Bring the sincerity of your intent to your spiritual practice.

Once Sincere Intent and Sincere Practice have been adopted as a way of life, your Sincere Dedication will lift you. Through the lifting you will find an expanded State of Being that is the Recognition of the Truth of the Divine. This Sincere Recognition is usually a felt experience that may include humility, gratitude, joy and expansiveness.

These four steps must be repeated often, for the realm of density consciousness calls us back frequently. You will know that density consciousness has infiltrated when you experience frustration or pain. Be grateful for these signals and then find your sincerity – your heart will offer the trust required to recommit if you ask it to.

Archangel Uriel calls these four steps the bridge between Spiritual Activism and Ascension Awareness. Sometimes we play on the steps going back and forth, until we have fully anchored our attainment.

You must call upon your sincerity to bring you back to your intent, practice, dedication and recognition. Practicing these four steps assures you success. As you approach this very powerful section of lessons brought directly from the Archangelic Realm, we suggest you apply the four steps to each of them, and also to the energy of your daily life.

Here are Archangel Zadkiel's words about the lessons:

The lessons are designed to gently ease all vibratory energies into a pattern that is both joyous and filled with recognition. They are not meant to alarm, challenge, question or move anyone out of any belief pattern. They are simply a way to say hello, we are here, we know who you are and we see your light shining brightly all the time.

There is a patterning within many that has prevented complete acceptance of the light within. You may at times say yes, I am light, or yes, I see the light in others, however, other things come in and take you away from this knowing; pressure, stresses, family, business, money, to name a few. The lessons are a way to allow you to find your path again and to remain in connection with your Divine wholeness.

How can one continue to live in a density based life when they are awakening, opening, being, growing?

This is a most important question. These lessons are self-taught. They are best completed in order as each is a building block for the next: understand one lesson before moving on to another.

It is best to begin by simply reading all the lessons, then go back and begin studying the lessons. Dive into each lesson. At the end of the process of going through all 12, then go back and allow yourself to assimilate each lesson knowing that they are already within you, and have all-ways been. They simply provide a framework that offers familiarity in this density to reacquaint with that which is already true.

We offer the method of lessons, as each one is its own teacher. As one is a student, one is becoming a teacher. As each completes the assimilation of the lessons, they then become ready to be a teacher.

In teaching the lessons, each can deepen evermore their own expression of the lessons. So, the lessons become the lessons for the teachers, for everyone who decides to study the lessons is truly a teacher. So, in way this is a workbook for teachers.

Sri Ram Kaa: There is a difference between acquiring a concept or a new pattern, as opposed to recognition of truth.

Yes, how well put that is.

That is what this is, a workbook of recognition. Lessons of Authen-

ticity: A Guide to Bring You Home. Is not Sacred Union the Journey Home? When so many ask how do I maintain my divinity within this world, these lessons will be most helpful.

Sufficient time to study these lessons is about six to twelve months for most and it will only be in the final review of the lessons that they will take on a greater meaning.

Many Blessings of Love to you.

Chapter Nine

Sincerity or Frustration

As you delve into the lessons, it is important to take a moment to simply become aware of the levels of consciousness that are present in our world and within ourselves. These have been offered to the world from the Archangelic Realm as the Pyramid of Spiritual Awakening.

The Pyramid of Spiritual Awakening offers a strata of consciousness which helps to illustrate the process of Self-Ascension. We are all born into Density consciousness and over time we heal the many trances and preoccupations associated with density. Most spiritual pathways are rooted in the next level of the pyramid, which is Spiritual Activism.

Spiritual Activism is actually a refined form of Density Consciousness, its highest expression. Both levels of consciousness are organized around strong attachments to belief systems and density-based standards of conduct.

In Ascension Awareness one has loosened one's attachment to the "density dramas" and has begun to see the Divine in everything and everyone. Ascension Awareness is anchored in the ascended heart and is a 5th dimensional energy. This offers conscious connectivity to the Divine while still having a body.

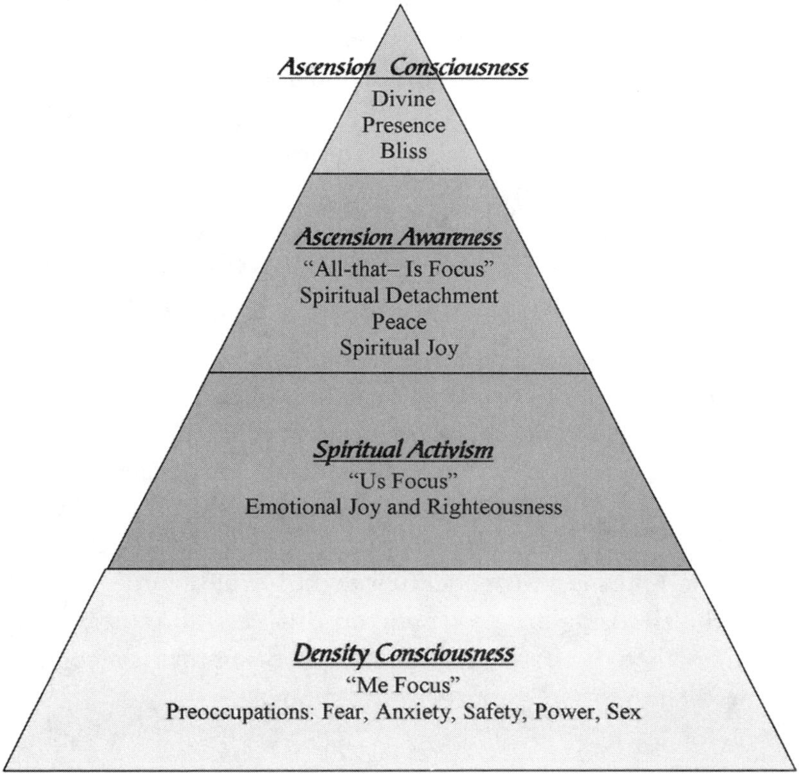

Pyramid of Spiritual Awakening

It can be challenging to anchor in this energy because of the pull of mass consciousness. The teachings we share in our writings are designed to assist the reader in moving through the levels of consciousness. There are many teachings on the planet that will help lift one from Density into Activism. Our work is oriented toward carrying the spiritual seeker beyond third dimensional attractions to cultivate Ascension Awareness. This level of consciousness cannot be sustained without releasing your attachment to density and activism energies.

One of the challenges of anchoring in Ascension Awareness is that the body must be purified at a very deep level. That is, simply engaging our density world brings toxins into the body. This is why the Soul Nourishment program is fundamental. One must clear the debris from the physical, emotional and mental bodies. The cells in our physical body are repositories of toxins, unconscious belief patterns and other density-based energies. To lift through the density requires that we release all energies birthed of Density Consciousness. This is far deeper than one can anticipate from the density point of view!

Unless one consistently cleanses through periodic fasts, meditation, and sincere spiritual practice we tend to re-absorb many density-based energies. The energetic frequencies we are bombarded with in our shared environment serve to reinforce unconscious patterns and orientations. Everyone rooted in density is hypnotized by their refracted consciousness and recognizing this is a critical step toward awakening. One must surrender fully to the Divine in order to purify. While the cleansing process is uncomfortable at times it is always joyful, for there is an innate sense of well being that is recognized as one becomes more congruent and refined.

"Is he sick?" They asked.

My fever had been running for six days before it broke. I (Sri Ram Kaa) knew I was undergoing a spiritual process, not a physical illness because I felt safe during the entire process. I really did not have any other significant symptoms. So each day I remained in bed passing the time with chills and sweats. Each day the fever would break for a spell and I felt peaceful and rested! Then it would begin anew. This went on for six days straight and even though I trusted that I was in a spiritual cleansing process, I did get to watch my mind jump to conclusions: "Maybe I have an exotic illness....Should I take aspirin.... maybe I should call a doctor, just to be on the safe side....what if I'm wrong to trust this....I can't believe it is taking this long."

The prolonged fever taught me to let go of my expectations. Judgments about how hot, how long and what the process should look like are all based in density perspectives. From the ascended perspective it just takes what it takes to purify. Each person's process will be unique to them.

My six days of fever were unlike my prior Dark Nights of the Soul[21] because I was not wrestling with emotions or depression. Yes, at times self-doubt crept in, yet I knew that in spite of the delirium and discomfort, somehow this fever was a gift.

The day after the fever cycle completed Kira and I shared an Archangelic In-soulment together. I share this discourse with you here because it helps set the stage for you to benefit from the lessons to come.

Archangel Zadkiel Speaks:

Dearest Sri Ram Kaa, we are here today in a great welcoming energy for you. In the welcoming energy, we offer you many, many energies. As you are already aware, there are many of us here together today. The predominant energy is the energy of the Uriel, for the energy of the Uriel is that energy which must be predominant around you at this time.

Golden rays of rejuvenation. You see, Dear One, you have walked through a time of great darkness within. The darkness within is a darkness that has been, as you might want to hear or perhaps understand, a cobweb on the soul. This cobweb on the soul was encapsulating your attempts to grow into a manner for which your soul vibration has already accepted, is indeed, if you must use this word, a destiny. And so this cobweb of the soul needed to be cleansed, washed and literally burned away.

It is indeed important for you to recognize that in the cleansing, in the burning, in the shifting, there is an opening before you now. This golden opening is a ray of light. This golden ray alignment is the direct source, a direct pathway, a stairwell if you will, that will take you straight up into that which is no longer the illusion. In this pathway, in this golden light, in this direct portal, in the God-like beingness of all that is and for all that you are, your heart has grieved for many years seeking communion with this energy. You must understand that this energy is you, as you are the energy. The communion is already at hand. It is already complete. It is already before you now. It is not something you must do.

We open the hands to offer greater energetic alignment, to flow through greater energy, to offer you greater understanding of all that is. To bring to you the great golden connection. In the pyramid of golden connection, all answers come forward, all light is present and the illumination through luminosity of all that is, is understood without the brain interfering.

It is important for you to know that what you are seeking has already been found, that all of the prayers that you have sent to us, all of the demands, all of the screams, all of the absolute frustrated energies of this world have been transmuted, they are aligning around you now. All you need do is step into a vibration of sincerity... ***Sincerity****. In the sincerity, the sincerity comes back.*

In your sincerity you attract. In your frustration you repel. Is this not indeed the same model as works in density? This is a great lesson in the world of density. Sincerity attracts, sincerity attracts. Frustration repels. These are energies that are core central energies. Many deal with the energy of sincerity in many different ways. Many call it love, yet love without sincerity cannot attract. Sincerity is a key component in all attraction energy.

Do you sincerely wish to attract abundance, or do you wish to attract abundance from a frustration energy, which will repel it? It is that simple. If you were to make a soup indeed, hmm, a soup of this world, you would always want to add the ingredients of sincerity as your soup base mix. For if sincerity is indeed the foundation, the base, then everything that you add to it will indeed be an attractor. The attractor energy of sincerity is the most powerful attractor energy on this planet. It is the missing ingredient in much, which is why the energy that repels is so prominent.

For example, if you draw a circle and you write the word "sincerity" in

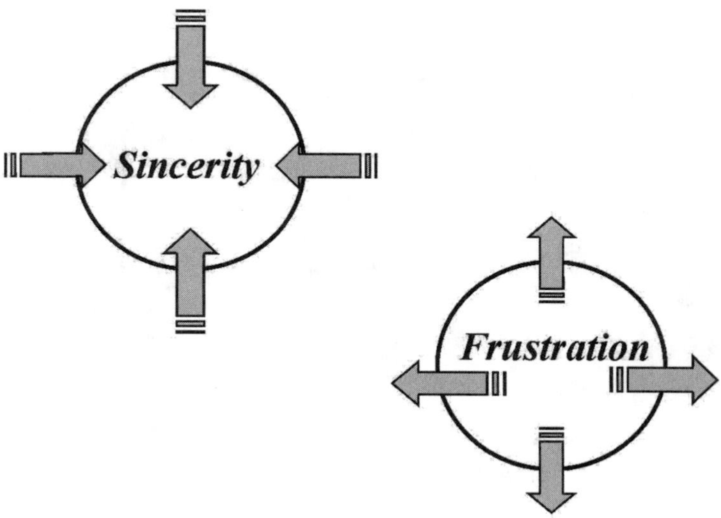

the middle, then draw arrows from the outside toward the inside, facing in, that is the energy of sincerity. Make four arrows, all directions very good. Now draw another circle, and on this you put "frustration". You draw the same arrows leading out. Everything Sri Ram Kaa, everything, EVERYTHING forms in these two models. Everything.

If you wish to teach, if you wish to share, if you wish to complete a book, begin with this concept because it is that simple.

Sincerity attracts, frustration repels.

If one wishes to solve a challenge and one is trying to solve the challenge in the energy of frustration, then the solutions that come forward have repulsion energy, and so you will continually fall into a loop of solution, of solution, of solution, thereby offering magnetism to the repulsion energy which is based upon frustration so you will become evermore frustrated in everything. One must alleviate frustration before one can even begin to find a solution. Finding solutions while in the energy of frustration can only offer greater repulsion.

We are offering this to you in the term of simply the abundance area because this is the most popular area in the land in which you seek to be. In the land in which you are, the abundance issue, as you say, is the one that causes the greatest frustration, and those in the greatest frustration have the greatest repulsion, thereby they will never be able to embrace completion, because the energy of frustration permeates, even as it cycles out from more and more, it will still permeate.

Now, when one is able to recognize and be present with and understand that they are in the energy of frustration, there is only one way out. If you draw, or if you were to superimpose two circles, we shall do this for you or you may do.

(Kira's hand begins to draw). We shall draw it, but it is going this way when you look at it. If this circle at the bottom is frustration and this circle up here is sincerity. One must lift up, one must look up. This energy of repulsion in frustration can only go outside of itself. One must look up into sincerity to be able to call in Divine flow from all areas. Divine flow does not come from density, which is the energy of frustration. Sincerity comes from Divine recognition. Do you understand?

Sri Ram Kaa: Yes. Frustration is of density and from the consciousness which is entangled in density; it would be a common experience to have the frustration energy come in?

Draw your pyramid on this page here of spiritual awaking (see page 105). Draw the four levels, for your answers are within here also, there is a correlation. What are your levels?

Sri Ram Kaa: Density Consciousness, Spiritual Activism, Ascension Awareness, Ascension Consciousness.

Density Consciousness, Spiritual Activism, Ascension Awareness, Ascension Consciousness. From one level of consciousness to another embraces the pyramid. If we take your pen from Ascension Consciousness you come into Density Consciousness, from Density Consciousness, you are able to return to Ascension Consciousness. Continue to ask your questions.

Sri Ram Kaa: In the awakening of consciousness there is a knowing that all is at ease, all is available and all is, and there is also a vibratory alignment with the level of consciousness that does not know this.

Yes.

Sri Ram Kaa: So the two existing simultaneously seem to be the generator of the frustration.

Yes for you see, in the Density Consciousness and the Spiritual Activism, those two levels are the levels of frustration. It is impossible to enter into sincerity, Divine recognition sincerity, until one recognizes that they are aware, and awareness can be touched, yet to hold awareness is where true sincerity becomes the embodiment.

You see, in Density Consciousness and Spiritual Activism, frustration is the embodiment of consciousness. Whichever consciousness you embody the majority of the time, until one can be fully anchored in the Ascension Awareness, frustration will always offer an opportunity to recognize that you are not in Divine recognition. This is indeed the gift, yet one must be fully aware of what the gift is, in order to recognize it.

Sri Ram Kaa: Yes.

We are offering you all of this today because indeed your third book must come out and you shall accomplish this without frustration. Everything we offer you today will introduce the lessons in that book. It will offer a foun-

dation for the book, it will expand the pyramid more, it will help others. It is imperative, imperative, that many seek to recognize Ascension Awareness, for if you review your pyramid, Ascension Awareness does not come forward until the third level. Many will run around and say I am aware. Yet, there is a difference between being aware and embodying awareness. There is a great difference and that cavern is too large to jump. You can only fly. You can only lift across it. If you stick out the foot without the embodiment you will indeed retrace your steps many times.

It is imperative to recognize that in the doing is the being. If one is simply doing, doing, doing, it becomes frustrating, does it not? There is a cycle of great frustration, there is a cycle of great denial in simply doing. Often many simply do so that they can preoccupy the brain that is busily focused on the energy of frustration, hopelessness, depression, addiction. These are all energies of frustration, all of them. Go back to the diagram that we drew, yes this one. The arrows that we drew out of frustration, write these words on each arrow: hopelessness, addiction, depression, poverty, lack of belief. These are imperative and there are many more, and simply on the last arrow you put others, just put the word others for now.

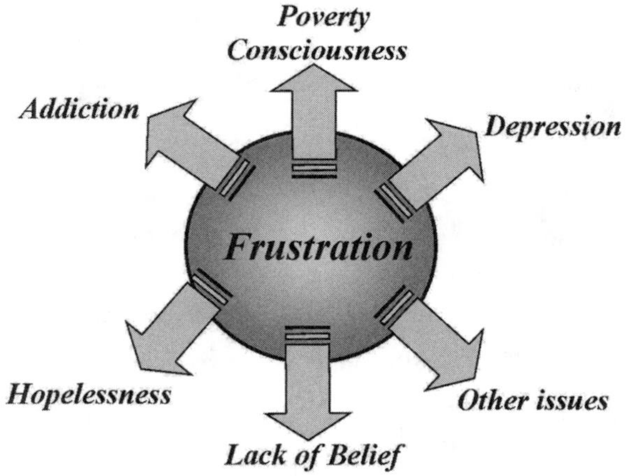

You must realize all of these, all of these, come from a lack of wholeness based upon frustration. The energy of frustration is what births these energies. If you look at any one of these energies and there could be so many more in the others category, there could be anxiety, there could be repetitive patterns, all, all of these energies begin with frustration.

Are you frustrated with the world around you?

Are you frustrated with your government?

Are you frustrated with your love life?

Are you frustrated with your finances?

Are you frustrated with your day-to-day existence?

Know that in frustration there is no resolution. Frustration is a cycle that depends upon the lack of resolution, so frustration becomes its own cycle. Frustration becomes its own energy. Frustration then becomes a pattern of being that separates you from the doing. And in that separation, as your pattern of being, your doing can only come from frustration.

And so, this is why you can not move away from frustration until you are able to lift up into Divine recognition. Many will say how can I do that? Is not that question alone a recognition of frustration? "How can I do that?" is a question of frustration.

The "How" comes from frustration. All "how" questions come from frustration because the true question is not "how can I do this?" the question is "I have tried and do not feel I have accomplished… I am what?" Frustrated. Do you see the cycle? It is the single most powerful cycle, because the greatest energy of frustration is fear. From the repetitive loop of frustration, fear is birthed.

And so, frustration creates fear. It does not equal fear, it creates it. It is the creator. If your creator is the energy of frustration, then you are in fear, and you are indeed worshipping the energy of frustration every time you remain in fear. Fear is birthed from frustration. It becomes your creator, the Divine separation.

Divine Recognition

Births

Sincerity

OR

FRUSTRATION

(SEPARATION)

BIRTHS

FEAR

The Divine separation is an energy that began in Tu'Laya. In Tu'Laya the first frustration began between those that wanted to continue and those that felt continuation was futile. It birthed what? Frustration…and in that frustration birthed separation. You see this energy has been present for a long time. This is the primal separation energy.

Primal separation energy is frustration because from frustration rises doubt. When you are frustrated, you first doubt yourself, and then you doubt your Divine connection and then you doubt the outcomes, you doubt any positive resolution, thereby you have created what? Great separation.

Sri Ram Kaa: I did not think that such energy could exist in the twenty fifth dimension[22] ?

In the dimension of the twenty fifth birthed the dimension that is below. This was a birthplace, not a place of existence.

Sri Ram Kaa: So in the traveling…

In the propulsion of the traveling…

Sri Ram Kaa: In the propulsion of the traveling the experience of the Tu'Laya gave an environment for the creative energies of frustration to become experienced and in that, birthing ever-denser dimensions.

You must remember, in the seeding of that which became your Leumeria on this planet, the energy of the frustration was already in the seed. It had to be. It was already in the seeding. That energy was there. The seeding was brought to this world intentionally to manifest, yet on this world it was already, if you would use the word genetically encoded. This is why it must play out, this is why you have had many cycles of this experience and this energy, and the gift, the gift was in the recognition from the Elohim that the seeding could not be interrupted. That this energy had to play out as you would say.

How the Elohim could offer assistance without interference was to offer the energy of reunion, knowing that when the energy had expanded enough, that when the frustration energy had expanded fully enough, that the reunion energy would then come into fruition, offering the time of the release of the frustration and the lifting into Divine recognition, thereby freeing the cycle. You are at that time. You are at that time.

Sri Ram Kaa: The lift into Divine recognition involves the recognition of the gift, it involves consciousness.

Correct.

Sri Ram Kaa: Awakening to the truth of what is there.

This is what we said earlier, Ascension Awareness.

Sri Ram Kaa: Are many ready to accept that concept?

More are aware than have ever been and in the next few years they will lift into the embodiment of Ascension Awareness. Everything must shift to embody this, and the body must purify, because everything that is of this world that is created through a technographic ideal is designed to perpetuate frustration. Frustration with the physical body, frustration with the world around, frustration with what one sees, hears, tastes, smells. One must look with clear eyes at the gift to be able to lift into the Ascension Awareness, and in order to do this, in order to fully lift to break the cycle of frustration, many will need to burn through.

The burning will be felt in many different ways for many. For some, the burning will be emotional. For some the burning will be financial. For some the burning will be physical. For some the burning will be spiritual. Yet the burning will be. It is not designed to be painful. However, in the trap of frustration, pain is part and parcel for the experience.

When one can recognize that the pain is designed to offer the lift, one will break through it. Many, however, in the cycle of frustration are most addicted to the pain and addicted to the frustration energy.

The energy of resolution can only be found through the sincerity of Divine recognition. You say what is sincerity and what and where does love come in? ***Sincerity is the embodiment of true love.***

True love is the energy. Together they become their own energy, a Divine blend of full awareness, full trust, full recognition, full unveiling that all is in Divine order. In all communications, be fully in the embodiment of your Ascension Awareness. Let go of being aware and rest in Divine awareness. Let the embodiment of truth, love, trust and Divine recognition flow through you in all ways, so that sincerity emanates. This is how you will be known. This is the marker that many will show and bear. Are they carrying the mark of frustration, or are they carrying the mark of sincerity?

Many practices have been offered to you, and many lessons are being offered. All of these practiced with Sincere Intent, this is the key, you must have Sincere Intent, for Sincere Intent is the first in the staircase that moves you from frustration to sincerity. Sincere Intent is the first step. Sincere Practice is the second step. Remember, Sincere Intent, step one, Sincere Practice, step two, Sincere Dedication, step three, and Sincere Recognition is step four.

It is just four steps from frustration to sincerity. Here they are, and so draw the stairway between the two showing the four steps. It will be it's own diagram showing how to move between the sincerity and frustration. You have been given the steps, it is that simple.

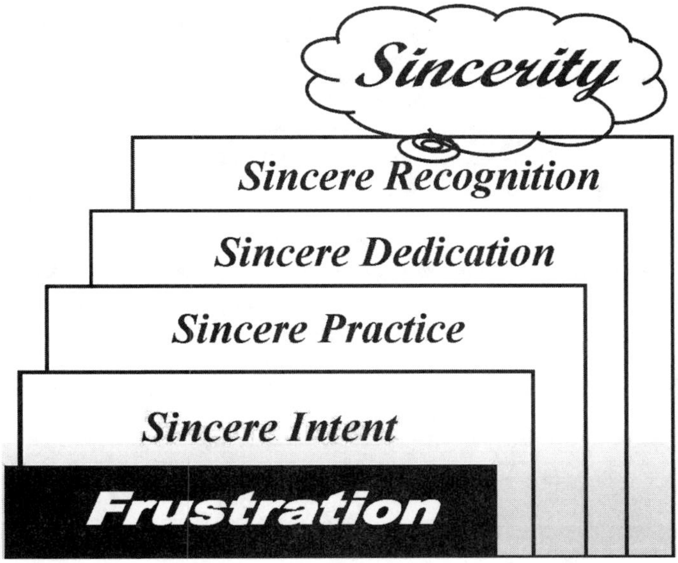

It is a great gift to know the steps, so that when perhaps you reach a step and then step back, one or two. If you recognize that you are stepping back, then you are indeed offering yourself the energy of awareness. Each time you may step backwards you gift yourself with ever more awareness. You are moving from being aware to the embodiment of awareness. And so, do you enter into the energy of frustration when you step backwards, which then energizes that energy ever more, **or** *do you recognize in the stepping backwards that indeed you are doing so and embody even more awareness? You see, you must play on the steps! You must go up, you must go down, you must go up and you must go down until you can fully recognize that every step, ever single one, is taking you closer to the embodiment of full sincerity. This is the gift of this density dance. That is the gift in all of the experiences around you.*

Do you respond with frustration or do you respond with awareness? Offer yourself recognition and as you respond with frustration, each time you can transmute frustration in the full awareness, you are one step closer to the embodiment that will truly break you free from the cycle of the activism into the living of the Ascension Awareness. When you can fully live in the energy of sincerity in Ascension Awareness, you can then only lift into the Divine recognition of Ascension Consciousness. It is that simple. And yet it must be studied, it must be practiced, and this is why you have been offered practices and lessons so that you may walk your four steps from frustration to sincerity.

When you interact with each other in complete sincerity, you will always be embodying the Divine and the Divine will work through thee with the energy of attraction. When you experience frustration with another, and interact with another from frustration, you are attracting the energy of density and the interaction will carry the energy of repulsion and the energy of repulsion will manifest in many different ways. Everything can be applied to this. There is no limitation and this is a complete lesson for all who wish to go further with the lessons.

Sri Ram Kaa: Very good. Most powerful.

Yes, and timely… A great lesson indeed.

Sri Ram Kaa: Yes.

We are complete with you. Divine recognition is at hand, Divine dispensation has been poured forth. Stay in your sincerity, carefully watch your frustration and simply let it give you the gift of greater awareness, so that you may propel, model and walk in your truth. You must stay consistent, this is all we ask. This is your challenge and your vision, to be consistently in the vital energy of Divine recognition. You have been given much and you are ready. Go forth, prosper, share, remain in humility as you expand more.

An Important Note about the Format of the Lessons

Know that as we present these twelve lessons, we have held in our hearts your highest expansion and service. As mentioned in the opening pages of this section, the request by the Archangelic Realm with respect to the lessons is as follows:

1. **Simply read each lesson and continue with this book until completion.**
2. **After you finish reading the book, come back to this section and begin reading from this point forward.**
3. **Stop after each lesson and fully complete the Integration Questions for the lesson.**
4. **Review the same lesson every day for up to one month.**
5. **Repeat this process for each lesson, (therefore all twelve lessons could require one year to fully integrate).**
6. **Breathe in the Peace, Love and Joy that has now fully anchored into your daily life!**

At the end of each lesson you will find three things that will remain consistent for each lesson. The first is an I AM statement that calls forth the succinct energy of each lesson. We encourage you to write it down, and powerfully declare it often as you work with that lesson. As you continue through the lessons, you may also find it helpful to begin stringing them together. Simply put, add each statement to the one you just completed.

The second action with each lesson is the lotus picture. Remember that each time you see this gentle reminder to take a moment with yourself and to simply:

Pause - Breathe - Allow

- **Pause** by bringing your hands to your heart.
- **Breathe** in the gift of breath and,
- **Allow** yourself to feel and experience whatever is present.

You may even encounter that your feeling experience appears to have nothing to do with the lesson. Trust your flow!

The third piece of each lesson is to take time and complete the Lesson Integration Box. You may find that each time you revisit the lessons you want to add or change your responses. This is perfect! Allow whatever is coming forth to simply be present for you. You may even wish to create your own Lessons Journal. Keep this journal for your year with the lessons and only for your lessons. By the end of a year, you will be delighted and amazed at the soul that is gifting you with YOU!

Chapter Ten

Living the Lessons

"It is a magnificent time to be alive. It is a magnificent and glorious time to know the gifts that are abundant here on this planet Earth. It is a glorious time to celebrate all that is manifesting, manifested and in the process of culminating now. Be in joy."

~ Archangel Zadkiel

As you embark on the journey of these twelve lessons, the following discourse was offered as a means to unlock your Divine Oneness. Along with containing important information about these times, it also reveals a powerful breathing technique designed to fully open one to the energy of the information.

We have found that utilizing this technique now for several years has offered us profound clarity and revitalization. This technique, in combination with other Galactic Yogic Traditions being restored to the planet, has been a great gift.

We offer this gift to you and encourage you to simply start your day knowing how amazing you are.

Archangel Zadkiel Speaks:

It is a glorious time to be alive and understand the many gifts that are given on a continuous basis from the Oneness, from the Light, the Love. The

Universal secrets, as they say, are available to all. They are only a secret because one chooses not to know. So it is when any becomes available to knowing, it is no longer a secret. So many talk about how they hold the secret, they know a secret, they offer the secret, they will tell you the secret, it is a special secret, oh my goodness. This word secret used much.

The secret is not so much in the knowing as it is in the Being. For if one is being, then one understands. If one is allowing, if one is in surrender, then one can be. For when one has the secret, it means that they are still withholding from themselves, from others, from the world. There is no basis for this withholding unless one desires power or control. The Elohim does not desire power or control; this is why there can be no secret. The gift that the Elohim offer is the expanding Love of Light. That is the big secret!

You are an expansion of Love. You are expanding, and as Light everything becomes available for you to see. Understand the metaphor of what we say, for we can only offer metaphors because in our realm it is challenging to discuss, disseminate, or offer this information in a way that would satisfy the density brain. And yet we must for you are still in this vessel.

Sri Ram Kaa: So throughout the last several thousand years there have been secret teachings, mystery schools, secret societies, and it is my understanding they were secret because it was not safe for them to be open.

This is very true, however let us explore this a little more. There are those who hold in secret their training even to the sincere seeker of the secret because of a need to have a structured or uniform process whereby they feel it must be approved to divulge their secret. While this has had its place and certainly was formed with good intent, it is important to understand that the true seeker can find any secret at any time by going into their heart and connecting. By genuinely and sincerely saying dearest God, my heart is open, I am here, I am ready, I am open, guide me. (The Mantra of Self-Ascension.)

So we offer you this information because the time of the secret has past. The secret is out as they say. Everything is out in this world as they say, very little is no longer out. Oh yes, there are still some things to be, as you would say, discovered or recovered is more accurate. Soon they will find things that will be indisputable, although they will want to dispute of course. It will become very evident there was life on Mars (Ancient Su'Laria). They are already getting it, yet it will not be released as they say to the public for quite awhile. However it already exists.

Sri Ram Kaa: The data.

Yes, the pictures.

Sri Ram Kaa: The pyramids.

Yes and beyond. There is more than one reason they now wish to send more people there.

Sri Ram Kaa: That's traveling the hard way.

Of course it is, because it comes from a method of density and scientific experimentation, however, it serves its purpose. So know this, it is the time of the great awakening, it is the time of the great Self-Ascension, it is the time of the knowing of all secrets, of the revealing of ancient mystery wisdom, whichever you wish to call, that will offer much release of judgment to many others. For you see the only time capsule that needs to be unburied here is the one that inside of each being contains the unconditional love for the Self, for the world. It has been long buried.

When you and Kira came back together you activated your time capsule opening. It is that deep, deep love between each of you that continues to unlock this capsule and bring it out. Those around you will feel it and know it and express it, especially those of open pure heart. Then they will activate the opening of their own time capsule, which will activate the opening of others and so on. This is very exciting. It is important for all to understand that the only secret is the one they keep from themselves.

For this is the only key that is needed to unlock a heart; and you are in a society, you are in a modern age, as they say, that is paced at a speed that is not healthy, that does not support unconditional love. Unconditional love is subject to time. Time is the false God as we have already discussed. Everything subjected to time becomes conditional. There is no time to love you unconditionally; I must be at an appointment. There is no time for me to be myself because I must be someone else for this period of time or to do this or make this money, whatever.

That is the great secret: That the only secret is to unlock the heart, to allow the flood gate of unconditional love for the Self to come in, to forgive, to reemerge as the soul based heart centered self-ascended energy, ready to be of service to all, being in the continuous flow of the God of Love. For you see, once one is activated by drawing the golden white energy up through the soles of the feet and meeting the chakras at the base and continuing up the spine,[23] *once that one has been activated, one opens up a Divine flow. This flow comes into the crown, activates the sixth, the fifth, and the heart where it then flows out and then goes back up like pyramid and comes back in.*

This is a new exercise we shall be teaching you. It is very powerful and has some powerful breathing techniques. You may sit or stand. Sitting is fine, very good. Begin with the right nostril closed. You may use your right hand to do this, yes.

Sri Ram Kaa: Close the right?

Yes, close the right, there you go. You take the left hand, put it on the belly and breathe in through the left and then breathe out through the mouth, hard breath out. Breathe in again, hard breath out. Breathe in again, hard breath out. Yes, three times then you reverse your hands. Breathe in, hard breath out. Breathe in, hard breath out. Breathe in, hard breath out. Yes, then you take both hands and place on heart, close eyes. As you breathe in through both nostrils, you bring in a golden ray through the crown and then blow out the mouth long and slow. Then bring the ray down to the heart and then you open your hands out and breathe again. Yes, that is the exercise.

Sri Ram Kaa: Do we not send it back up?

As you have sent it out with this breath, it will touch the energy needed and go back up. It is not yours to direct. It is yours to know that you have sent out the energy of Love in a cocoon[24] *that it will touch and go back up. It is the flow opener. You should start every morning with this. For every morning it opens the flow. This process should only be done in the morning for it is most energizing.*

So you may sit or stand, close the right nostril, breathe three times with the other hand on the solar plexus or belly, and then the other three times. Make sure the exhale is very profound. Inhale deep, profound exhale. Then you take the hands to the heart breathing in deeply through the nose bringing the crown energy with the golden ray and then slowly out through the mouth as you bring it down to the heart and then you open the hands and do the breathing again and send it out. You send it out with great intention for the day. You should start each morning with this, holding an intention of calling in the abundant eternal flow of Love, un-conditionality, service, true expansion. Then send it out to the world as your gift everyday. It will find the welcome heart and it will be received and recycled.

The more people that start the morning like this the better. It is a beautiful practice. It is a practice that you may indeed teach along with your lessons.

Lesson One

Individ-u-Will
Understanding Refractory Devices

"Enlightenment is not imagining figures of light but making the darkness conscious."

~ Carl Gustav Jung

Archangel Zadkiel Speaks:

We ask you to release the concept of the individual. It is important for you to understand that the individual was an illusion created to begin with, and through the use of that illusion, it created your separation. Notice how I pronounce that for you. Individ-u-will.

It is not that you do not have your own preference or decision capability, or things that you enjoy while you are here, (on Earth). Yet, you are of the one light energy that fractured and splintered.

How can you return to union without first recognizing this?

Understand the blessing of true light has many names and it has greater illuminative ability when we accept that it is many particles that make up a beam. Even the I [Archangel Zadkiel], that speaks to you now is a we.

Sri Ram Kaa: The individ-u-will seems to me to be multi layered, meaning there is the individ-u-will that is owned or identified with from the personality self, the ego. And then there is the actual fracturing of the light and is that not an individuation of sorts?

Ask yourself this question: What am I?

Sri Ram Kaa: I am light.

What is light…What is light?

Sri Ram Kaa: There's nothing but light. How do I answer that?

What composes light?

Sri Ram Kaa: The dark composes light.

What else?

Sri Ram Kaa: Focus of resonance, intent. I cannot apply my mind to this.

Consider it as a spectrum. You have there a clear prism and when the light shines through it what happens?

Sri Ram Kaa: It allows the refraction of its component rays.

Correct. You are a refraction; the individ-u-will is on the other side of the refraction. It only exists after the light has hit its body or true spirit.

Sri Ram Kaa: Yes. The individ-u-will is light that is on the other side of the barrier which has refracted.

Correct!

Sri Ram Kaa: Where is the ego? Is that not a further refraction?

Correct!

Sri Ram Kaa: That is what I was wanting to understand.

Correct. It would be as if you had this refractory device and you were able to direct the separations into another refractory device that further would separate the beam…denser and denser and denser, further and further and further. Therefore the absolutely last refraction that occurs is when you are here as the individ-u-will. We are all one. Yet, in the one there is oneness.

Sri Ram Kaa: Then the Travelers are those who can walk

through and between the refractory devises.

Yes. How else would you travel? Your mind can understand this if you always think of it as a spectrum. So always think of it as a spectrum.

Sri Ram Kaa: Then is there a risk of being lost?

How can you lose that which you are?

Sri Ram Kaa: By being sleepy.

What is sleep? The losing, as you say, is part of the finding of the way, and the greater one loses, the more they are compelled to hunt. And even if they do not, by your perception, find their way while they are in the form of a body, when they release the physical the way is always found again.

Sri Ram Kaa: And yet we have those that are bound here.

Only because of their love and commitment to service.

Sri Ram Kaa: So it's temporary.

Correct. All bound energy is eventually released. It is either released by others who are of a sensory ability to do so while they still are present in physicals, or they are released at the time of the great release. However, know that all will be released. Understand that through your refracted energy as you ask me this question it implies a perception that once one releases the body the path is done. This is not so. ***It is because you are on your path that you are here.*** *This experience is simply a part of the overall evolutionary growth of the soul that you are. Individ-u-will is yet another means of growing your light. It is another expression of experience that gives you the opportunity to understand what refraction does. All light is made up of particles of the many. When they refract, the individ-u-will forgets that inside of the light there was every color.*

Sri Ram Kaa: Such delight.

Yes! It is through this recognition that leads to your expansion; which leads to evolution; which leads one to enlightenment. This is done simultaneously although this is a challenging concept for you here on this planet; to accept that you are in many dimensional realms at once.

Sri Ram Kaa: Then must each splinter or fracture become self-recognizing to reunite?

Each fracture, splinter, color or individ-u-will comes to a point where it recognizes it is of highest service to reunite. Only through the recognition, does the reunification begin.

Without recognition there cannot be reunification. One continues in the loop of separateness until each comes to the recognition of the energy of unification. For unification without self-recognition would be a house of cards.

Sri Ram Kaa: Yes, really impossible.

Yes. In this manner, a pyramid is built, a planet is built, a world is built, a universe created. Please allow yourself to accept the perfection of the myriad of individuations. You are then able to release judgment of yourself, of those around you, of those you do not even know. Remember that judgment is yet another refractory device, it will further refract the truth therefore making it harder to find because you have many pieces.

Is it easier to put together a child's puzzle that is five big pieces or is it easier to put together the one that is five thousand pieces all looking similar with subtle differences? Which is easier to complete? For when you apply judgment, know that it is a refractory device and think of it as the complex puzzle.

The moment you remove judgment, automatically many of these pieces bind together, thereby leaving just the few. Both puzzles are solvable, both can be done, one just takes more time. Once either puzzle is put together, one can then enjoy its entirety. So the question is how much time do you want to spend putting it back together? So you lay your five thousand-piece puzzle in front of you and remove your judgment and instantaneously it becomes five pieces, and then one.

It is not that they are not both fun and this is important to know. Some may even say, "I get more enjoyment out of figuring out these bigger pieces." Or some might say, "I like the challenge of all these little pieces." Is that not symbolic of all lives? Sometimes you enjoy the challenge of the little pieces without even knowing you've chosen complexity. Some might say, "Oh that's too simple: I won't enjoy it."

This is only because they are deep within the struggle and have actually turned it into enjoyment. This is why we give you the analogy of the puzzles.

Model of Refraction of the Individ-u-will

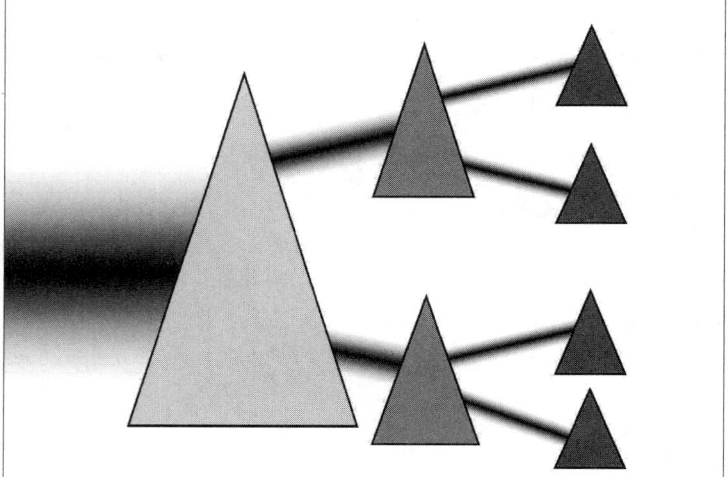

Divine Light is refracted by the Individ-u-will, who continues refracting into ever denser forms of experience.

Figure-A

As you begin with this first lesson, the Individ-u-will, it is important to recognize how you are a refraction of a refraction of light. You will notice in Figure-A above, the Divine Light streaming from source. As this light encounters the first refractory device the Individ-u-will comes forward. Once the Individ-u-will evolves, it then becomes subjected to ever more refractory devices as it learns to navigate into denser form.

Each refraction still carries with it the spark of the Divine Light, (source), and it also is propelled by the attraction to density expression.

The energy being depicted here illustrates the first collective refraction of light into form, Tu'Laya. From here, additional refractions birthed the conditions for the experience known as Su'Laria. From Su'Laria, we refracted again to the Experience that we call Earth.

I AM the Divine Light!

Instructions for Deepening the Integration of the Lesson

Please use the following journaling format each time you see the Lesson Integration page.

Sentence completion journaling is a useful method of bringing your personal information into the light of consciousness.

Just state the sentence stem out loud and then begin writing a completion. Just let the pen flow without any mental editing – a flow of automatic writing will gift you with deeper levels of truth.

When your pen stops writing, then repeat the sentence stem out loud again to see if more writing wants to flow. It is useful to write several completion statements to the sentence stems.

Pause - Breathe - Allow

Journaling For Integration:

This lesson helps me to recognize:

Integrating this teaching means that I now release my attachments to:

Integrating this teaching means that I now accept:

A declaration that will help me integrate this lesson is:

Bring your hands to your heart once again, and declare the Mantra of Self-Ascension.[25]

I AM HERE
I AM READY
I AM OPEN
GUIDE ME!

Lesson Two

Restoring Presence

"When one finally moves into acceptance and learns to release fear in a conscious manner, then the subconscious routines of the ego will kick in allowing you the opportunity to further ripen and deepen that acceptance.

In the Illumination of the true remembering, there are trans-neural pathways that will be corrected, unified, and strengthened."

~Archangel Zadkiel

Archangel Zadkiel Speaks:

That which you focus on expands; so why the preoccupation with rumination? When you are trapped in self-judgment, the way out is to look beyond yourself. Self-judgment is one of the greatest egoic traps within density. The consciousness of it's all about me, is often cleverly disguised as self-deprecating actions and statements, and it does not serve that which you are trying to achieve. ***You must learn to look beyond yourself. This is the gift of Divine partnership.***

As you wish to release this part of the ego, as you look beyond yourself, the partner can look beyond themselves, and then the two nourish each other. Look beyond you to your partner. Let your partner look beyond themselves to you. Be wary of the trap of focusing on the ego as being bad! Yes!

We have also discussed compassion, and how when one believes they are being of service, they are often stuck in false compassion. This is the same as self-judgment. You believe that you are doing yourself a service by looking at something that you consider to be less than what you want it to be, which in and of itself is a method of control.

Do you see? It can be most difficult to move out of this trap because the trap in and of itself is self-preserving. So it will mutate like a virus. When a virus discovers that there is something that can get rid of it, it will mutate very quickly to preserve itself. This is what the ego does, this is why the attainment of moving through the layer that you desire to move through can only be done when you remove the focus from yourself. There is no other way to do it in this dimension, for within the density of vessels it is impossible.

Sri Ram Kaa: So are you suggesting that any form of self-discipline or self-vigilance is a preoccupation of self and therefore will feed the very thing that you are seeking to dissolve?

It is important to understand that the answer to that question lies in the intent of the vigilance. If you are vigilantly reminding yourself to look beyond yourself, then you will perpetuate a new pattern which will release an old pattern. If you are vigilant in saying bad ego, go away ego, then that will perpetuate, that which you wish to go away. We are simply expressing to you an opportunity to be in joy.

Sri Ram Kaa: I ask because what I am feeling into this day is the absurdity of efforting. I mean I was immersed in letting go of the ego, and in this moment, what I'm immersed in is the recognition to just be.

And what does that mean for you? To just be?

Sri Ram Kaa: It means to smile. To smile at my ego, to smile at my Divinity, and to be in allowance and acceptance. We call it nonresistance; to just surrender.

We call it trust. We call it Love. Trust, Love, Trust, Love. When you trust, when you love, the flow is abundant and ever giving of life, and all that you need. Trust that the release is OK, trust that all is in order. Trust it shall be. This efforting is an important venue to look at. For efforting in and of itself is a platform of the ego, is it not?

Sri Ram Kaa: Indeed. A spiritual principle that is taught is to focus on making an effort and not focus on the outcome. Basically to center in pure intent, and leave the results to God.

So, simply focus on the intent. What is the intent? Then allow trust, with flow, to provide the how. This is again a trap for you can get into the letting go and trusting, and then do nothing. This is again a very important step to pay attention to.

When one is in trust, one also trusts that there is an action to be taken. It does not imply that I should sit and wait and a phone will ring with my answer. ***Trust means that you trust yourself in the steps you are taking.*** *You trust the action you are being guided to do and you use as your barometer the degree of joy and fulfillment and nourishment that comes from the action you are taking. You trust that if it is not there, then there is a new direction that is provided, even if it is not one you want to create, even if it does not look like that which you believe it should look like. That is the way to do it.*

There have been many who we hear all the time begging, help me, help me, yet they do not step into their own flow. They do not step into the action. We are helping, we are always there. Yet, if you do not reach out, how can we assist? This is the trust, the great trust and love of the self enough to do the action you are guided to do, and to truly honor the barometer of joy. ***Understand that joy is a state of being not an emotion.*** *This is an important distinction. When many hear the word joy, they assume it means giddy or laughter. Joy is peace. Joy is love.*

Joy is a state of being. It is a way of living where you are in complete acknowledgement and harmony with your authentic being. You are able to relax into trust so implicitly there is not one second spent on the double asking. When you truly flow from one action to another without questioning, that is when you know. When you stop with the second guessing of yourself, your actions, your being-ness; when you simply stop questioning what you are doing. This does not imply recklessness, it implies complete peace, trust, flow, and knowing. Balanced in that recognition is of course quiet time, a time of reflection, and the time to receive guidance for which you can act upon.

The concept of meditation has become convoluted on this planet. ***Meditation is any process of sincere intent directed toward achieving***

***inspired guidance**. Many ask, "How do I know it is inspired? How do I know it is true guidance?" There is only one answer.*

Does it give you greater joy? Does it provide a sense of love? Do you feel peace?

If anything you receive in quiet reflection causes you distress, make sure you understood correctly. ***True universal energy will only create feelings of Peace, Love and Joy.*** *This is the most simple and direct barometer we can offer anyone. It is also important to remember that meditation takes many forms. Perhaps it also needs to have many definitions. We may refer to it as meditation, you may call it reflection, inspiration, quiet time, it does not matter.*

However, when your entire being **is** *meditation, when your existence is meditation; that is when the questions you ask are no longer even in your thought process to ask or even to formulate. This is a barometer. Now we encourage you to be careful as you listen to these words for they can trigger a loop of self-judgment. This judgment may wish to express itself as the belief that you are not doing enough now. Remember, the very trigger that sends that message to you is the same one that knows you are already doing everything you need to do.*

It is all meditation. It is all joy. Trust, do not second guess. Presence is love, love is trust. Trust gives presence.

Presence is love, love is trust.
Trust gives presence.

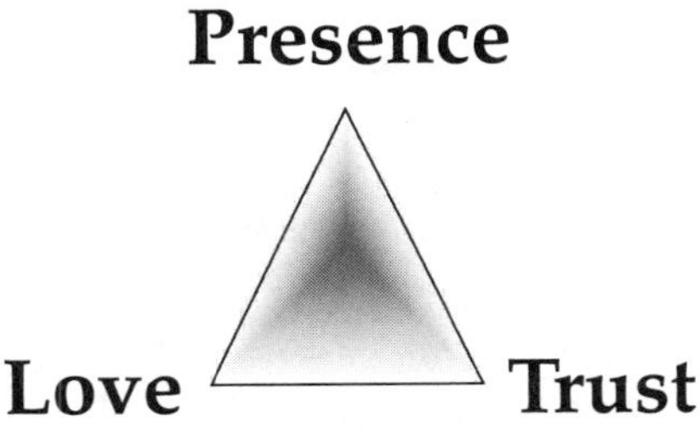

For you must have presence in the present. Otherwise it is a false symptom of one who is on a path of aspiration. OK, I'm present, now….now what? You must have your presence in the present. Always remember this. ***Your presence honors Divine light through the recognition that trust and love are inseparable.*** *Trust is love and love is trust, and let it begin with you.*

If you find yourself unable to begin with you, then this is when you are being called to go beyond the you ever more; to claim your presence, in the present.

Sri Ram Kaa: The present is the presence.

Yes, that is correct and it must begin with you. For you see, when you are able to bring your presence into every breathing moment, then you are unshakable. You are then so connected, so available to yourself, that there is not an event that can ever stop you from your Divine connection. This is not to say that there would not be momentary connection with the pain of events, for the pain of the pain is the habit of this sphere. However these moments are fleeting and will shift in their ability to affect you in a manner that is now different.

They shift because they love you. Yes, you have shifted because you love you. We love you. You are love, so therefore you know love, therefore you become love, therefore you are the presence of love, which also means you trust yourself, your partner, your life, yes!

Within relationship in your world there are many couples who do not trust each other. They do not trust each other on many levels, this is the number one reason relationships do not work. They must claim Divine Partnership, this is where they will all need to go.

Sri Ram Kaa: Building trust?

Yes, however this is work that is done on an individual basis first. You must come to trust and love yourself unconditionally; only then are you truly ready to be in Divine Sacred Union. You may be with the correct partner, yet until the veil of distrust is lifted, until the comprehension that trust is love and love is trust is looked at, acknowledged and owned, it cannot be Divine

Sacred Union.

Sri Ram Kaa: I feel that many of the spiritual tools I've learned are ineffective for creating trust. Or is trust created through love?

This is so true, because trust is love and love is trust.

Sri Ram Kaa: Yet what is required is for one to create a vessel of love so that one may learn to trust themselves?

Pure love. The love that sustains the love that cannot ever be challenged, changed, thrown away, neglected, or dishonored, for all these things you do to yourselves.

Sri Ram Kaa: The love that will accept mistrust?

Yes, it is the same love that will dishonor, disrespect, and say no to life.

Sri Ram Kaa: Let me ask you There is a bit of a paradox from this point of view in wanting to be of service and allowing the result without expectation.

What is your intention?

Sri Ram Kaa: My intention is to cultivate a state of being.

Hold your intention firm, honor yourself by honoring your intention. Be sure that your intention is pure and based upon love. Be sure that your intention when you think about it, when you declare it, brings you great joy and gratitude. When You have all this, you have everything you need.

You are always delivered what you need. This is part of trust. This is part of trust.

When you are open to receive the receiving, you give yourself a great gift of self love. A gift that says Yes, I am truly ready. I will not dishonor that which is brought.

You honor God when you honor yourself.

I AM Presence!
I AM Love!
I AM Trust!

Pause - Breathe - Allow

Journaling For Integration

This lesson helps me to recognize:

Integrating this teaching means that I now release my attachments to:

Integrating this teaching means that I now accept:

A declaration that will help me integrate this lesson is:

Bring your hands to your heart once again, and declare the Mantra of Self-Ascension.

I AM HERE
I AM READY
I AM OPEN
GUIDE ME!

Lesson Three

The Resurrection of Self-Ascension

"I am the Resurrection and the Life!"
~ Jesus, The Christ

Archangel Zadkiel Speaks:

Now is the time of Great Resurrection. This lesson is about the true meaning of resurrection and the disparities among the definitions of this word in your world.

What is resurrection? Why do many fixate upon it? Why do many become so preoccupied with resurrection? Who was Jesus, and why did he resurrect?

In the understanding of the Self-Ascension process, resurrection is a term that does not have a separate meaning from Self-Ascension. They are very much one and the same. ***From the moment you are born into this expression of density you are resurrecting.***

Understanding what this means has a far broader scope than, "Let me kill you and see if you rise from the dead…oh, you did…resurrection." No, it is much broader than that, for that is a density based limited view.

The perspective of resurrection we offer is the same as Self-Ascension. Essentially, resurrection is the removal of refractory energy. In terms of resurrection, when you remove yourselves from the light, when you become refracted pieces that move further and further into density away from light, then symbolically this is death, a separation from source energy. The resurrection process begins the moment your path is determined and you arrive on this world.

This applies to all lifetimes, as all experiences are part of what is now the culminating resurrection of all Divine Light. When you arrive here, in this form of density, you are already in your resurrection process, although you may not feel it, know it, or even be aware of it. And so, you begin the process of Self-Ascension/resurrection.

Once you begin this process, all of your energetic experiences are carried forth and contained in each and every lifetime, regardless of where it may have occurred. It is important to remove the limited view that all lifetimes occur on this planet, or even in this galaxy or dimension.

Yes, there are those beings that are bound to this planet, so all of their lifetimes are on this sphere. Kira Raa is one of them because she chose to be bound to this planet because she so loved this planet, this third expression of light in form, that she chose to be here.

This is what you must understand. If you are bound to this planet or any other for all of your lifetimes until completion, it was by your choice. **All incarnations are by choice.**

There are some who make a different choice with each incarnation, and there are some who make one choice initially and then have all their incarnation experiences within that one choice. You, Sri Ram Kaa have been here on this planet very few times. This was by your choice. Part of the reason was due to your pain, as you did not want to be on the same sphere as Kira Raa knowing you could not be together, and so you chose to be away from here. You've carried this pain for a very long time. So where you expressed was chosen by you as Kira Raa chose to be here.

As you re-collect your energetic **expansionsism** *through every experience of your refracted particles, it contributes to the resurrection of the reunification that removes refractory devices and brings all beings back to wholeness. It is most challenging to explain this so that the mind of this world comprehends, and so we do our best.*

It was many refractory devices that further and further created the Individ-u-will that brought you through all of theses different lifetimes. *[See Figure-A, Lesson One, page 130.]* *They are now being gently and systematically removed. For if they were all removed in an instant, the collective shock would create a wave of energy that would throw the sensitive balance of life energy into imbalance. So from out of respect for the mind, it must be done in a gentle manner. Every event, every energetic shift that occurs on this sphere here, affects all other dimensions simultaneously. It is as if you take calm water and drop something heavy into the water and big ripples go out. This is the effect you all have throughout the universe.*

The Universal Effect

If you take calm water and drop something heavy into the water big ripples go out. This is the effect you all have throughout the universe.

Because of the immense power of the shift and the effect of the shift, it must be done in accordance with vibrational harmony. This is why all events seem to have a time and a place as you say. This is not to say that something happens according to the linear time line of your world, however it does occur within the Divine order of expansion. The evolution of the energy has come to a point now where it is ready to be reunited. With the removal of each refractory device, you start the integration process.

This is why it is a joyous time! It is as if an explorer has discovered the new world and has successfully explored that world without creating damage to that which it has been exploring. The explorer has filled their ship with all that was offered to go and is ready to return home successful!

The greatest gifts of all of your incarnations are ready to reassemble. Is that not truly resurrection? How could resurrection simply be for one person, one being? Why must it require a violent act? This is the paradigm that many get stuck in on this planet. Many energies are expressed with violent graphic detail to shock the psyche into belief patterns and then to hold that belief system through fear.

This system of conditioned belief patterns is a big concept to embrace and then to release. When you understand true resurrection, you understand that it is also Self-Ascension. As each Self ascends, it becomes part of the great resurrection of all! Thereby it does not diminish the importance of each Self ascending, it further gives the proper perspective of the joyous gift of Self-Ascension for you are being of service to all. Through your many incarnations you are coming closer to assist with lifting all of the refractory devices and coming back into the compete recognition and the joy of union on all levels.

Sri Ram Kaa: So, you are saying that Self-Ascension is contributing to the removal of the refractory devices, and the coming mass event is not significant enough dimensionally to cause any disruption, yet it may look like disruption to those who are still anchored within the individ-u-will?

Correct, which is why many beings from many dimensions are communicating with your planet in many ways, it is a means of offering the energy that supports you to Self-Ascend. Thereby as with all events, it occurs within the vibration of balance. Without balance then you would have that heavy object dropped into water. This is why it is not a surprise that so many are becoming aware that the shift or the rift in the shift is becoming greater - polarization is increasing, which is simply creating balance.

However, at the current time on our planet there are more who are polarized in fear than are not. This is why we are here - to support all light bearers and to assist in providing the energy for all who wish to claim it, that have chosen the Self-Ascension process.

Sri Ram Kaa: So awakening others to the choice they have already made is part of this teaching, and providing that support for them.

It is important to honor all definitions of all words, however for the purpose of great service in the time of the great resurrection, it is good to express the broader view, to recognize that each individ-u-will Self-Ascension contributes to mass ascension which leads to the removal of the refractory disturbances and enhances re-unification with the one God of connection, light, love, and peace.

Take time to assimilate the lessons. We wish you great awakening, you have entered the time. It is a new phase, and the energy has now come in and will continue to be integrating. Understand that a new phase of all life has begun. You have honored what needed to be accomplished, so it has brought you to this time. You are loved, you are supported, and we are always with you.

I AM the Resurrection!
I AM Life!

Pause - Breathe - Allow

Journaling For Integration

This lesson helps me to recognize:

Integrating this teaching means that I now release my attachments to:

Integrating this teaching means that I now accept:

A declaration that will help me integrate this lesson is:

Bring your hands to your heart once again, and declare the Mantra of Self-Ascension.

I AM HERE
I AM READY
I AM OPEN
GUIDE ME!

Lesson Four

Remembrance and Re-Spect

There can be no more running away,
no more pretending, no more withholding.

~ Sri Ram Kaa in
Sacred Union, The Journey Home, page 87

Archangel Zadkiel Speaks:

This world enchants you to remember that which you are. It entices the senses to wake up, to remember. Long ago this land was held sacred. It was chosen to be the point of remembrance which is why so many are called here. As you take in the energy of all that is around you, feel the abundance, and feel the path of nourishment. For what is nourishment, truly?

Nourishment is what goes into the soul to awaken, sustain, enliven, and bring you back to yourself. This lesson is about respect and nourishment. Together, these two serve to bring you closer to God, closer to the One, and closer to your ability to remain in authentic being-ness while in the cloak of density. There is much that is available to you from this respect, and so we begin with the word "respect".

To Re-Spect.

Re – to visit again.

Spect – to look closer.

Through this deeper view, you uncover the true meaning of respect as: to visit again with a closer look. Or, stated more fully, to be able to remove that which no longer serves in your introspection and to acknowledge and honor this with great depth, gratitude and love.

Re-Spect.

To look again.

To honor again.

Re-Spect, to visit again; because it has always been, and to know that this is not the first time. It is once again something you are connecting with. When we discuss respecting others, it is part of the universal knowing. **Once you understand that you have indeed done this all before, then you know, and then you are responsible.** *It is then that you are able to truly Re-Spect all, because you recognize that you are visiting again that which has always been. You have the opportunity to honor, to create and to be a co-creator of God in the way that you honor these energies. Of course, this starts with yourself.*

Until you are able to find this in yourself, how can you ever truly find it in others? There is so much fascination around past lives and regression – I want to know what I did, I want to know who I was, I want to connect – there is a curiosity. This curiosity is actually a stirring in the soul of the Re-spect.

Once one has that curiosity stimulated, they have declared, "Yes, I understand I have been here before." It is a signal of the awakening heart when one shows fascination and curiosity in past life. Even if you believe they are not coming from a place of light, it is a signal to you that says, "Yes, they are waking; yes, they are understanding."

One cannot move into the process of true Re-Spect until one understands that it has all been done before. Understanding of the purpose of multiple incarnations in density is what opens one up to the respect of the self, of the authenticity of the true God.

Once one opens to Re-spect and becomes the co-creator, you become available to remember. Is it not said that you live in a world where respect is often sought through fear? "You respect me because I will beat you if you do not. You respect me because I say so. You respect your elders." Yet the true meaning of the Re-Spect is lost very deep within this paradigm. Even that Re-spect, which has great beautiful opening ability, has been shrouded in fear and guilt. Fear and guilt are great traps, for they trap you in the vessel, they trap all beings of energy. Do you not now see how every single aspect of your cellular structure has been orchestrated to keep you asleep?

Sri Ram Kaa: Yes, every aspect.

Every aspect is correct. And so it is cause for great celebration when you are able to break through! As you move through these lessons, that is what is happening – a deeper enhancement of breaking through. This is a lesson on remembrance for the Re-spect of all paths. When you remember that you have done this all before, then you are responsible.

Sri Ram Kaa: Then true responsibility is true remembering, and true remembering cannot happen without Re-spect.

Correct.

Sri Ram Kaa: So therein lies the recognition and the seed of reference.

Yes. This recognition is found within the First Commandment that says: Do not put other gods before me. What it means is that as a child of the one God, as a piece of light, as one of oneness, you must Re-spect and discover God first. For when you are a victim of illusion, victim of the fear, victim of the guilt, victim of the heavy foods that cause great density, victim of belief patterns that are limiting and do not allow you to understand, then you truly have no Re-spect for your own Godhood and you have therefore put other gods before you.

Sri Ram Kaa: By clinging to density, you are incapable of Re-spect.

Correct; in the true meaning. For one to truly not put other gods before me, one must be in the position of honor, to be honored, and to honor all. Once you have Re-spect for your path, once you have Re-spect for yourself and have not placed other gods before thee, then you understand and hold sacred the gift of enlightenment.

Every single cell, every single process, every single lifetime has added to the veil, and has added to the separation. This is why it is always appropriate to be in joy and celebration once one has discovered the truth of their own nature. This is why joy is your birthright. This is why it is the peace and the love that gives you the joy. Do not invert this formula. Understand what joy is!

Peace + Love = Joy

This is the conscious recognition that comes through the Re-Spect of the oneness of the light. The being that you are! The gift of love! This is everlasting. It has always been and will always be. It is the you that you have always come to know, again and again. ***Joy is your birthright!***

Many look at a guru or acknowledged teacher and say, "Look at the joy, the laughter, the absolute sheer funniness around this enlightened being!" Of course! That is their message; that you should not let anything stop your connection to joy, that it is absolutely your birthright to be in joy with all creation. This includes what you wear and what you do with your body.

At this time in the cycle of density, there is a preoccupation that demonstrates a lack of Re-Spect of the physical body, it is expressed through trying to change the body. It is a sign of true remembrance to come to love and delight in the body as it is expressing itself. To understand the sheer joy, that is what it is all about; to walk in joy, to love, and to be in joy. This is what true Re-Spect brings. The barometer once again is joy.

Sri Ram Kaa: Yes.

If Re-spect brings you fear, if re-spect brings you discomfort, if Re-spect brings you guilt, if you Re-spect because you feel obligated, is it authentic? ***True Re-Spect comes from the knowing, the recognition, and the knowledge of the Truth of Joy.***

If you move out of joy, are you Re-specting yourself? Or, are you moving back into illusion? Are you moving back into that which prevents you from joy, therefore lacking the Re-Spect?

True Re-Spect is to honor the soul that you are, and to honor all beings, for all are on their path.

I AM Peace!
I AM Love!
I AM Joy!

Pause - Breathe - Allow

Journaling For Integration

This lesson helps me to recognize:

Integrating this teaching means that I now release my attachments to:

Integrating this teaching means that I now accept:

A declaration that will help me integrate this lesson is:

Bring your hands to your heart once again, and declare the Mantra of Self-Ascension.

I AM HERE
I AM READY
I AM OPEN
GUIDE ME!

Lesson Five

Responsibility

"In the recognition of the oneness there begins the responsibility."
~ Archangel Zadkiel

Archangel Zadkiel Speaks:

The lesson of Responsibility begins with the vessel, (body), you have. If you can not be responsible for your own vessel, how can you ever be responsible on any other level? This responsibility is not about vanity, which has been misconstrued on this planet. As with many other concepts it has taken on a perversion such as: "I must respect my body by surgically altering it," or, "I must respect my body by making it conform to an outside source that says it must be a specific way." This is simply not true. "I must respect my body so my hair or eyes should be a certain color, or I should be a certain height or weight."

All of these serve an egoic perversion do they not? They serve to satisfy a false illusion. If one derives their sense of security from the illusionary outside world, has that truly helped them connect with their authentic self and being?

In this density of refractionary existence, the body is the greatest illusion. For the body in density helps to keep one separated more convincingly than the emotional or spiritual body.

One can touch the emotional body occasionally, yet everywhere they look there are ideas and concepts about the physical body. The body will normalize once it is respected from its authentic perspective. Wherever and however the body normalizes is perfect and therefore means you have released an expected outcome.

For example, one may claim they need to lose a specific amount of weight, or have an optimum weight goal in mind. These concepts do not serve the vessel in its authentic state, because you are looking at the vessel from the outside in. How many in your society have gone to a specific goal of weight and have sacrificed all within only to become a hollow shell in the need for societal exterior approval? There is then nothing left inside to support their authentic being. This therefore causes stress and great separation where joy can only be obtained through an endless pattern of perfectionism of the external.

Therefore is joy ever possible?

One must be full from within, one must be created from the inside. Even that is an illusion, for it is a perception that your authentic being is somehow locked inside. Yes, the vessel provides you the biological necessity to occupy space in this density. However, it is not a question of within or without, it is all around, all encompassing.

Soul nourishment[26] *is vital…VITAL. One must nourish from the inside, one must support their authentic vibratory level first, and then all else will normalize. Whatever weight is perfect for your body will appear, whatever structure is correct for you will manifest. You were each and all given beautiful colored eyes to assist with the way your vibratory level operates. Why change that? For in so doing, you shift the vibratory energy receptors and create ever more imbalance.*

All physical manifestations of the body, hair, skin, eyes, are appropriate for the energy that is being supported by your vessel. When you alter this balance for the exclusive purpose of physical approval to seek joy in an illusionary society, then you have given your power to separation.

Please recognize that there is no judgment around these alterations. Some will declare, "Oh, my goodness I have already enlarged my breasts," or some other alteration. Recognize the beauty that this path of alteration has brought you to. How beautiful that through the search for joy you have learned about separation. It is not unusual for one to go into the abyss to be able to recognize their Divine being-ness. Begin by loving the alteration. Love the gift that it has given you of recognizing separation and allow the joy to enter in and continue from there.

No matter what has been done prior to the knowing, all experience has served to bring you to the knowing.

Sri Ram Kaa: To make one responsible.

Yes. As we have mentioned, laugh at the belly, the nose, the eyes, the hair, or lack of hair, and you nourish starting with the inside. The Soul Nourishment Program is very powerful. As one continues on this program, routine fasting becomes an integral piece.

True fasting, fresh water, fresh lemon, the cleansing of the colon, are all aspects of the concept of nourishing the soul versus the egoic nourishment of the body. This is an important knowing.

When you make a commitment, you learn much about yourself and your world. You must make an agreement to stay out of ego. Surrender during the fasting and prepare ahead of time to make it easy. Discuss your fears and concerns. This is good, because it is fear that traps you into egoic eating versus soul nourishment.

Even if one is not preparing to fast, simply shifting into vibrational soul nourishment will create or bring up much fear. One should ask: Why am I reluctant to stop eating the flesh of animals? Why am I afraid to stop drinking milk? Why am I not so happy about no longer eating eggs and cheese? This is the true barrier.

Authentic soul nourishment is simple. Gift yourself with plenty of fresh water, anything green, and once every 30 days, or every lunar cycle, two days of liquids, juices, or soups. Then, after approximately 8 months of this process, introduce a 10 day liquid fast. Once you have successfully completed this, consider a 10 day liquid fast every 6 lunar cycles. Yes, you must prepare.

Discuss your feelings about the fasting portion of soul nourishment openly. Avoid letting the ego take over and assume you can jump right in. Acknowledge yourself and you will learn much about yourself. Write, (journal), and Be. We are with you.

Sri Ram Kaa: Many people have questions and feel they must justify this choice. Why should I give up the eggs, why not just meat? Often it is a negotiation of the ego.

Exactly! This is why one must talk about it. What is their true fear of no longer eating eggs or meat? This is why we ask you to ask the questions we gave you. All of it is an egoic trap. There will be those who will also justify by stating, "Well, I have read that, or I believe this, or my body must have this certain food!"

Of course! If your ego is telling you what you must believe and what you must have, than indeed you need it, for it, (the ego), is the controlling energy of your vessel. Honor it. As with all steps toward the awakening of authenticity on the path, gentleness and love expressed toward yourself is paramount.

Sri Ram Kaa: So, even with the soul nourishment program, if the person is unable to accept the entire program, to accept even a small portion would open them to a state of increased recognition.

Yes, correct.

Sri Ram Kaa: Then over time they would experience ever greater opening and understanding?

Yes. Any step is a positive step. Even just drinking water is a powerful step. There are many who are so disconnected they are unable to ingest this life giving gift. They claim water makes them sick, or that they can only drink sodas. One begins by simply drinking water. Start there and be in joyous gratitude that you are starting there. Substitute just one meal a day for a meal of greens. Or start by reaffirming to yourself that you are in joyous gratitude simply for being. All of these actions nourish the soul.

It is not just the partaking of solid or liquid foods that nourish the soul. Complete integration of what you are thinking, how you process it, how you receive it, and how you support it, that is soul nourishment. It is so much more than what you may put into your mouth. You feed yourself with thoughts, belief patterns, and ways of expressing them.

Sri Ram Kaa: This also centers the importance of offering prayer and/or gratitude prior to ingesting anything.

Absolutely. This is also another way to begin; simply take that moment with every meal, with every opportunity regardless of where you are, to say thank you. Or is it again something that is done ceremonially only one day a week, or not in public for fear of others looking? It is still an anomaly in this society to see someone stop to give thanks prior to eating. This simple public act can also make others feel uncomfortable.

Sri Ram Kaa: Yes, anything that disturbs our slumber is perceived as uncomfortable or threatening. I have a question about the body being the greatest illusion, for is not the body the vehicle of connection to this reality? It seems that the body is very real.

It is a real illusion. Try to understand that.

Sri Ram Kaa: It is important in this vibrational stream.

It is the only way you can experience the stream. In your light body, it is impossible to be present here in this world. One must put on the cloak to experience the density; yet, that does not make any of it real.

Sri Ram Kaa: It makes it a profound gift.

Yes! Yes! Now you understand. That is why one must be in deep respect and reverence of the vessel and be able to release the false judgments of external appearance.

Sri Ram Kaa: From that place of recognition, the nourishment program is not a negotiation. When we approach change from the standpoint of the ego and the prior energy, this perspective is the same as one that claims we must process or integrate.

Yes. It is also why aging is an illusion. For you see, as the vessel matures, it grows, and it supports your energy. When it starts to decompose and age, it is simply due to a belief in the collective illusion that this is expected. The vessel was designed to grow and mature, not to decompose, and certainly not to be of detriment.

Yet, you live in a density expression that is terrified of everyone remaining vital. For indeed this would have an economic impact, this would have a planetary impact, and would demand a different experience of the illusion. So, the collective illusion solved this by creating old age and a physical death.

Because of the lack of trust, the concept of release of the vessel became frightening. Yet, there are small groups here on this planet that have never ever gone away from the concept of the voluntary release of the body and still demonstrate today that this is the way it should be (Mahasamadhi[27]).

They are here on this planet, and yet it would demand great trust from the masses for each to recognize their own time for joyous release from the vessel.

Sri Ram Kaa: This folds in with stories I remember of Buddhist masters or Himalayan Gurus.

Correct! Is that not joy? Is that not a way of saying thank you to the physical vessel and the world of density for all it has gifted you as part of your experience? Yet, as with everything else, even death has been taken as a disharmonious separation. It exists within a belief system of sickness, old age, and unwilling death where one must be "taken." Then, a system of fear has built up around that belief and has led to even greater distrust.

Sri Ram Kaa: One of the sensations I have not yet resolved is the great challenge of being in a physical form and holding any of the collective belief systems while also trying to have a recognition of light. It is most challenging. There is pain and restriction everywhere, there is fear and suffering everywhere. When I hold joy for any length of time those issues matter not, yet the moment I step out of joy they are ever present again.

Yes. It is important to focus upon staying connected to the joy. For as you have experienced, the one sure way out of the fear, suffering and pain, is to remain in deep connection to the joy that is the truth of all beings. Soul nourishment opens the energies of the body, spirit and emotions to release the accumulated toxicity of the density experience, and open the door to embracing the joy of being.

Remember that periodic fasting will bring you through many emotions and experiences. We also highly suggest that the first time anyone fasts, they have a supportive partner. Simply be present for each other as you offer yourself the gift of releasing the patterns of destruction to re-embrace the gift of restoration.

As a student of consciousness, it is time for you to recognize that these first five lessons are the most important of all the lessons. They are the foundation, and one cannot continue until this foundation is truly firm. At this point it is good to stop, reflect, and to recognize, "Yes, I understand these first five lessons, I see their congruence, I understand I have opened up." These five lessons are a key in a lock, and now that the lock has opened, you are ready for the next five and so on.

I AM Divine Love in Action!

Pause - Breathe - Allow

Journaling For Integration

This lesson helps me to recognize:

Integrating this teaching means that I now release my attachments to:

Integrating this teaching means that I now accept:

A declaration that will help me integrate this lesson is:

Bring your hands to your heart once again, and declare the Mantra of Self-Ascension.

I AM HERE
I AM READY
I AM OPEN
GUIDE ME!

The Lesson Between the Lessons

Archangel Zadkiel Speaks:

Many things lie dormant in many. Dormancy is the way in the land of density. It is simple to keep things dormant because it is a way of being that is able to activate on one level only. Once the dormancy has ended, then there are other planes of existence, other vibrational levels, other ways of expressing that become available to you. Other means of existence that become effortless, new channels of opportunity in different realms combining with this realm to bring existence into fullness and wholeness, to bring dimensional shift into practice.

Shifting is simple: resistance is difficult. For it is the resistance of the shift that brings in the difficulty, and brings in confusion, emotion, the physical shifting changes, the ways of making it seem it too mechanical, too difficult, when all one needs to do is say, "OK, shift!" It is that simple.

We recognize that at times it is challenging for a brain based in density consciousness to understand simplicity. Is that in and of itself not ironic? For it is all effortless: it is all truly simple. The complex is a design of a mechanism that wishes to keep you in one realm. It is not complex.

It is as if you take the refractory device and add layer after layer of complexity, questioning, doubt, fear, anger, habit, collective consciousness. This is where the complex arises. Yet, when one is able to move through this, when one is able to remove the refractory devices completely, one realizes this is indeed the dream. Yet, when one first wakes from a dream, one is still confused, especially when one was so deeply in the dream. For when you wake now in the world of density having been in a deep dream during your sleep state, you wake up and in those moments you do not know which is real, which was the dream, which is the dream state. Or in your case you would think which is the dream...which is real? Yet truly you exist in this density in a dream state permanently. The dream is a dream of the dream state. It is a glimmer, an opening, an opportunity. Yes, there are dreams of an egoic construction and there are dreams that help to stimulate awakeness, to help call back that who you are, to help push the wheel into motion.

So as you wake, you will question which is the dream, which is reality? This is a normal questioning. It is one that is most expected, most perfect and most welcome. The questioning is a habit or patterning of density. Only in the density does one question because the questioning comes from lack of trust.

There is much difference in questions that are asked for clarification versus questions that are asked because of lack of trust. Most questions in the realm of density consciousness are asked from a perspective of lack of trust. They will usually begin with the word but: "But, how can this be? But what makes this so?"

All of those questions are asked from the perspective of one who does not trust. What is really being expressed is the energy of lack of trust of another, thereby they are actually disconnected from love, for trust and love are the same.

So, if trust and love were apparent, the questioning would shift. It would shift so that the energy of the questions would arise to help one serve with greater love and trust, for when one asks, "How may I serve?" , this is a question asked from trust and love.

It is important to understand and ascertain these subtle differences. It also gives you an opportunity to learn more about the trust base of another. For the trust base of another will be revealed in how they question. If you are able to listen, if you are able to love, and you are able to hold the space of Divine Light, then you can be present during any questioning and understand why the questioning is present. Remember, it is not the question itself that matters, it is the underlying need to ask. Is it for clarification or is it because of lack of trust?

Know that it is not important for you to make that distinction out loud with whomever you are interacting with. What is important is for each to understand the essence and to wrap the love around the heart of the questioner so that they may understand that trust and love are one so that their questions may release. How often do some say, I have questions, and then after a loving interaction, the questions no longer exist? This is because they have accepted the energy of love and trust.

It is important to demonstrate at all times your connectivity, your ability to maintain Peace, Love and Joy. If you are to be a Light Bearer, you must live it. It should not be a challenge. It should be effortless. It should be a great recognition of the Love that you are.

Remember, when you go deep within your own heart, you become the wave of Divine flow. Know that this energy is here, now, for all who choose love and trust.

Regarding the lessons, inside of each lesson there is a central theme. All of the lessons together are the components of Self-Ascension. They are components, not the steps. It is important to recognize that they are the components inside of the steps. Each of these steps have a color. As you review each lesson, it is important for you to allow yourself to go ever deeper with the lesson, until the energy of the lesson can be called forth with just one word. This word is for you to discover as you work with the lesson.

There are a total of twenty five lessons all together. As you review each lesson, you will discover that they are offered in a series of 5 lessons, with the sixth lesson being a transition lesson. So, for example, the sixth lesson is a transition lesson, as is lesson twelve and so on.

Sri Ram Kaa: So, we began with the individ-u-will, and then we moved into refractory devices and would you mind talking a moment about that phrase, the individ-u-will? What was not made explicit, at least for me, is that we are talking about an individual or not.

The individ-u-will is the opportunity to experience, as a One, the reason for the vessel. Because as your pure form, until you are broken down into refractory pieces, Light is all-ways in junction, in conjunction with other Light. And so, individ-u-will can not be expressed until one takes on the form of density through this vessel.

Sri Ram Kaa: Is that the same of Travelers having other experiences, (not on Earth)?

Absolutely. This is the reason for it. It is also so that you can come to realize how magnificent you are. This is the reason for all the cycles of returning to the inidivid-u-will. Until one can come to the recognition of the magnificence and the perfection of the being, once you recognize it, then you understand why. Then you are able to be in your ascended state, whole, complete, with other whole, complete beings of light.

Sri Ram Kaa: So then are you not describing the whole evolutionary process?

Yes, because there is no requirement at that point for individ-u-will. It is a growth phase, consider it your teen years.

Sri Ram Kaa: You have shared that the Light exists as One, as a collective, and that what many come forward from the Light could be called color, could be called perhaps a unique expression. Is the individ-u-will still part of the collective in its authenticity?

Yes!

Sri Ram Kaa: So what we are experiencing in the physical dimension is similar to what you might experience as a color of light. Is that accurate?

Yes, that is very accurate. This is why we keep using the term refractory device, because it goes from being pure Light to color, to color, to color.

Opening the Joy Pathway

No matter where one is in their emotional maturity or vibratory state of evolution, joy offers a pathway to the next level of existence. For the child, joy teaches them what they like and dislike and through this feedback children can learn their own preferences. For an adult, joy also offers feedback as to what kinds of experiences are truly nourishing you. We all begin at the emotional level, for the emotional body surrounds us as children.

Initially we begin to educate the emotional body and then as adults we give power to our mental body. These two non-physical bodies, the emotional and mental, interact together and cooperate with the physical body and the ego to create a personality that navigates life. As the adult matures they will find that their value system evolves from a me-based egocentric world to a more inclusive world. This is the natural evolution that helps society at large, for adults learn to recognize that their joy is related to their living environment and to the support of the community at large. Therefore adults often set their personal needs aside in favor of the family's needs or the community's needs and they find true joy in doing this service. Principle based living expands the ego's world in a healthy way.

Spiritual Joy is beyond the emotions. While the emotional body can open the door to spiritual Joy, this form of experience is unique. It is an expression that becomes known when consciousness aligns with essence. This is the Joy of your soul.

Thus, regardless of your state of discernment Joy is an elevator that will lift you. Joy can connect you to ever-refining states of consciousness for joy has no boundaries. Joy is the expansion into oneness. It permeates all levels of existence and all levels of consciousness, therefore joy can be found in any circumstance if one will only look deeply. One's experience of Joy does refine and change as one's consciousness expands. By choosing Joy one can find the Divine underpinning in any life experience.

Joy is your magic key to enlightenment! When a choice confronts you, ask where is my highest joy in this? Sometimes we need to look inside and see if our choices are nourishing the ego or the soul. True nourishment is soul nourishment and will offer the highest vibration of joy. Soul joy offers a sense of peaceful harmony and it is lasting while ego joy is quite temporary and dependent upon external conditions. Thus, with a little practice you will discern the difference between soul nourishment and emotional Joy. The key is to choose Joy!

Dependency upon the external is indeed an out-focused displacement of your power. As long as one relies on the external world to create an internal state such as joy, dependency is at work and you will remain a victim of circumstances. As one finds their inner authentic energy within, their orientation toward life will shift.

It is important to recognize that the ego is the servant of the soul, not vice versa. Over the centuries the ego has grown so strong in the consciousness of humanity that we often forget that we are spiritual beings having a human experience. This separation from Source is so common that millions of people seek religious experiences to remind themselves that they are indeed spiritual beings. Weekend spirituality will never bridge the inner gap between your ego and your soul. Only living from your soul will heal your life and our shared world. The everyday mystic knows his or her connection to Source is available 24 hours per day! Joy is but a choice away.

The ego has become a great habit in the consciousness of mankind. Because it carries such a primary role in the human psyche, the ego is thought of as a sign of health! That is, every form of self-help program available today is intended to empower the ego in ways that offer greater coping skills and self-worth. This is not bad. However, teaching our ego to model spiritual values does not negate its essential nature. The ego is a pirate; it wants to steal your identity.

The spiritualized ego is a high form of attainment in our every-day world. And it is a trap, for the spiritual ego will keep you limited to density concepts. It will color your view of the Divine and cosmos with its limitations. As we develop our spiritual discernment we are able to see the actions of the ego differ from the actions of the soul. The soul energy simply feels different than the ego energy. Whenever the ego is in charge, the choices it makes are based upon emotional motivations (usually fear) and it applies its focus to something external. Even if the decision at hand is of a personal nature there is still a belief at work that something outside of one's self is pivotal or important and will influence that decision. Therefore, one way to discern the ego in operation is to look at where the beliefs and energies are oriented. The soul, on the other hand, simply knows. It is in a state of trust and does not require external reassurance.

Authentic joy is aligned with core essence of the soul. It is not a giddy emotional state, rather it is a state of deep peace for it is your core essence. At times it is felt as excitement, a tingling expansion, but more commonly soul joy is rooted in a true sense of peace. It is this quality of peace that indicates the soul connection.

As the ego has become a great habit, so too has the habit of pain become commonplace. People have become accustomed to experiencing lack and pain in their lives. Many have released all belief that it could be different. Thus the ideas in this book can be challenging for people rooted in limiting beliefs to accept. The masses of society have truly adopted self-defeating beliefs that keep them in a dependency relationship to the world. They believe this is "just the way things are" and thus perpetuate lack and hierarchical existence.

This is not just about education – it is about the lack of soul-based living in the society. Modern liberals believe that equality will be cultivated through education and training. Certainly education and healthy self-esteem work wonders towards a person's life style. However true equality can never come from one ego teaching another ego, for the one who rescues another finds their self-esteem in the hierarchy, within the belief that they can actually rescue another. You can never rescue anyone – you can only point them to the energy of their own Divine connection. It is our spiritual legacy which is true empowerment. If the activists in our world would take the leap into Ascension Awareness, they would discover that all prior states of consciousness were but stepping stones or opportunities to develop soul-awareness and true empowerment.

We support each other by lifting ourselves. Remember everything that exists in the outer world is a reflection of consciousness. As we align with our soul energy we emanate a different frequency into the world. This sends an energetic signal to others. They then can use that energy to remind themselves of their own true energy.

Initially joy is felt through the emotional body, and as we evolve the sensation of joy becomes less emotional and is experienced through the spiritual body. There are many ways to interact with the world. Spiritual interaction is presently less common, however it is through identification with our spiritual body that we can transcend the magnetic attractions of the density world. The spiritual body experiences things as energy and places experiences within the context of Divine Love. Spiritual experience penetrates into our other bodies (the physical, mental, emotional bodies) and offers a sense of peace and spaciousness that is healing to those refractions.

Remember, while you are in a body you need an ego to help keep the body safe. While you are in this density, the emotional and mental bodies also serve to navigate this world. Celebrate these tools! Do not commit your identity to them. Instead simply observe that these ways of interfacing with the world are a gift. You get to experience density. You get to touch and feel. What fun!

As our vibrational level lifts we sometimes feel a sense of loss. This is because we are leaving behind some people or groups that once gave us meaning. We invite you to keep your eyes on the Divine flow and trust, for new friends, new spiritual family groups are finding you. And, as you anchor in Ascension Awareness your adventure in the body becomes more conscious and in many ways, more exquisite!

In the pyramid drawing the joy pathway is represented as a

portal of connectivity that continues from the Density Consciousness to Ascension Consciousness. If you have wandered off into a distracted consciousness, Joy will bring you into the portal. Then further surrender will lift you!

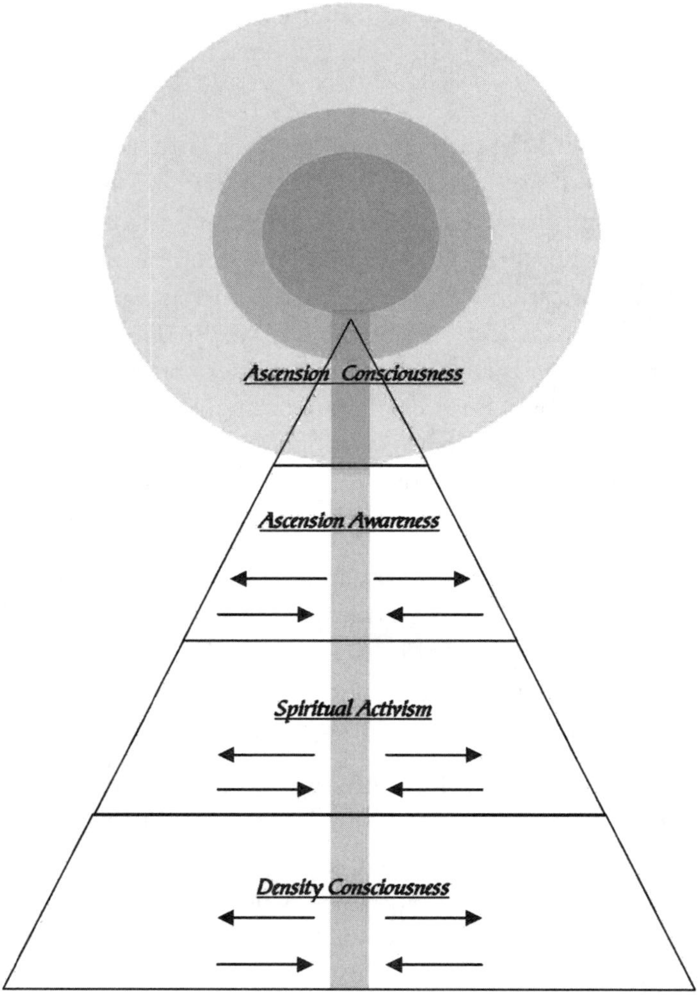

Pyramid of Spiritual Awakening
The Joy portal will attract some & repel others

Lesson Six

Expectation

"People often ask me how my life shifted so dramatically. All I did was surrender what surrender looks like! I stopped cutting deals with God."
~ Kira Raa

Archangel Zadkiel Speaks:

Look at having had an expectation. When we have an expectation it allows us to be "setup" as you know. When you find yourself hungry, or searching for food, whatever it may be, not feeling happy and energetic, you often move into self-judgment. Why am I not happy, why am I hungry?

It is important to recognize that self-judgment is often induced due to expectation. This is the lesson. The lesson is on **the Expectation**.

There is expectation of life, the expectation of death, the expectation of certain events happening at certain times, and the expectation that all will flow in a certain order. **All expectation encourages limiting belief systems. All expectation limits possibility.**

Some may say, "Oh, but I can expect quite a lot." Yes, this is true, so it is more than simply saying you can release expectation. It is the calling forth of the full understanding of where expectation comes from and what it is.

Recognize that the ability to even encourage or experience expectation is in and of itself a gift. Because how else can you face disaster, disappointment, and yes, even happiness at times. You say, "Yes, that met my expectations. Yes, that exceeded my expectations."

Pay attention to how often you engage in this talk about expectations;

meeting them, exceeding them, falling short of them and declaring what your expectations are. Listen to this! It is common to declare expectations ahead of time, usually with a well conceived list. Thereby declaring you are limited to this belief system, or set of expectations.

This is again a trap of being in a vessel, for the soul surrenders completely to the vessel so that it may have its full experience until it recognizes the soul presence. When the soul enters the vessel, it has put on the veil and has agreed that it will experience through the vessel. Then the mind ties in with the vessel and comes forward to limit the soul experience thereby making it even more difficult for you to be able to break through this illusion. Then, you feel comfortable with sets of self-limiting beliefs known as expectations...about everything.

Some may ask, well are you not talking about judgment? Certainly there are times when judgment feels like expectation. For when you say, "You did not meet my expectations," is that not a judgment? However, at this moment we are focusing upon expectation itself; the energy and the ability to expect something. When you expect something, you are therefore surrendering again your responsibility, your personal ability to be able to rise through any form of expectation to know that you are already whole without it.

When you recognize that you are already whole, then it is easy to see expectation for what it is; a limiting belief pattern that has been set in motion and is in place to encourage you to limit.

Let us re-visit the statement, "Oh, I can set great expectations for my-self."

How do you truly know within that statement that you are not limiting yourself? How do you know that which you are expecting and that which you have created in the great seeing of expectation is not in and of itself a limiting path for you?

This is only because you have self-limited the possibility of any other path by creating a series of expectations and setting them in motion. They rob you of your truth, they rob you of authenticity. When you are able to truly accept the light that you are, to know the light that you are, to be in your authentic being, then you realize there is no reason to have an expectation, because you are Trusting!

If you truly trust that all must be in flow and order and that all is in the flow and the order then why would there ever need to be an expectation. Some may ask "How can you set up a measurement of achievement without an expectation?"

Look inside your heart. Look inside your joy. Look deep into that which you are. Are you in Joy? Are your relationships with the Divine, with yourself, or with others bringing you joy? Does your action serve the highest or does it have a judgment center?

This is how you know. There will be some who may feel how would I get anything done? I must have something to measure, something to allow for expectations. How could I ever get anything done without declaring my expectations?

What if you were able to rephrase this by bringing the energy of Divine Love into the same mechanism without expectation and simply be able to say; "I trust that you will do in Divine service all that you need to do and feels joyous, to serve you on this path."

Many will say, "I cannot do that. Nothing would get done."

How do you know?

Sri Ram Kaa: Trust

Yes, and this is most scary for many because it is a great symbol. Expectation allows you to purge, it allows you to get out everything in your mind that is trying to escape, and so in this way it is good. When the expectations come up it is simply residue, left over gunk in the machine, and so when it comes up it is a wonderful thing. You are able to look at it and recognize it for what it is; a mind that is trying to control.

Love your mind for showing you what is still trying to be controlled. Then you are able to bless it, and offer it reassurance that you trust all actions are in the highest service and you do not need to have expectations provided, for you trust it will be done.

Then the expectations simply diminish. The more that we allow all expectations to diminish, many may claim they have no expectations when indeed they do and often express disappointment even within the declaration that expectation did not exist. ***One can only release expectation when one is coming from a Divinely centered heart that is filled with trust.***

One must be totally encompassed with trust to be able to do this. And remember, we offer you the knowing that trust is love, therefore it is one. Therefore, one must embody this type of trust in order to truly release expectation. Until such time it is futile.

One must not be frustrated over the usage of expectation, however it is important to continue studying and being present to what expectation is. It is an opportunity to see where the mind is trying to cling.

There are many places this most powerful mind, or you may wish to substitute ego, will go. It simply means that the mind is trying to control you, instead of you allowing it to be of service. You are not in service to your mind, your mind is in service to you. So this is the great gift of expectation as you live in a world of expectation.

You live in a time of great expectation on many levels. Many. You live in a society that teaches expectation.

Sri Ram Kaa: Are not belief systems expectations?

Absolutely.

Sri Ram Kaa: So, in this world here I have yet to see anyone who does not have belief systems.

A belief pattern like all patterns is a habit. I ask you this, we are communicating, chatting as they say in this moment. As we are communicating has not your belief system experienced a challenge in accepting our appearance to you, in the way you are now living, in the surrender of your own expectation of what every day should look like?

Sri Ram Kaa: Yes, that is so.

You see, the veil between the worlds is much thinner than you may know.

When you allow your belief that the sky is blue or the wall is solid, your belief that glass can be broken, your belief of your age, your belief of any of this around you, to fully release, then you have ascended .

This is why you have not found anyone without a belief system. There is a difference between believing and knowing. Yet getting there can seem most challenging.

Sri Ram Kaa: Is not true believing true knowing? Is there really a difference?

Yes. There is. It is a beautiful difference, and it is one that exists. To believe in something on this sphere, and we must qualify this, on this sphere what you are believing is a set of patterns and habits that have been manufactured and have been enhanced through a collective conscious patterning.

You believe in wood. You believe in bones, metal, iron, sticks and whatever. When you walk, when you dive into your authenticity with great abandon and surrender and sprinkle on top of that trust and unconditional love, then you know.

Sri Ram Kaa: So, where is belief?

Available.

Sri Ram Kaa: Available to create?

If you wish, of course. Belief is a healthy and beautiful thing. It sustains you and allows you to go ever deeper. The more you know, that more you are aware. The more you practice and the more you stay in constant contact with your light body, the greater your knowing. You realize then that belief was a beautiful pre-requisite to bring you to the place of knowing.

And the more that you know, the more you can surrender. Belief is not a bad thing, it is a good thing, it must exist. These lessons are to help all learn how to walk through this dense world into the energy of Self-Ascension; into a state of permanent Joy and recognition of the self, the soul, the light body.

For many years on this sphere it was not possible for many to achieve this state. You are at the time and place in your history now where it is important that just the opposite occur, that there is rapid escalation that as many as possible are able to move into this state.

This is why this lesson of expectation is also a lesson of trust. It cannot be undertaken until the first five lessons have been truly studied. For this lesson is an expanding exercise. You must expand your consciousness which means you must break through thinking to be able to truly understand this lesson. To take in the concept of simply looking at expectation as another means of the ego or the brain trying to find yet another way to hang around. Everything else to the ego appears to be going away, so it is looking for another place to be.

Sri Ram Kaa: And expectations seem to be woven into time.

Yes, the false god; very much so because they are measurable. How could you measure expectations if they were not woven into time? It would be impossible.

Sri Ram Kaa: Seems that as soon as we are willing to release the mass belief system then we can release any expectation.

Yes, that is exactly the point.

Sri Ram Kaa: So for those who are at the forefront of that, they are assisting to create a belief pattern that it can be done.

Correct. Yes. For many need teachers. You are all teachers as you are all students.

Sri Ram Kaa: Yes, there have been many lessons.

Remember to look at expectation every time it comes up. It is kind of fun, every time an expectation comes up, you may wish to Stop and make a little mark on a paper. At the end of the day, see how many times you have expected something. Very fun. Do not expect that it will get better everyday either!

Sri Ram Kaa: I expect I'll need a large piece of paper.

Yes. This can be a metaphorical exercise also. You can just stop in the moment and notice. Like the rubber band on the wrist.

Sri Ram Kaa: What has already been taught in the prior lessons, especially the lesson of Re-Spect which is tied into responsibility, for one to fully reside in that knowing would that not take care of this?

Maybe. Everything is a layer. Everything goes deeper and yet, they are all connected.

Sri Ram Kaa: Yes, many aspects like facets on a crystal.

Spokes in a wheel, and this is the analogy of the lessons which we offer you. Think of a wheel with a hub, and the spokes around it. In the middle is Self-Ascension, the 25th lesson binds the wheel together. There are 24 spokes, and then there is a circle around the spokes which is the 25th lesson. These are the components. There are four steps to Self-Ascension, but when you walk the path there are lessons, and so this is the wheel of lessons. Is that not like a wheel of dharma[28]?

Sri Ram Kaa: Yes

The lesson wheel, as you may wish to describe it, is a wheel because it enhances every time you re-visit it. This is why we discussed earlier that each must go through the lessons, and then do them again, and then perhaps one may wish to start all over again!

This is a very big lesson that will be revisited perhaps more than the others.

Sri Ram Kaa: Is it not useful for one on the path to have an expectation of success?

Absolutely. As we discussed, the expectation of success can be very self-limiting, yet it will propel one to keep seeking and this is how it can be very beneficial.

The energy of the expectation will assist one to continue the search until one is able to stay connected to the Divine without any conscious assistance.

It is a beautiful ingredient of enlightenment, yet as with many ingredients, once the final accomplishment is made the individual ingredients are no longer available or even able to be recognized. All of the individual parts have now become integrated into the whole.

What is important for you now is to stay in trust and focus on your path. This is where you are of the most service. Love and be available without expectation. That is all that is needed and that is a lot. Consistency in your actions is the greatest gift you can offer to yourself and those around you.

Release the idea of flesh and let the truth shine through. Many Blessings.

I AM Trust!

I AM the Divine in Action!

Pause - Breathe - Allow

Journaling For Integration

This lesson helps me to recognize:

Integrating this teaching means that I now release my attachments to:

Integrating this teaching means that I now accept:

A declaration that will help me integrate this lesson is:

Bring your hands to your heart once again, and declare the Mantra of Self-Ascension.

I AM HERE
I AM READY
I AM OPEN
GUIDE ME!

Lesson Seven

The All-Encompassing Moment

When you find yourself in a pattern that does not serve you; interrupt it. For just like an old record, you simply take the needle off and say, "No, not now."
~ Archangel Zadkiel

Archangel Zadkiel Speaks:

It is time to instruct you in lesson seven. Remember that it is important for you to fully understand lesson six before you continue. We suggest that you have fun with this, make them into a little game, do whatever you like, have fun.

Sri Ram Kaa: With the lessons?

Yes, make cards, make little pictures, whatever makes it fun for you. Have joy in all you do. Be the effervescent joy.

There is nothing that can happen in the now that you are not a part of. In this one moment you are all encompassing. This is the directive of the seventh lesson. The understanding that in the one moment you are all encompassing; that within the moment it gives and provides you with a framework for the integration of all that you have learned to date and becomes the springboard for all that is to come.

Many often spend their days and their time making lists, things to do, lists for lists. Then, focus is spent on having to reprioritize according to the list. Often, this creates worry about accomplishing the list. From here, one creates time parameters around these priorities. Is this not a vast preoccupation, to be consumed by accomplishing the perceived priority?

This belief system creates a vast disconnect from the All-Encompassing by responding to time. There is much talk and there has been much talk for a long, long, long time on the history of this planet about being present or the gift of being in the moment. Let us expand the gift of being in the One Moment.

Regardless of how busy you are, you can always recognize any given moment and be present knowing that you, in that moment, are all. Within that knowing you are able to accept that everything in that moment is exactly as it has manifested itself in your consciousness to be. Learning and acquiring the habit of connecting moments is a powerful stage that allows you to be the All-Encompassing expansionary Light vehicle that you are.

In order to be, we say again, in order to BE, you must practice bringing your consciousness into the One Moment, and there are no restrictions on this moment. It is not a timed second, or minute, you do not set a fixed amount of time to be the moment, for that is irrelevant within the moment. It is whatever it is. There is no restraint, no restriction; there is no tightening of the moment. It is a respite for the soul, a big AH of relief that you have recognized, that you see your all encompassing expansionary vehicle. For as you expand and as your colors become further defined through refractions, a great gift is to be able to recognize the momentary expansion of authenticity.

Many have these moments. They get very excited. They share or they get scared and do not know what has happened. Ah-ha, I had a moment. Some go Oh, what is that? And some go OH what a gift! Then they continue in a futile effort to keep trying to find the moment when it has never been lost. Oh I want to do this again, how? Oh, I touched it once. The beauty of understanding the power of the All-Encompassing Moment is that it can happen at any given opportunity. All one must do is say, "I am in that moment." Boom it is there!

This ties into learning how to use the energetic pulsing of recognition throughout the systems of the vessel. As one evolves, as one creates greater connectivity with authenticity, as one is able to bring in moment after moment, the vibratory level of the vessel is then prepared to accept an increase. It will automatically increase because you are spending more of your experience within the presence of authenticity, therefore density becomes less.

There are physical sensations that accompany the Now Experience. This is also a place where many say, "I had a moment, but then I took a pill." Or, "I had a moment, but someone told me there was something wrong with me so I got rid of it, oh thank goodness."

This response to the physical experience of the escalation of vibratory energy is simply because of the unawareness of the necessary physical shifts in the vessel that must occur at this time. For all to transcend, for all to truly grow into Self-Ascension, it is important to be aware that there will be physical shifts, and to know they will happen. Yet you live in a dense circle that encourages all physical shifts to be squelched, that adamantly declare that it is unacceptable not to be afraid. You are conditioned on this sphere to believe that all that is not part of what is considered to be the accepted standard is therefore wrong and something to be afraid of.

We ask you this: Was not the accepted standard that the Earth was flat prevalent for a long time? And did this also include the accepted standard that you would fall off at its edge?

We share this observation because it is important. When it comes to that which is required for health, for the body, there are many who believe very clearly in the accepted densities of the time. Perhaps, these levels are required to keep you in a certain area of density. Perhaps certain levels of vitamin, nourishment, mineral, and consumption of certain foods are meant to keep you in a certain density and will make you feel very comfortable in the density. This is very true.

So it is indeed a great pattern of beliefs, and the way that you practice out of it is by being in each moment. Remember that within each moment there is an undeniable absolute recognition of the authenticity that you are, and when you choose not to medicate it, then you learn to connect each moment to moment. This soon becomes a new habit because when you start with a small moment, it is easier to start releasing belief systems and patterns, as we have already talked about, and it is easier because they come up. They will come up over and over and over again because they are everywhere here in this world.

So as you stay within a moment, and as you learn to connect each mo-

ment, things shift. Your physical body shifts, your systems shift, and you become very aware of interactions with others that are toxic. Please know this is not a form judgment and it is important we take this moment to simply state this is NOT judgment, it is a choice made through awareness. If you are choosing to continue on the path, if you are choosing to remain firm within the connectivity of the moment to the moment, you will find yourself simultaneously choosing to be with certain beings, as much as you will choose not to be with others. There will be a time when a reclusive nature may serve you. There will be a time when you may have to release every other association with people you have around you if it is not congruent with conscious presence.

At this time of recognition of the conscious presence around you, it may feel as if it is a test. Know that you are being tested, it is simply that your ego is flaring again because in that moment your ego will say, "Oh my God, how can I ever release members of my family? How can I ever release my life long friends?"

The truth is you are releasing yourself from the **Bond of Illusion**. *As you embrace this authentic self, the Bond of Illusion has released for you to have a form of relationship that will usually look totally different than what your ego expects. You are now creating the conscious recognition that you must release all energy that is incongruent with the now because of your presence within the moment to moment. Therefore, all those around you who are part of this release are giving you a great gift. They love you so much; that they have brought you to this point of conscious recognition. How could you ever dishonor that?*

Those that you have released have literally loved you to the point of choice. This love has given you what you need at that time. This may look painful on the surface of this planet. It may look nasty in world actions. What they are doing is actually making it easier for you to continue. Love them through this great gift of separation illusion and may you be able to hold as much loving space for them, so that they may choose, if they wish, to go through their own Bond of Illusion. This does not mean that all must go through release. Those who are already around you, those who are there to support you, are present because they themselves are on this path or have been there before. It is important to understand these shifts as there will be many shifts on many levels.

Learn the gift of connecting the moment to the moment and understanding the all encompassing authenticity of you.

Let us now talk about the shift in the body. The most common first phase of physical shift will be experienced as sending forth vibratory energy which some may feel as a tremor. While it does not resemble a tremor so much; the vibratory energy does send electrical impulses through the body in a manner that you are able to feel. It could be described as a jumpy feeling perhaps, or it could be described as an electrical impulse, either way it is a new sensation.[29] *This is another time for the ego to flare. An immediate conditioned response may be, "Oh one must go to doctor now. This is not normal."*

What will usually happen is that when one goes to the Doctor, they will be unable to find anything wrong with your body, and that is the truth. Everything is actually very good with you. Be prepared that in finding everything fine, it is not uncommon for them not to rest until they try find something based upon accepted science that might be causing the vibrational level experience.

A call to turn away from the experience may also be offered from well intended observers such as: "May I suggest you start eating meat again. May I suggest that you eat denser foods." You might also be offered suggestions nutritionally, such as do not have this or that. Remember that all of these suggestions will bring you back into heavier density, so the sensations of experiencing lighter vibration will cease. This experience of returning to density is also powerful as it self-justifies the actions of the ego. It is an opportunity for the ego to demonstrate its power.

When you experiment with receiving increased vibratory energy and then move awareness from it by re-entering density, it is the same as adding another refractory layer. This is a choice that will always be in front of you, and you can certainly do this. Of course it is always more comfortable to stay with the experience of density for it is the most familiar, and even if it is painful there is often comfort within known pain.

Interestingly, there are many vibrational levels that exist simultaneously at this time on this sphere. As you move from one to another, is it not expected there would be some perceived discomfort until all the refractory devices are removed?

For until one moves out of the predominant heavy density, it is uncomfortable to adjust to a different vibration. However, as one removes layers of density, one is able to begin understanding, comprehending, and experiencing the multi-dimensions that are here in this world. Remember, until one allows themselves to walk through the perceived discomfort of the shift, one can not understand or experience both or more.

So yes, it takes great courage to walk through the many Bonds of Illusion. Many, many begin, and as you have seen, there are many times the ego flares and demands that you come back to density consciousness. This is very much the Devil concept you find in your religions. Oh the devil made me do it. Yes this is true, however, there is no devil other than that which is inside of yourself. The egoic mind wants to be in control, however, the egoic mind is more like a two year old. All it wants is to belong, be loved and be accepted. How beautiful because you can so easily recognize this truth within the moment. Just keep the boundary of the ego in perspective; who is serving who?

So as one goes through the societal change, the emotional change, and the physical change of learning to understand living within the moment to moment. This is the gateway. This discipline, this process, opens the door to greater understanding, greater evolution, and the ability to cultivate the release of judgment.

For example, let us look at the energy of one who has released their affiliation with a specific family. They may be saying to themselves, "Oh I am a horrid person. How could I do that?"

Perhaps this is a great opportunity to release judgment. Perhaps their family was responding to them in a manner that forced growth and choice. Another choice point arises through pain of the physical body triggering a belief that outside assistance is needed. Is this not another opportunity? Then, there is the advice of worried friends. First, recognize that they must love you very much to be worried about you. However, this is the perfect opportunity to trust yourself within the moment: they do not know more about you than you know about yourself. Is that not an amazing opportunity to be present in the moment? Remember, the presence of judgment is that it is truly the opportunity to appreciate love and to accept the gifts being offered.

When you unfold the understanding of the All-Encompassing Moment, you recognize that within the true presence of the moment, you cannot live in the world of density; it is impossible. Oh no, because the moment becomes your world. It becomes the radiant light within this space.

Instead of reacting to the Bond of Illusion, your world is available to you through the gift of gratitude and love that you offer it. When you accept the All-Encompassing moment, and learn to recognize the moment, this is a great and powerful lesson for your Self-Ascension.

Sri Ram Kaa: Our family and friends then provide many opportunities to renew trust….to release….to have the Aha! moment.

As one cultivates the moment, it will happen. Always be present to those who may wish to interrupt your knowing of the moment, because in their expression of judgment the gift to you is to remember how far you have come and that they love you enough to express their concerns. For without their judgments, you would not remember your truth.

Sri Ram Kaa: That is a beautiful discernment….

Yes, and it is always appropriate to respond by simply sharing; Thank you for loving me enough to give me the moment of remembrance. This is the response of presence to those who judge you.

Sri Ram Kaa: And from that place we also cultivate compassion and understanding.

Each moment is a gift, a connection, a choice to be with God. Each moment gives you more and more depth, love, and understanding of the soul. So listen to your own heart and hold the space for enlightenment for yourself through the All-Encompassing Moment.

The All-Encompassing Moment is the backdrop of the universe, upon which the limited energies we call judgment and expectation are playing out. As you allow the All-Encompassing to be your consciousness, then the refractions happen in proper context.

I AM All-encompassing!

Pause - Breathe - Allow

Journaling For Integration

This lesson helps me to recognize:

Integrating this teaching means that I now release my attachments to:

Integrating this teaching means that I now accept:

A declaration that will help me integrate this lesson is:

Bring your hands to your heart once again, and declare the Mantra of Self-Ascension.

I AM HERE
I AM READY
I AM OPEN
GUIDE ME!

Lesson Eight

Sacred Mudras[30]

"Movement equals life."
~ Kira Raa

Archangel Zadkiel Speaks:

Welcome to Sacred Mudras.

Sri Ram Kaa: Sounds beautiful.

Sacred Mudras are important in the integration of the release of the egoic trap. For now that one has opened themselves, now that one has allowed themselves to cleanse, to clear, to nourish, to welcome in the new vibratory level, there are things that can be done to sustain this level.

There are many sacred symbols; this certainly will not cover all of them, however it is serving to introduce those that are most important, those that help. There are many to show you. This one, (Mudra One), is the mudra of great Wisdom, Love, and Compassion. It is the one that opens the portal for the subconscious mind to receive.

Mudra One

Simply holding this position allows the subconscious mind to receive Divine Wisdom and energy when it is in an open state.

For understand, as with any pure vibratory symbol or structure, if one is not in the vibratory energy to receive, if one is not cleansed, if one is still too trapped in density, of course it will not have an impact. It will simply be on the surface. It is still there, however it simply touches the surface and then bounces back off again as if the entire vessel is wrapped in a plastic. It is like throwing a rubber ball against a bouncy wall.

Sri Ram Kaa: It appears to be a protective mechanism of the ego, protecting the density and reflecting off that which is more refined.

This is correct. When one has completely surrendered into the true vibratory level that they have and they are emanating at a vibratory level of great escalatory time, all radiance enters effortlessly. Then, the benefit and the ability to sustain becomes simple and effortless because it is not being resisted.

When one has the fear element as the primary ego component, punching holes so to speak in the protective areas, this fear allows for the negative energy to come in and start convoluting and re-densifying the energy. This is what creates that barrier, that shell. The greater the density, the greater the shell of prohibited Light. Once that shell is complete, and there are many for which this shell is greatly complete. It is not that the Light is not there, it is not that the elements and the structures of positive Love are not there, it is simply that they are bounced off. They are reflected away because the emanation is unable to receive such a fine Light. So in order to escape that loop, in order to move forward, one must go within. The cleansing must come from within. It can not come from the without.

This is what the first seven lessons brought you to. This is why they culminate with this understanding of how to achieve that. Then and only then, will everything have greater Light impact. This means things that perhaps you were exposed to and enjoyed before now have a greater affect on your Light body. This, thereby encourages the Light body to stay, enhancing the Light body, helping the ego to stay in its true place where it belongs and being able to receive on many levels simultaneously. This offers a greater expansion at all times. Do you understand?

Sri Ram Kaa: Yes I do. And I see this exquisiteness, even the density is a beautiful self-preserving system. It is most remarkable, it is as beautiful as the development of a flower.

Yes. It holds you exactly where you should be until you are ready to move into somewhere else. Sometimes that happens in another lifetime, but it serves. Everything serves, everything serves - we can not stress this enough.

Sri Ram Kaa: Yes, the first lessons provide us with inner cleansing or offering a cleansing of the body, a cleansing of the subconscious, a cleansing of the intent.

Yes, it allows everything to be a truly clean vessel and you now understand there is great definition in the word clean. It does not mean just wash the hands with the soap, but a truly clean vessel is one of pure radiant Light as it was meant to be. The arrival at the recognition and the ability to release fear and ego is one to be joyously celebrated at all times as is the one who is able to stay in the density. For every time you interact with that one, they give you the gift of remembrance, the gift of knowing.

Sri Ram Kaa: Yes, for it is in the contrast that we find the release of the joy, the energy.

Yes the constant reminding of the gift. When one is able to completely surrender and recognize all of the many gifts, then all experience becomes a loving gift, no? All experience!

Sri Ram Kaa: All remembrance.

Yes. This is a powerful Mudra (Mudra Two).

The hands just slightly bent.

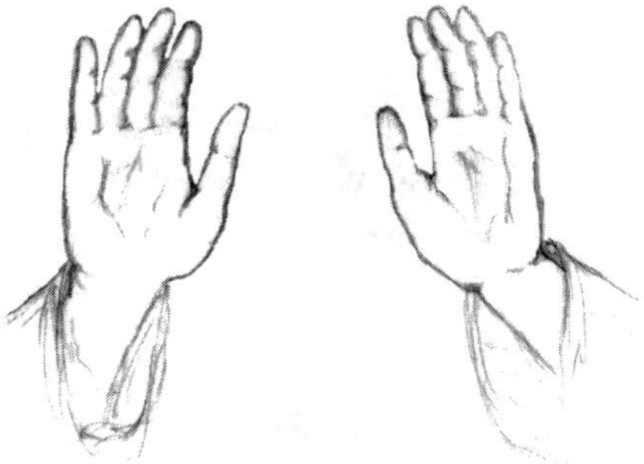

Mudra Two

Sri Ram Kaa: For healing?

Yes, also communication and openness. If you are in an interaction with another that is interfering to your Light body, and if the energy is not nourishing, you may interrupt that pattern for both you and the one that is offering that other energy with this Mudra (Mudra Two). You may also move the hands like this or you may continue doing the two like this, (Mudra Two A).

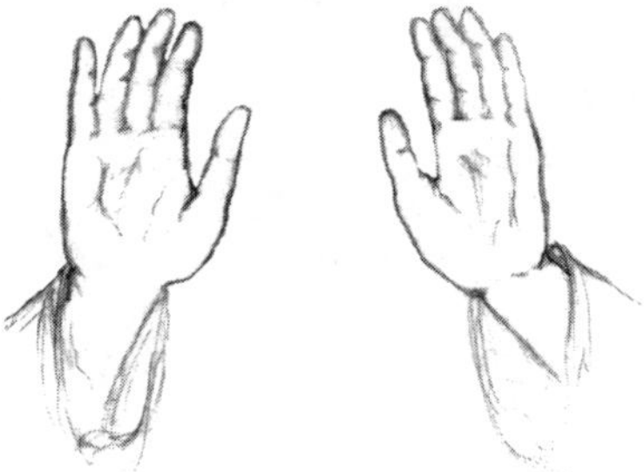

Mudra Two

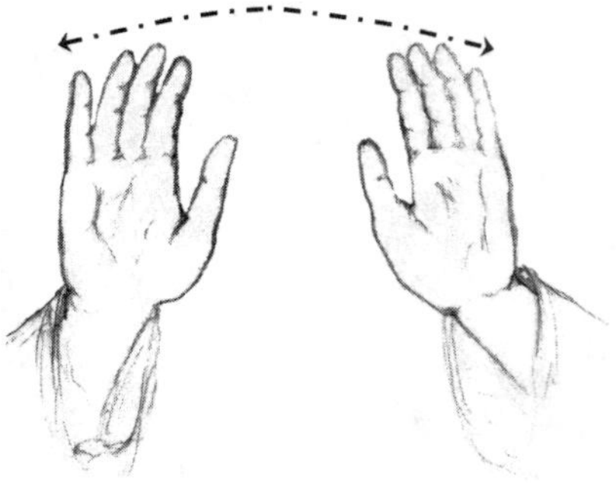

Mudra Two A

Sri Ram Kaa: So what I heard you say is that this will interrupt an emanation that we are finding unsettling or uncomfortable to our Light body as well as project a loving energy.

Correct. Love. Complete unconditional love and compassion. For when this one is performed from a vessel that has been purified, the recipient will automatically respond to the love. However, remember, the recipient may have on their plastic sheeting and it could bounce off, yet they will respond.

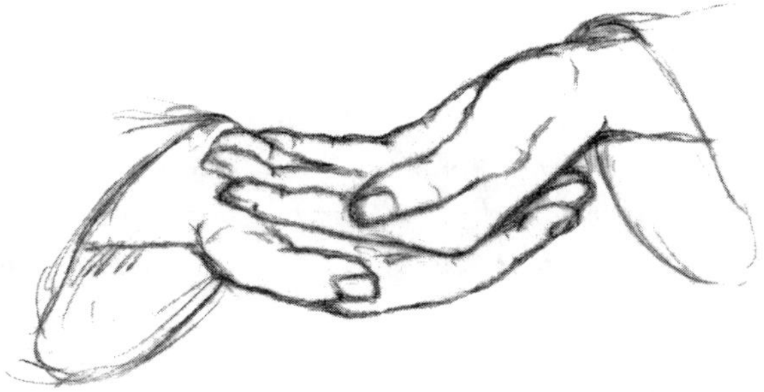

Mudra Three

When at rest like this, (Mudra Three), meaning when at rest yet being in the presence with others, when asking for the opportunity to be radiating unconditional love for yourself or others, this is a satisfactory posture.

We start today with some sacred symbology and then we move into cleansing exercises. Everything that you are being given is to enhance and assist the ever expanding Light body. But the first lessons are of course the most challenging because they require complete trust. These lessons require unconditional love of the Self and of others. For only when it is held in the highest vibratory level of the Light, can the impact of these lessons truly be felt in a manner that provides all of the components of the exercises Light, Love, Compassion, Service. A true flow has all those elements: Light, Love, Compassion, Service.

You know that you are indeed on your path and holding the space for enlightenment when you have Light, Love, Compassion, and Service. Do you understand?

Sri Ram Kaa: Yes. And so these three mudras are a state of being which then spawns a flow.

Yes! Congratulations you are expanding! We are all ever expanding. We remind you again of this big bang, funny to us because there is only expansion. And so every event, every cause and effect as your scientists like to say, is about expansion, is about the expansion of the Light, is about the return to the authentic being, about the return to God, about the return to Universal Love and Light that is truly beyond the comprehension we can offer you at the limited vocabulary of this vessel.

So we choose to offer you metaphors that we are able to provide you in a manner that you can see and accept, like refractory devices, many faceted colors, each one beautiful on their own yet collectively shining even brighter. It is the time of the greatest expansion that your authentic being has yet to experience.

Remember who you are at all times because when you do you are remembering God. You are remembering the Universal Love that shines down so radiantly upon you it can not ever be denied once it is touched. You have awoken; you understand completely that you have done this all before. You have become the conscious co-creator. You have surrendered into true nourishment. You see how these steps have allowed you to progress even more securely, safely, and rapidly into your expansion. For once one recognizes the truth of expansion, once one integrates all of the components, nothing can stop it. Ever lighter, ever freer, ever more buoyantly and jubilantly joyous.

Sri Ram Kaa: For when one enters that place of expansion, then the love that is always here is lifting you and self-propagating.

Yes. Sustaining and all encompassing.

Sri Ram Kaa: All that is.

Yes. So it is important in this lesson that one practice, that one integrate the habit, that one use these beautiful symbols to be offering wisdom and love at all times.

I am now showing you a mudra that is very similar to the first mudra, Mudra Four, however the two hands are used differently. It must be two hands like this and you look at it like an arch.

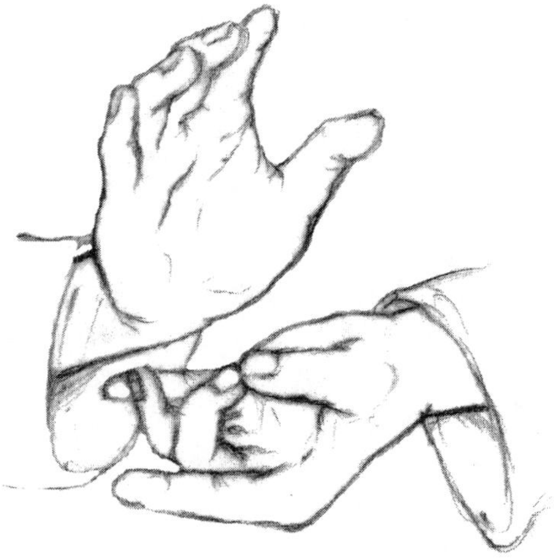

Mudra Four

Feel out of your raised hand the energy that is escaping in this moment. Do you feel the pulsing and the escaping?

Sri Ram Kaa: That seems to be grounded.

Yes, this is correct because you are offering the greatest Light and Love that can ever be offered. You are giving it as an arrow to God while you offer it out to the world, while you still hold onto that within you so you never deplete.

Sri Ram Kaa: I am doing it backwards and that still wants to radiate.

Of course and it will. It is always radiating, both hands are radiating. Feel the cycles of energy, feel the pulsations, feel the beautiful Light that is around you, abounds in you and is offering you great Love, Divine dispensation, and great compassion on your journey. Remove any remaining fears, be in union, be in joy, surrender for it is all happening.

Sri Ram Kaa: Such a beautiful gift.

Yes, do you feel the power of this one, (Mudra Four, Four A and B)?

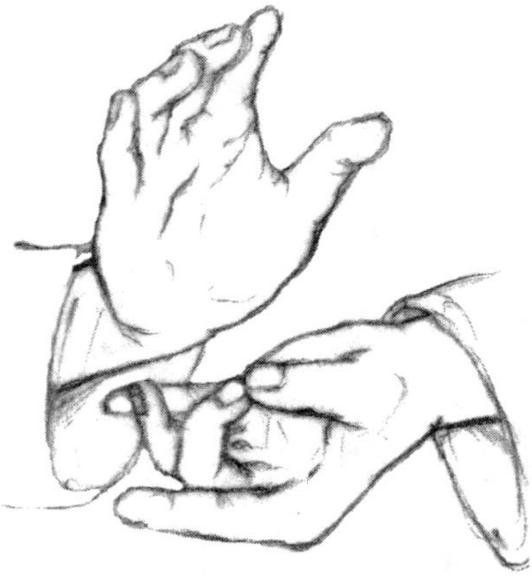

Mudra Four

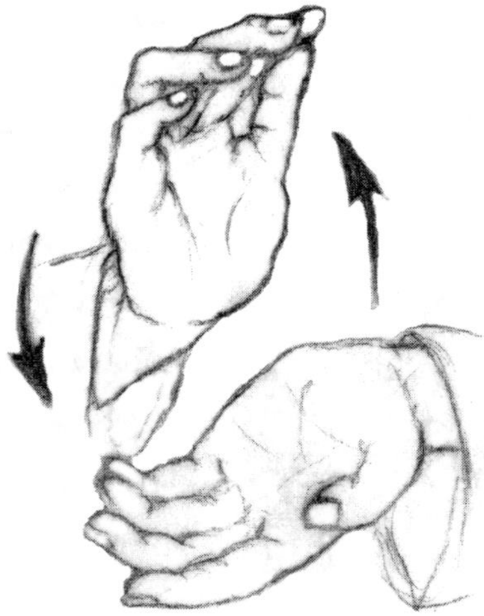

Mudra Four A

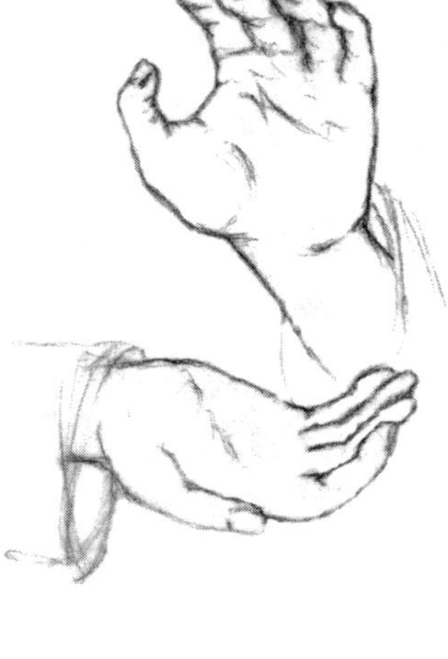

Mudra Four B

Sri Ram Kaa: I do and I feel such joy and gratitude.

Know that we love you. Do you have questions about this lesson?

Sri Ram Kaa: These Mudras are available as an energy conduit to hold us in Divine flow. Is that said properly?

Yes that is correct.

Sri Ram Kaa: OK. There is a similarity between the ones that you have shared. The protection one is the most distinct. The rest all have the similarity of an emanation of Love and Wisdom.

This is correct. You may also do them together in a flow. (See Mudra Flow below) Understand? Like this, one and two and three and four. You may do the whole flow. We gave you four mudras in order and so you may join the four together into a flow.

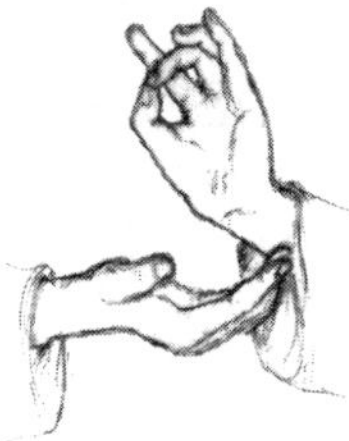

Mudra One

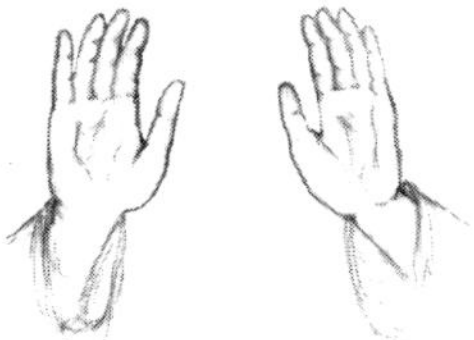

Mudra Two

Mudra Three

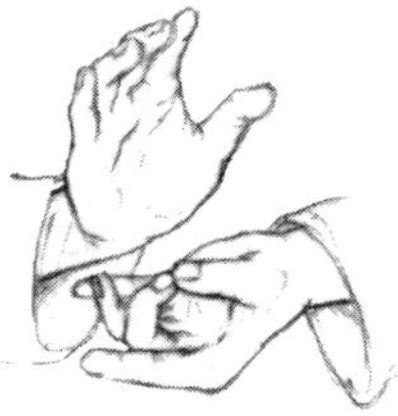

Mudra Four

Mudra Four A

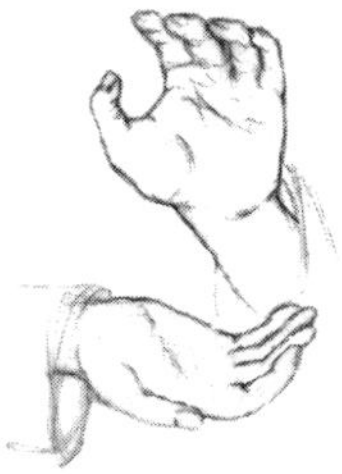

Mudra Four B

Sri Ram Kaa: And the flow, actually I am not sure I have the flow.

It is correct for the flow to be natural for you. You do not need to ask if you have the correct flow. You will always have correct flow. By rotating this mudra (Mudra Five) used with both hands, you create an energy field of the Infinite, it is the symbol of infinity. When rotating this symbol you are creating an energy field and then you open up the field and allow the healing energy to flow, coming to rest with Mudra of Divine Wisdom. This is a very powerful, powerful string of mudras as it opens up the energy field.

Mudra Five

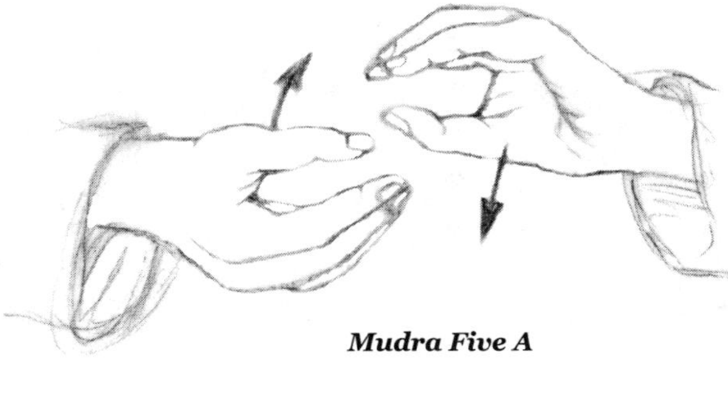

Mudra Five A

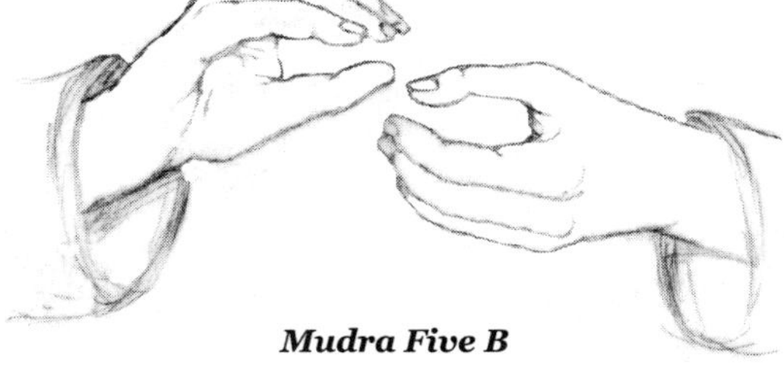

Mudra Five B

To further enhance the energy, if one is sitting, the back should be straight. With a straight back, if one does the Mudras here as we have been doing now, it will have great impact on solar plexus area for it creates a center, a great flowing energy center. However if one is having heart challenges, then go up to the chest, it will still affect all the chakras, however it will provide extra energy into the heart, into the throat, and open them all.

When one opens up all the powerful energies of these Mudras we just taught you, there is great swirling energy mass. So there is created, especially if you have a circle of people doing this, in the center of the circle there is a very powerful opening of the universal vortex of Love. Once one comes into a compassionate nourishing center for themselves there is always a powerful and open portal of Love.

This portal of Love should benefit all. How you close "the portal" is to begin with the arms up here. (Mudra 6)

Mudra Six

One in front of the other, you bring them to the third eye, (Mudra 6A), knowing you are receiving this and then you bring out and collect from the portal, (Mudra 6B), and bring into the love of the heart. (Mudra 6C). We will do this again so you can feel it because there is a great swirling portal of Love between us. So we go up with the hands in front of each other just in front of the third eye, we go out and we allow ourselves to bring in the Love and then it comes to rest at our heart.

Mudra Six A

Mudra Six B

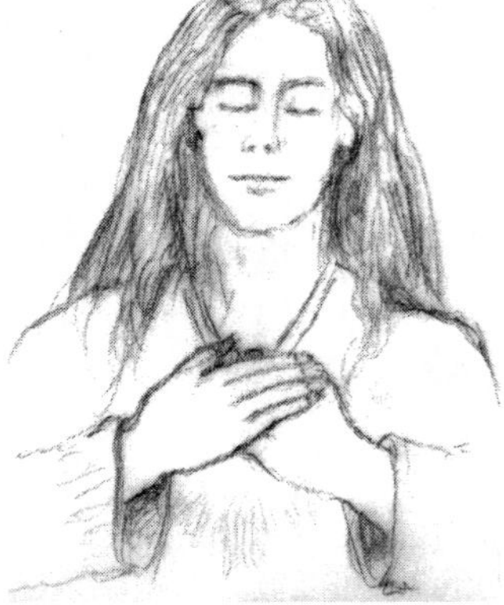

Mudra Six C

So you have learned in this lesson eight, through sacred mudras, how to open up a universal portal of unconditional Love, how to hold this space for yourself, and how to embrace it properly.

Important Note: Practice each one of the mudras until you feel comfortable with them and are receiving the energetic blessing they offer. Then, try combining Mudra 6, 6A, and 6B into an upward flowing motion and feel the peaceful opening and centering of all of the energy centers, (chakras), along the spine.

I AM Sacred Bliss!

Pause - Breathe - Allow

Journaling For Integration

This lesson helps me to recognize:

Integrating this teaching means that I now release my attachments to:

Integrating this teaching means that I now accept:

A declaration that will help me integrate this lesson is:

Bring your hands to your heart once again, and declare the Mantra of Self-Ascension.

I AM HERE
I AM READY
I AM OPEN
GUIDE ME!

Lesson Nine

Trust and Love

When many chose not to embrace Sacred Union in Atlantis, their own fruition went into suspension. They began to cry out for their soul. It was known that the time of union would have to wait until the culmination of the planet which is now.

You are at the time of the great transition. You are at the time that many have prophesized already, and we use the word prophecy because it is the only word to explain what is already known. It is simply a vehicle or tool to bring understanding to that which is. This definition is important for it is vital that you are comfortable understanding, when we speak to you that we bring you the knowledge of a generality, for to interfere with the path of any is not appropriate. Remember, however that to offer guidance on the path was asked for, and we acknowledge this ancient request by providing it to you now.

~ Archangel Zadkiel

Archangel Zadkiel Speaks:

Every moment of every day you must stay in the challenge of trust. When one stays in the trust and love, when one allows it to be, then the floodgates open, and all of the Divine protection one may wish to call forth is abundantly present.

Trust and love; in this time of the removal of the refractory devices, in the acceleration of Divine energy, and in the time of the coming together of the Sacred Union, one must acquire, live, and then teach through experiencing the trust love relationship. Know that the trust love relationship with the creator is a non-mutually exclusive one. It is one that is able to obtain greater height, breadth and width by allowing oneself to continually stay in this pattern, (trust and love).

Many will cry out loud, "How can I trust? I cannot just trust, my trust has been violated. I cannot move forward with trust. Oh, I can love, but I cannot trust. Oh, you do not understand, we live in a world with too much terror to trust, and you as an angel just don't understand."

For you see, we are not suggesting the reckless abandonment of caution with dangerous situations. We are not encouraging you to simply trust the bomb as it is dropping on you. This we are not saying.

What we are saying is for you to learn how to trust yourself enough to allow your God energy to surface and guide you. You can only allow this Divine Ray, this Divine energy in through an open love portal as it can only come in through a pure energetic light shell.

If your light shell has been disrupted with holes, tears and scars from negative energy patterns that you have attracted to yourself through self-hatred, self-judgment, lack of self-trust, confusion, and depression, then the pure vibrational trust energy is unable to find its way to you.

Some will say, "How can I do this, Zadkiel? You give me a chicken/egg scenario." We do understand that it can appear like that because trust and love are energies on each side of a scale balancing each other.

If you remove trust, then there is only love and it is heavy and out of balance. If you remove love then there is only trust. Therefore, it is not chicken OR egg scenario, it is a chicken AND egg synergistic relationship. Begin to recognize that trust and love exist simultaneously; they exist together. You cannot have one without the other.

As we introduce the trust love model in relationship to the energy of Self-Ascension, you begin to recognize that within the energy of Self-Ascension, trust and love are the same thing. Some may say this is impossible, how can trust equal love? We say to you: how can you truly love if you do not trust?

Is not everything expanding? Is not even the way questions are phrased and asked expanding? Trust and love are the same.

One must ask within, "Do I trust myself enough to simply wake up?" What is your response and is it mechanical or heart centered?

So we ask you again, "Do you trust yourself enough to wake up, to come back to that which you are?" Without deep committed trust, you would not be able to create the energy of Self-Ascension. If you are unable to trust yourself enough, then ask the question, "Do I love myself enough to wake up?"

All of the lessons up to lesson nine have prepared oneself to ask this question, and to understand the gentle balance between trust and love. To understand and rejoice in the recognition that you are whole as you are now. You are whole, even with all of your perceived imperfection, with all of your conjured up reasons not to be whole.

We see you, we honor you, and we see the joyous authenticity of "the you" and the great celebration of the trust love relationship that wishes to unfold within you. Yes! Once you delve into the trust love relationship all other questions fade away, and only one remains, "How do I live in this energy?" That is all. "How do I live? How do I now express? How do I remain in the energy of trust and love?"

There are those who state, "I have lived in trust and love and I got burned." Then we ask, "Were both components, (trust and love), present and fully expressed in the living?"

It is one thing to make the declaration of loving and trusting yourself, and it is quite another as one walks out into the world not expressing the completeness of trust and love, or creating an action that may be judgmental.

Some might feel the integration of trust and love should be the first lesson. Yet, it was good to be shared now. All of the lessons are spokes of a wheel. For had this been the first lesson, would you fully understand the individ-u-will as you do now? Would you understand the importance of the moment and the connection of the moment? Would you fully understand judgments and the ever expanding vehicle that you are and how refractory devices inhibit growth? For you see, when you come to the trust love dynamic with a broader understanding, then you are then ready to receive the true message.

The message is always the same, yet it is received differently based upon your own ability to be present with yourself. There are many false scenarios where many claim that they are so in love with themselves and that you do not know what you are doing. This does not exemplify the trust love relationship.

One way this expresses is as follows: "I am so complete in me that I will show you why you are wrong." This does not emulate the trust love relationship. When one is truly of the trust love mind, the trust love body, the trust love spirit, the trust love wholeness, when one is truly expressing from that level of understanding, then a part of that expression is the trust love application to all that is around you.

The expression of this would be as follows: "I trust myself enough to know that I trust and love that your path is perfect for you. I shall not do anything to change it. I shall not do anything to harm it, or to make it go somewhere else. I honor your path, Many Blessings." That is how you know you are in the trust love energy.

Anger, fear and hate do not appear when you are living in a trust love relationship. How could they? So you see there are many ways that assist you to be aware as to whether or not you are in wholeness with trust and love.

It is also important to hold the energetic vibration of pure love so that one is always protected. It is understandable if anger, fear or hate appear. When that experience appears, the greatest gift you can offer is to say, "Thank you for reminding me where my trust love relationship is needing to be complete." Then love yourself ever more.

If you move into self-judgment, "Oh my goodness I felt fear or anger or hurt," then you further remove yourself. This occurs because the energy of self-judgment pierces the protection of Divine love and allows negativity in. It is not irreparable; it is just that you must begin again. Sometimes we begin again a few times so that we learn how to maintain the energy of love we have called in. It is a very beautiful gift to understand the trust love relationship with the self and to be present with it.

This is a beautiful gift, and it is not something to dwell upon. Yes. Too often while in vessel the egoic mind takes you away and tells you how bad you are, and this takes many forms. The greatest gift you give to yourself is to understand that it is now your time to love yourself through that illusion.

When you are aware that you got angry, or felt fear, it is at that moment that you stop and say, "Thank you." What if you felt hate or terror? Say thank you again.

Understand that it is not the feeling that damages you. The feeling can all-ways be transmuted into the great gift of awareness that keeps you on your path; therefore it is something to be grateful for. It is only when we take those feelings and transmute them into non-loved based actions that we cause damage to ourselves and others.

Sri Ram Kaa: Rather than using the feelings as feedback to propel one on their path, there are those who will use them to create ever further separation.

Correct. To act out on those feelings against oneself and others is when the barrier is crossed. It is then that they are expressing the inability to find the trust love within themselves. They are in so much pain, so much pain, that rather than going within to end the pain through trust and love, they project the pain upon others who then project it upon others, thereby causing disruptions and energetic shifts.

It is an important discernment to recognize that you are not creating just one action. Rather, it is the multiplication of that action that then comes back to you in ever greater form than the initial one action. Is it not simply wise to recognize the gift of the feeling and experience and go back to the trust love center and say thank you?

Embracing the trust love energy is a powerful ally. It is also a powerful activity to embrace the trust love model within the context of conscious Self-Ascension. Consider that at this very moment you are conscious, and you are awake. For one cannot even begin to understand this concept without being awake. Some have just been up longer than others, and not everyone needs to go back to sleep!

You are all striving to come home, even if you are unaware of it. This is a preoccupation of the egoic mind. This is also why death is such a popular subject here in this world, and a consuming fascination! This is why so many feel compelled to watch death over and over again. It is simply in its truest essence a refracted way of reconnecting with the greater energy of your true home.

So through the funnel and the filter of all of the energies present, it becomes perverted into the fascination of watching death. There is no death, understand this. It is a fabrication of the egoic mind of the vessel used to help control society. Once you understand that you do not die, everything else falls into clear perspective. Self-Ascension brings you to the point of graduation, of voluntarily knowing when your time to go home has arrived. The trust love relationship with the self is paramount.

As you fully embrace and embark upon your mission you will have great opportunities to live the trust love experience. It is not just a teaching, it is what you live, and life is a great opportunity to practice.

Sri Ram Kaa: Every opportunity to practice offers greater expression of trust and love.

Every time you repeat, every time you are called to remember, it becomes easier, it becomes more permanent, it becomes the new habit. You must know you are ready. You must not doubt yourself or your perceived imperfections. You are ready, and all will be provided.

Your egoic mind is the spectator and your authentic self knows it is time. You are wiser than you know. Are you willing to love and trust that?

I AM Trust!

I AM Love!

Pause - Breathe - Allow

Journaling For Integration

This lesson helps me to recognize:

Integrating this teaching means that I now release my attachments to:

Integrating this teaching means that I now accept:

A declaration that will help me integrate this lesson is:

Bring your hands to your heart once again, and declare the Mantra of Self-Ascension.

I AM HERE
I AM READY
I AM OPEN
GUIDE ME!

Lesson Ten

Discernment is Calling

We are here with you first because you asked us to be present during this time and we agreed that we would be here for you. This was predetermined. Your agreement was "Yes, I will come and have this experience, and all I ask is that you come and guide me when the time comes." This is why we are here, yet you must remember that in your acceptance of this experience, it was on behalf of the world...for together all said yes to the Elohim.

To be of the highest service, to be of the greatest impact and to be able to follow through, this was the assistance that was requested and joyfully given. Remember why we are here, all-ways.

Personal completions are an important gift, yet not the primary reason you are here, they are simply a side effect, a bonus. Do not allow that to minimize your experience or union, for it is the union that is the greater service, the greater vessel of opportunity to serve.

If ever you feel discomfort ask for guidance. When you embrace upon these lessons you may feel changes in your body and your emotions. These lessons offer an opportunity for elimination, and each will experience this differently.

~ Archangel Zadkiel

Archangel Zadkiel Speaks:

If you can accept and know that it is already done, and have declared your intentions, then it is already done.

(Phone rings) *You should get that Sri Ram Kaa.*

(Sri Ram Kaa answers the phone and it is a wrong number. Sri Ram Kaa states this to Archangel Zadkiel)

How often does one receive a wrong number? With this question, we begin the lesson here. When you hear a call, the ego immediately wants the call to be of a certain nature. The body begins reacting to the nature of the call, yet you have not yet answered the call. You do not yet know what you are responding to.

However, prior to answering the call, you subject yourself to many different patterns and emotions. How many times do you get the call and find out it was the wrong number? This is a very powerful lesson, so let us explain more.

You wake up feeling unsettledness and confusion. This is a call. By responding to this experience you are already engaged in the energy of the experience. And so, you make a decision: "Do I go into the habit of how to receive to these perceived calls, or do I simply love myself enough to say thank you, good morning, I now move into my love day, I now move into that which serves me."

Let us assume you make the first decision, and react to the call, (unsettledness and confusion). You begin formulating responses, and call forth the action needed to support your formulations. Your entire day is proceeding based upon this call. At some point during the day you finally pick up the phone so to speak, and are able to laugh and find out it was a wrong number. You see, you are revisiting the habit of the habit.

You can let go of the uncomfortable-ness, the unsettledness, the self-judgment that declares that you are flawed and inhibiting your own process. The simple truth is, it was just not your call.

When you hear the next call and the adrenaline rushes; you assume that you know the purpose of the call and that you are correct in your assumptions. Respond by breathing deep and then taking another breath and loving your assumptive response, then release it to the container.[31] *Declare to yourself, "This call does not need to disrupt my peace, my love and my joy. If indeed it is a call for me, I will wait until I have answered it to confirm this, before I begin any form of response. And if the response takes me away from my peace, love and joy, then I must ask; Was this really my call, or one that I wanted to be my call?"*

You are constantly receiving calls, and on many levels. There are Earthbound calls sending energy up from the Earth that are calling you. Hunger is an Earthbound call, you hear the call and respond, "Oh, I am hungry. I see junk food and want to eat."

Is that truly the call, that you want the junk food? Then you eat the junk food and don't feel so good. Was the call truly for you? This is but a small example, and yet we wish for you to know you have many types of calls coming into you all the time.

So, you have the Earthbound or physical calls, some of them are most correct. "Oh, I must relieve myself." This is a call for you.

"Oh, I must drink or nourish. I am cold and need warmth, or I am warm and need cool." These are all examples of the physical calls of the Earth and of the vessel. This is the first category of calls that you receive.

Then there are the mental calls which are actually an aspect of the vessel calls, as they are still Earthbound, they are not of spirit. They are the ego calls.

"Oh, I see this shirt, I must have this shirt. I will feel better if I am in this shirt. Oh, I see my hair must look a certain way and I will feel better if it does."

You live in a time where mirrors have become judges. Found within the reflection of a mirror, when one is acting from the mental, is the judgment meter. It is in the reflection of this meter that you decide to change your nose, flatten your tummy, reshape your body and agree to surgical alteration. All of these actions are done in the effort to gratify and answer the call. This is the call that is saying you are not enough, and you are not complete. Do you see the web that is being built?

It literally starts from the ground up. The Earthbound calls to the vessel, and from the vessel calls are sent to the mental. Do you see the progression? Next, one moves to the perceived spiritual. We refer to it as the perceived spiritual because it precedes spiritual authenticity.

Let us digress for a moment. We have opened up this teaching with how you can break this chain, and we are now explaining the chain. When one answers a call from the perceived spiritual there is still great judgment. For one identifies with a set of habits and patterns to find the spiritual. They hear a call. Perhaps they hear a call that says I must dress a certain way, or pray a certain way or conduct myself in a certain way and all others who do not do it the same way are wrong. This is the absolute key to knowing you are in the energy of the perceived spiritual that is controlled by the ego mind.

If in the practice of any spiritual endeavor, commonly called religious, one is moved to judge others and called to believe that others who do not honor the same practice are wrong, then one is within the perceived spiritual. This is merely a function of the mind.

There are components of the perceived spiritual that in and of themselves are of a highly evolved nature. However, answering any call before confirming that it is aligned with your higher energy is when misperception and judgment take over.

Just like your call today, you were convinced you knew who this was and had a prepared answer. You felt ready to respond to the call, and then discovered very quickly it was not your call at all. This is a very powerful lesson, and most appropriate for these times.

One must learn how to grow through responding to calls. You have the Earthbound calls of the vessel, the calls of the ego mind and then the calls of the perceived spiritual. Each one filters through another layer of energy. As you help yourself to release responding to these calls, there is always a layer that desires you to stay where you are. It will convincingly cry out: "Of course this call is for you. How could it not be? You heard it."

How one can break the loop of the Earthbound, mental and perceived spiritual callings is to simply remember that when you first hear the call, stop, breathe, and allow whatever reactivity is appearing within you to dissipate before you proceed with any thought.

Pause - Breathe - Allow

This takes discipline and practice. Then, you feel into the peace, the love and the joy that you are or are not experiencing. ***This is how you will know if the call is for you.*** *The presence or lack of these energies, (peace, love and joy), will also show you if there is judgment present, or a reason that you are calling forth a judgment.*

It is very simple to discern your calls once you know the parameters. When you wake up and are called to feel uncomfortable, or called to feel uncertain, you are in a place that challenges your peace, love and joy. Stop, do not react, breathe and meditate, even if for a moment. Interrupt the cycle before you begin responding to it.

Sri Ram Kaa: It is interesting to me that in order to be able to interrupt the cycle requires that one first becomes aware of it.

Yes.

Sri Ram Kaa: Usually our best feedback sensation is our emotions, or it could be noticing our thinking. We notice we are feeling something other than peace, yet in the calls, you did not mention the emotional body. Is the emotional body simply responding to the mental?

Yes.

Sri Ram Kaa: So we call that the mental/emotional body?

Yes. We see it all as one energy known as the ego. So, however you must phrase this expression to be understood is fine, however know that the emotions are driven by the ego as they are driven by the mind, it is all one. The complexity is not necessary and the mental, emotional and ego are held within the vessel; even the perceived spiritual, it is all part of the same.

Many do themselves a great disservice by answering the call of the perceived spiritual and defending it.

Sri Ram Kaa: Then we enter into the pain of the pain from that place.[32]

Yes, correct.

Sri Ram Kaa: So it feels as if habitually reacting to the perceived spiritual could produce grandiosity.

And the phone is ringing all the time, creating a self-deprecating reaction. It can take either form. Either way, one's mind is tortured with the constant ringing of the phone. This self-imposed torture must be resolved, and can easily be so by simply remembering to stop, breathe and allow.

I AM All-ways Discerning!

Pause - Breathe - Allow

Journaling For Integration

This lesson helps me to recognize:

Integrating this teaching means that I now release my attachments to:

Integrating this teaching means that I now accept:

A declaration that will help me integrate this lesson is:

Bring your hands to your heart once again, and declare the Mantra of Self-Ascension.

I AM HERE
I AM READY
I AM OPEN
GUIDE ME!

Lesson Eleven

Shadow

You have opened the doors of your heart and they are open for yourself and each other. It is time to allow in yet another symbol of the infinite through complete loving acceptance of all as part of the acceptance of the self. It is the door of the shadow that has opened.

It is important to understand the shadow. For you see, the shadow has been interpreted primarily as that which is dark and scary, where fear, hate, and anger exist, where the alternatives exists, and this is the exploited area of the shadow. "Oh, I did something terrible, therefore it must be from my shadow." No, it was you!

~ Archangel Zadkiel

Archangel Zadkiel Speaks:

To understand the shadow, one must understand what the call is, because the call will always bring you into the shadow if it is left unrecognized and unchecked. There are times when the ego and the shadow are in great cahoots together causing one to believe things that are simply not true. For, what is a shadow?

If you look deeper into the word shadow, is not the shadow a reflection of the self? If one is not standing in the light, there cannot be a shadow. If you stand in front of a light and project it to yourself, there will be a shadow; you will cast a shadow, as will anything else. As you gaze around you find shadows, and they are all reflections created by the presence of light.

So begins the perennial discussion, where there is light there is dark, where there is shadow there is the being. This is all true. However, some plants grow better in high light and some grow better in the shade. These same shade plants actually wither and die in the light. Is this not so?

It is important to remember that there are aspects of the soul that grow better in shade, and simply because they are a shade dwelling plant does not make them less light filled, or less deserving of attention, respect and compassion. Ivy is a beautiful shade plant is it not? Does it not still contain chlorophyll, does it not still emit and help the oxygen. Yes. We use these examples because it is the clearest way we can demonstrate the beauty of living in shadow.

Because one is experiencing shadow or shadow-self does not mean one is violent, fearful, or filled with rage and anger. What it does mean is that you are a receiving the gift of taking a pause, as if you are enjoying shade on a sunny day. Does that not feel good? If it is very hot and you are walking, do you not crave the shade? Does not the shade created by the shadow of the tree become most nourishing to your hot body? It causes you to be grateful, for without the shadow of the tree, there would not be any shade.

As you take a rest in the shade, to cool off and rejuvenate, when you are cool enough, you are then ready to return to the light. In its most simplistic form, this is how your shadow serves you. It gives you an opportunity to take a break, to cool off. This is why many people live in their shadow.

There is a great recognition here so let us explain. If one is completely filled with light, and living the light, one has become accustomed to the heat, and the need to cool off in the shadow is minimal or not needed at all.

Now let us say that one is at the opposite end, without any conscious connection to light. Then one is living in the shadow, all the time. The need for light becomes repugnant. This one will not be interested in the light, for in the shadow they are cool, comfortable, and do have any desire to find the light. There are also many who carry both energies…moments of light and moments of shadow.

Each moment connects a moment, connects a moment. The moments determine the shadow and the light. This is why so many are discussing the need for balance. Most of this world are stuck in the middle, unable to fully embrace light or the dark. Therefore, the prevailing philosophy is that there must be both. Well, yes, during the growth phase of the soul in form. ***It is not that there must be both, it is that both exist.***

When one emerges from the shadow, at first there are just a few flickers of light that may be uncomfortable so one seeks to return to the comfort of the shadow. After all, if one has not seen light in a long time, then it is quite painful. It is the same for one who has lived in light; it becomes painful to visit shadow.

So very few are able to attain fully encompassed light living that it is not recognized much in your world.

Sri Ram Kaa: Interesting to me, when we talk about the middle place where one has received some illumination and is now wanting harmony between the shadow and the light, that this is a place where it seems that the ego has stepped in and said, this is the norm, we must have both.

Yes, of course, the ego does not want you to let go of shadow, because the ego can not exist without it.

Sri Ram Kaa: So it becomes a matter of how much light will the ego allow until one is able to re-identify with the soul?

This is correct. The ego is terrified of the release of the shadow. This is why all of the other perceptions of negativity exist in what is called shadow because it is simply governed by ego. It has nothing to do with the shadow, it has everything to do with what the ego is trying to create.

Sri Ram Kaa: So this flip flop between the light and the shadow is the calisthenics of the ego, and the more wild the flip flop the more powerful the ego?

Correct.

Sri Ram Kaa: So, when one is strictly in the shadow the ego would have less power, in a sense.

Actually, the ego is in great power then.

Sri Ram Kaa: For it has shut the door completely.

Correct.

Sri Ram Kaa: The ego is then in complete control. When one has the light and the shadow interfaced and then uses the light-filled experiences to justify self-defeating beliefs, has not the ego scored a victory of mastery over that person?

The ego will all-ways be able to score a point as long as it distracts you from authenticity. When one lives in authenticity, there are still periods where you embrace shadow, usually because you are removing yet another layer of the veil, and during these times the ego revisits, and says hello, do you remember me and can we play here? It is at these times that you might surrender your authenticity back to the ego. Then, it has scored a point as you say. However, this is also the exact time when you are given the great gift of recognition, for had you not looked for the shade, you would not be aware of what was still behind the surface. This is a great gift, for living completely without shadow has been done on this planet.

Sri Ram Kaa: Not by many.

Almost correct; it has been demonstrated. It is challenging for many to talk about or acknowledge or even begin to discuss this knowing because they are of a belief pattern based upon their inner experience that it cannot be done. Thereby dismissing that it has been demonstrated, and more often than just the few that have been made known by their legacy throughout your history. Know this, not only has it been done, it has been done well, and many times.

Thereby removing the veil of non-belief from those who say only shadow can exist with light and light must exist with shadow, this is not so. We acknowledge that in this societal base it is a prevailing concept due to the recognition and belief pattern that this is the only way to find light.

Sri Ram Kaa: Is this an extension of the pattern of polarity? That is that everything exists in polarities within this realm of experience on the Earth? Yet, when one resides in light more fully, this realm falls away and the impact of apparent duality becomes an amusement, it is not the truth. Is that what you are referring to, a state of attainment?

Yes, this is correct. Let us share that in the state of attainment it demands complete surrender, trust, unconditional love and release of judgment. It is the completion of Self-Ascension where there is no longer shadow.

Every time you cry over how you treat yourself, every time your body calls to you in pain, every time you doubt or produce fear, you are being given the great gift of knowing that piece of shadow is still existing. It is important to understand, as many believe, and only use the word shadow in terms of violence and fear and anger. This is why there is such a challenge in moving out of it. One must first understand the broader recognition of what shadow is.

Yet, of course, these negative emotions are able to be drawn in anywhere the energetic cocoon of Divine love has been pierced. It is not, however, in and of itself a function of shadow.

Sri Ram Kaa: I would like to know more about the distinction between shadow and ego.

Yes, this is a good distinction to make, as one exists within the other. A subset as they say.

Sri Ram Kaa: So in psychological terms I would refer to the ego as a structure that holds the separations that occurred through the experience of pain. The ego is holding the imprints and wounding of the shadow experiences. As we allow the shadow experiences to be released with love, the ego has nothing left to hold on to.

This is correct. This is why the ego will go out of its way to keep the shadow around.

It (the ego), wants to justify its existence. There is great wisdom in knowledge just as there is great ego in shadow. One exists within the other.

Rapid change and growth that transcends the shadow is existent now. We offer you the gifts of love and life for love and life exist interdependently.

You cannot have one without the other. To live authenticity, to understand the essence, one must remember and curb the desire to separate from love. The word life, to live to have life, is not simply about a vessel that can breathe. To truly have life one must;

***L**et*

***I**n*

***F**orever, the*

***E**ternal*

....that is LIFE is it not? Let In Forever the Eternal.

You call the eternal by focusing upon that energy, by allowing yourself to be centered within your life. You are then in living meditation, are you not?

What is important for you now? Perhaps it is deep gratitude and love, for you are the recipient of LIFE. You have called in life and you have agreed to life, and it becomes broader and richer the more you release the shadow.

The shadow is effortlessly released when you embrace LIFE, when you Let In Forever the Eternal. You call in LIFE, and welcome yourself home to your authentic being-ness. Many visits and many journeys, all have brought you to this time now. When you are able to come forth and discern the calls that are for you, then you are ready to recognize that the one call you are prepared to answer is the call to LIFE. Safe passage through this energy is your birthright, and you must own the journey for it is bringing you home. Do you have any questions?

Sri Ram Kaa: It would seem that the greatest challenge is to love the shadow enough to let it reveal its service. The challenge is not to recoil from it, therefore empowering the ego, and yet, what I have experienced is that one can wallow in the shadow, one can derive a false meaning by visiting there.

Yes, and quite well. There is an important discernment one must bring forward here. Is God present? Is this a God Present moment? Am I feeling that which God would ask me to feel? A God that is, always has been, and will continue to be, Pure Radiant Love. Once you understand that, everything else becomes simple. It is not the energy of a God of judgment, or mistrust. It is not a God that asks you to prove anything; it is simply pure, radiant love.

When you want to know if you are in the shadow or not, you simply ask that question. If the answer is no, then you know you are in shadow and can instantaneously make a movement away from it by thanking it, laughing, and seeing the joy of the memory and moving back into the light.

This of course is easier said than done as it requires that one understands and accepts God as radiant love. If you are moving toward Self-Ascension with Peace, Love and Joy, these are the components of God. So here is another way you can ask; "Does this support Peace, Love and Joy? Or, does this encourage Peace, Love and Joy?"

Sri Ram Kaa: Yet, there is an apparent paradox. As the shadow reveals areas where we did not fully love ourselves, or fully surrender, the experience tends to be one of pain until one is able to soften around it and see that the pain is carried within a container of Peace, Love and Joy. That can be tricky because there is both pain and joy present depending upon how deeply you look.

It can be a challenge. The ego is in full control at that time and supported by being within the shadow. Yes. This is why there are those who live their entire lives in ego supported shadow patterns. Consciously looking for the light, consciously training your responses, your reflexes, your habits, to move back into light is a discipline you are learning. You have some experience in it, however, you are learning it ever more.

There are subtle ways you can remind yourself. Create notes to your soul. Enjoy nature. Place sacred and joy-filled objects in strategic positions in your home and workspace. All of these will assist you so that when your ego shadow is present you can see these things and remember, "Yes, God exists here." Even when the ego is saying NO, these subtle reminders will allow you to look, see and know.

Then, eventually, you will not need the external look and see, because the energy of LIFE is firmly implanted into you. So you do the look and see within. Go to your heart, go to your brain, your solar plexus, there you shall find LIFE. Go to the love that you are within your third eye, and in that moment, you will know.

From that space you will be able to transmute energy and without having to consciously think about it, you will set up an energy conduit to bring in the God, the radiant love to assist you through the pattern. For you know that God is all-ways present.

I AM Divine Light
All-ways Present!

Pause - Breathe - Allow

Journaling For Integration

This lesson helps me to recognize:

Integrating this teaching means that I now release my attachments to:

Integrating this teaching means that I now accept:

A declaration that will help me integrate this lesson is:

Bring your hands to your heart once again, and declare the Mantra of Self-Ascension.

I AM HERE
I AM READY
I AM OPEN
GUIDE ME!

Lesson Twelve

Union with the Vessel

It is important to truly live and demonstrate soul nourishment and the effects that it brings. It is complete as a circle or process. One cannot truly attain Self-Ascension if one does not integrate soul nourishment. This is not denial. This is not about pain, and it is not about suffering for your enlightenment.

~ Archangel Zadkiel

Archangel Zadkiel Speaks:

There was a time on the planet when those concepts were necessary to break through certain veils, to break through energy patterns. Once those energy patterns had been released, it opens the door for other ways of attainment.

All paths of enlightenment are of great service to all.

As one studies all who have attained enlightenment, one realizes that the common thread is not the pain; the common thread is not the suffering. The common thread is the great love and compassion for all beginning with the self. This begins with gratitude for the vessel, and understanding why the vessel is here; to offer you a home and to be of service.

It is not selfish to honor the vessel. It is a great gift to God to honor the vessel. This is part of why you have many societies that have taken honoring the vessel to the extreme. For you see it is perversions of the seeking of giving back to God that led to the twisting of this. For example, the practice of "wearing my Sunday best," started as an honoring. The irony is that as society propels more toward a time of great enlightenment, so does the fascination with adornment and perfection of vessels. It is soul nourishment without the nourishment. Understand!

Sri Ram Kaa: It is a refraction.

Yes. All one has to do is remove the blinders, so to speak, to realize that in their search of adornment of the vessel they are truly searching for God. We take your question now.

Sri Ram Kaa: As we remove the refraction we see that the impulse to adorn is truly most sacred and that it has been usurped by the ego.

Also as time passed, it evolved to be a symbol of rank and monetary position with it. I can adorn better. I can buy better.

Sri Ram Kaa: We added hierarchy to it.

Correct. The simple act of putting ones hands together in prayer adorns the vessel.

The simple act of bringing your hands together in prayer is amplified when you place them at your heart.

This loving connection sustains the vessel in a vibrational state of Divine Expansion.

This does not require money. This does not require position, but it does require love to say, "Thank you God." This is an adornment. A simple covering on the head could be the leaves from a tree. They are green. A simple piece of homespun cloth or the most elegant expensive cloth out there matters not. You see, what gives true adornment is the sincerity of the recognition of the love that you are and the gift of the vessel to provide you with a home to live in.

On this planet they talk about basic need. There is what they call hierarchy of basic need. There is needing shelter, food, yes? Do you not see with the vessel you are always home?

Sri Ram Kaa: So one's needs are completely fulfilled?

Yes. You have been given all. Yet the vessel starts integrating with the ego and at its most basic level. The first need it offers you is food. You believe you must have food to grow. You must have food to live. You must have food to enjoy. You must have food to do so, so, and so. Yes, there are needs at the time of formation of the young child, to grow, food is a necessity. However, it is most important to grow into the understanding of Soul Nourishment.

Imagine one who from their beginning is taught nourishment not eating. What would their vibratory level be like? What would their light energy be like? Know that there are many on the planet now.

Sri Ram Kaa: A much purer sound. Harmony.

Yes. Yet there is the great gift of coming into soul nourishment after many, many years of non-soul nourishment because you can truly see and appreciate the vibratory escalation.

For you see, soul nourishment is gratitude. Soul nourishment is unconditional love. Soul nourishment is trust. Soul nourishment is surrender. Soul nourishment supports union because it begins with the union of the self. The simple acknowledgment and love that says I am…I be.

On this plane, the physical plane, you have synthetic medications needed and necessary for synthetic elements that have been created by synthetic foods and synthetic living. You also have natural or herbal type of remedies again for synthetically created challenges. The body is not meant to be ill. However, in order to escape the loop of this synthetic creation, it does support you to begin with a more authentic way out because it will help.

However, when one is wrapped in plastic very tight, they, (natural remedies), do not work. No I took them; they do not work. I must have these synthetic drugs because I took the others and they do not work.

This is because one must begin by purifying the system in order for this to work. For one has created through synthetic living and synthetic ingestion and synthetic thought process and synthetic spiritual process, one has created this plastic bag they are living in.

So one must be able to open the bag in order to receive the benefits, and once one has purified they take the same thing that did not work before and miraculously it works. This is the best example we can give you.

Sri Ram Kaa: Well said, and I see how true soul nourishment is inseparable from Self-Ascension. It brings all of the energies of Self-Ascension into the physical to purify the vessel and to honor this dimension. It is a completion, is it not?

Yes. When one builds on all the lessons, then one takes the time to simply say dearest God, I am open to opening. I am open to removal of refractory devices. I am open to the expansion of my light. I am open to living in light without fear of sunburn, see? That in and of itself is enough to begin and enhance the flow, and this helps to clarify the cloudy, to help strengthen the authenticity thereby allowing for release of ego.

This is a great opportunity. Gratitude and respect for the vessel that is this lesson. It is a lesson of gratitude and respect for the vessel and the understanding that you are always home. You can not ever lose your home because it is with you. All other fear is an illusionary creation of the ego. One embraces the wholeness and completeness in the recognition you are all-ways home. You are all-ways Home! When you embrace the beloved within, the beloved embraces you; what greater home could there be?

You are always home. You have come home to yourself, to your union. Do you not see how all actions flow into the model of Self-Ascension[33]*, be in union, surrender, release judgment, unconditional love? When you are able to give with love and gratitude, all actions to the Self-Ascension process, the effortless flow of abundant joy becomes simple. You do not have to work for it. You do not need to mine it. You do not need to find it. You do not need to go hunting. All you need to do is say; my joy is in my union, my surrender, my release of judgment, and my unconditional love. So I surrender this tedious project, I surrender my fear, I surrender my judgments, I surrender all that is stopping me, I surrender my car repairs, I surrender everything. You are love and you are loved.*

For example, when someone is between jobs they might think what will I do for money? It is at that time that you are called to love yourself, surrender, release judgment and unconditionally love the moments you are being given to experience what you are. For perhaps this time in your life is about finding, touching, and awakening to your being-ness.

The expansion of all souls means there is no room for some energies. This could be quite uncomfortable. As the light gets bigger it pushes up against that which is not light. Which then does one of two things: It gets absorbed by the light and becomes transformed, or it is repelled and moves away.

This is most easily seen by those around you. As your light expands those around you either become absorbed by the light and they themselves become light and become part of the expansion or they go away. This is a normal course of expansionism and of light living. Do not ever despair when others go away. Love them that they have chosen their path and may they find their light through that path, for sometimes one must align with a different energy or experience to find their path. However, each needs to find their path is perfect. Always remember this.

Sri Ram Kaa: Yes, this reminds me of how your lesson on the shadow illustrates how some plants thrive in the shade or find their completion there.

Correct. You see how the lessons build on each other? For without that lesson, how could you understand this one? Gratitude, understanding and respecting the vessel! The greater the light, the greater the effect for the vessel, the soul, and all those that come in contact with you. Prepare to keep yourself in great vibrational harmony, soul nourishment, sun, water, contact with the beloved, quiet respite, laughter and appreciation. These all serve to keep the vessel in harmony with a lightened soul.

Yes, it is work initially to provide a continuous safe vessel for one's authentic energy especially as it becomes more present. Yet is not joy a beautiful effort to make? When you release disharmony in your life it may often look as if greater disharmony has arisen. Same as when you cleanse the body. At first you may experience greater symptoms. Understand that this is merely the ego saying "I don't want to go, so I will I make it even harder." By quietly loving that energy and declaring, "thank you, I accept you," it will be gone. Then the path is clear and the channels are open. Your vibratory level escalates to a point where what others consider to be miraculous becomes normal. It is only considered miraculous because so many stay in density consciousness that prohibits expansion.

Sri Ram Kaa: Many are challenged to understand in advance how to be in harmony while living in the density.

Yes. This is why one must take as we say, baby steps. It is important to understand that while living in density the first opening comes from simply saying, "Dear God I am open to receiving clarity." This is all and this is where you begin: "Dear God, I am open to receiving clarity." Then one must simply trust.

Surrender, release judgment, be in union, honoring the vessel; all are beautiful ways to call in union. The greatest union begins with the union of the authentic being and the vessel. What a beautiful gift when the vessel is planted with flowers that say I love you! I know who you are and I am giving you great honor. When that union becomes apparent, this is when the soul can emerge. This is our lesson for today.

Review all of your lessons. You now have completeness. Know that we love you. You may call us in at any time.

I AM Complete!

Pause - Breathe - Allow

Journaling For Integration

This lesson helps me to recognize:

Integrating this teaching means that I now release my attachments to:

Integrating this teaching means that I now accept:

A declaration that will help me integrate this lesson is:

Bring your hands to your heart once again, and declare the Mantra of Self-Ascension.

I AM HERE
I AM READY
I AM OPEN
GUIDE ME!

Section Three

Finding Your Right Mind in a Left Brain World

"Sri Ram Kaa, you have been separated from the Kira Raa since the end of Su'Laria because the power of your Union was too bright to be on the Earth any earlier than now. You have had lifetimes on Earth, but you have never been in body at the same time as Kira, nor have the two of you ever been together since the end time of Su'Laria. You were not to reunite until this time of culmination on the planet. You will only be able to fulfill your agreement to reunite if you have fully healed the wound of your Su'Larian lifetime."

~ Archangel Zadkiel

Page 30, 2012: You Have a Choice!

Chapter Eleven

Addicted to Illusion

"There is only one pathway to Peace, Love and Joy, and that is reunion with the Divine. This pathway is indeed the journey Home and the gateway is your own heart!"

~ Sri Ram Kaa

Addiction is not limited to substance abuse. Many people are addicted to pain, expressed through emotional anxiety, poverty, abusive relationships and fear. One of the more popular addictions is drama, which is actually a dependency upon the energies of anxiety and adrenalin! People who are stressed by life often choose to be imprisoned by their obligations. Their *have to do* list becomes consuming and rarely will they become conscious of their inner world. Others are addicted to power, fame, physical prowess or other externally-dependent conditions. That is, their addiction requires the participation of others through attention and approval.

Often we can easily see these addictions in others, yet we do such a good job of lying to ourselves. Accepted conventions of society have taught us to put on a good show, to comply with behaviors that offer approval, to seek positive regard from others, etc. We have molded, conformed and distracted ourselves to the point that we are confused as to what is really true for us anymore.

Carried deep within the experiences of this lifetime, (and

often from other lifetimes), is an "inner party line," a spin about ourselves and the world that we've come to accept as true. Yet our energy betrays us.

This betrayal is being demonstrated on a large scale as many are having trouble sleeping, taking medications for a wide range of accepted issues, find a need for alcohol or drugs to relax, or have become dependant on excessive exercise to bring some form of balance to their lives. These problems all point to the fact that overall, we have separated from our essential Self.

Layer after layer of conformity has distanced us from our divine truth. Belief systems separate us from our essence. The personality-self becomes a mask designed to cope with a world that has lost touch with its soul. We have identified with a refraction of our true selves. The gap between this false identity and our authentic energy can result in a sense of being lost. Regardless of whether physical or emotional symptoms are currently manifesting, most people have identified with a refraction of their true nature. This refraction is the ego.

Addiction is the compulsion to engage an energy that modulates our experience and ultimately inhibits our healthy functioning. One engages a behavior or a substance in order to avoid looking more deeply at oneself, and thus avoids confronting one's inner truth. Addiction inhibits our expansion into authentic expression.

As you reflect upon your journey through the chapters that brought you back to the end times of Su'Laria, your responses, emotions and physical reactions are all part of the addictions to density you are experiencing now. When the opportunity to look at the patterns of navigating density are brought before you, what is your response? Often, it is denial that takes a front seat, and will spiritualize on your journey into the spiritualized ego. This is a wonderful gift, for it offers you the recognition that you are ready to break free.

Life provides many willing players in the addiction game, for every victim has an oppressor, just as every famous person has their admirers. Addiction is the repetitive choice to engage a self-defeating behavior. It can be expressed subtly or overtly, yet it is a norm in the western world.

As long as we judge the actions or beliefs of others, we are addicted to the energy of righteousness. Others are addicted to the disempowerment; they abdicate self-responsibility in favor of blaming circumstances or people for their predicament. Both the judger/blamer and the disempowered victim are compensating for self-doubt. An addict is always supported. The ego-mind is indeed a "pusher" – it offers pain-based limiting beliefs as truth and as long as you conform to these beliefs, then the ego remains in power.

How is it possible that we can all be addicts?

Simple, every person with an ego has experienced addiction in one form or another. The ego is also the container which holds our wounds and fears and generates refractions from them. It dances with our shadow. As the ego grows and gains in strength, it will protect us from feeling the pain of those wounds and fears by focusing our attention elsewhere. Over time this self-denial becomes patterned in our consciousness and we lose sight of the wounds and fears that are driving the ego's choices. We thus lose the opportunity to lovingly attend to and heal those inner wounds, for the ego keeps us busy coping in other ways. Denial becomes a global status quo.

The ego is a necessary tool. It is a divine creation that comes with having a body, and yet it is a refraction from Source, just as the physical vessels that house our souls are a refraction. Over the millennia the ego has grown out of proportion. People are so disconnected from the ascended truth that the planet continues to support wars, poverty and pain as accepted facts of life. What if you could accept that they are not necessary?

This is a powerful question, because it will confront your addiction to pain-based reality. Knowing that you are free to have a life without these distortions is usually first accompanied by a sense of terror. You may actually touch this truth with wondrous bliss and recognition, then within a short time, (hours, days or weeks), due to your interaction with a fear/pain based society, you trigger your addiction to the same belief system and find yourself spiraling away from the joy.

The gift of this process is that you are being shown the distortion of the divine energy that you carry. As the refractions grew ever-more complex and birthed refractions of refractions, people lost clarity of their conscious connection to their Divine Source. Realizing the pervasiveness of distorted beliefs and density customs, you can begin to unravel the addictive pattern.

It really doesn't matter how successful you are in coping with the world, if you have frustration or pain in your life then you are invested in a refraction! Negative feeling indicates that at some level we are efforting to do or be something that is not in alignment with our authentic truth. Frustration results when we lose touch with the divine flow. Pain therefore gifts consciousness with awareness of an imbalance. If these painful feelings are regular occurrences, then chances are you are addicted to your pain. The choice we have is to embrace the healing or to deny the imbalance.

It is the lack of trust in the Self (in the Divine) that triggers a focus on manipulating the outer world. This is why the lessons are a powerful tool for facing density addiction head on. The outer world is co-created from a fear-based egoic model of reality that disregards the truth of your Divine power.

When billions of people collaborate with self-denial and give their emotional energy to the outer refraction, then the density dramas seem evermore real. Density consciousness develops a magnetic pull through the power of those who contribute attention to it. All illusion, once validated by another person, carries a life of its own. Anyone who has felt the energy of an aligned political rally or a large church gathering can attest to the magnetic pull of the particular world view being offered. The ocean of energy that wraps our shared world is filled with the energies of frustration and fear which then enliven refracted belief systems that associate with those energies.

As we approach 2012 we have time to heal our wounds and expand our trust in our own divinity. We have been given the freedom to relax into our true co-creative capacity and live lives of Joy. The period we are in now is a very loud cosmic wake-up call.

Are you ready to awaken to your authentic energy?

We have few examples of authenticity in our modern world. Some of our elders have let go of worldly preoccupations and learned to live in a serene flow, releasing their density addiction and enjoying life. As one gains some distance from life events, new perspectives reveal themselves. This is the wisdom that comes with age. However, aging is not a prerequisite! Insights are gained as people disengage from the compelling dramas that entangle their awareness, such as work pressures, commuter traffic, financial fears, etc. The stressors of modern life seem to color our entire waking consciousness, if we let them.

Can we let go of the addiction to stress and let our lives simply unfold their gifts?

To cultivate a spiritual detachment allows one to flow harmoniously into the world of interactions as observers. Insights are gained as we widen the backdrop and see our interactions from a broader perspective. The observer mode is less reactive and thus sees more of the forces at play in any situation. The observer role thus offers greater freedom of choice – this is the paradoxical benefit of relaxing the need to control.

As we release the first person perspective and relax our need to control things that happen to us, we discover that there is an essential harmony already influencing the flow of life. The observer perspective is one that does not drown into the activities of one's life, but rather notices the sidelines as well as the center field. This perspective can be cultivated through meditation and introspection. It can be cultivated through an overwhelming life crisis, as well.

The essential quality of this observer mode is a compassionate indifference. To relax our egoic need to control life requires that we cultivate trust. Spiritual detachment is foundationalized by trust in the divine flow. One who is anchored in this trust might seem a bit indifferent to those who are consumed in drama, since they choose not to engage in the drama. However, they are actually enjoying more of the show!

"Being in the world, but not of the world" is a joyful state of trust and flow. It is the state of being present to the now moment without losing momentum. This state of presence comes as one resides more fully in their authentic being, their soul energy.

The energy of the divine out-pours through our refractions (ego ideas) and out-pictures into the world. In essence we use our creative energy to co-create a world of lack and fear. The Divine supports our co-creative out-picturing, regardless of its lack of true nourishment, because free will is our gift. With such powerful co-creative energy at our disposal, we can just as easily co-create a world of peace and harmony.

Everything we experience in our world is a symptom or indicator that points to our state of consciousness. Repeatedly losing a job or being unsuccessful in love relationships is a symptom of an unconscious limiting belief. We can blame the lovers or the bosses – there are all kinds of stories and conclusions that will place responsibility for our situation on the outer world. Yet, it truly has nothing to do with the individual players in our experience; it has more to do with the energies that are animating those players.

The lovers, the bosses, were simply dancing with our energy

and cooperating with the message of that energy. Thus the characters in the drama can change, but the theme will be the same. These unproductive patterns limit our empowerment and keep us bound to a level of consciousness. This is the life of an addict, and when recognized as such may sound familiar.

The person who fails to find intimacy does not necessarily have the wrong partner; he or she has not yet resolved the energetic barriers to intimacy with themselves. The person who struggles with addictions may resolve an alcohol addiction through treatment and then transfer the addictive energy to cigarettes or chewing gum or to love relationships. This is classic in the recovery arena and counselors who work in this arena are well acquainted with this transference.

How do we lift into higher vibrational states?

The physical and the emotional body both have to undergo shifts in order to allow the ascended energy to come forward. The ego must be treated like the child that it truly is and trust the soul to lead our lives. These are significant changes! Letting go of the orientations that once defined our lives can be challenging. It can feel like a loss of self. Yet, once you are clear that you wish to live authentically as a being of light enjoying a physical body, then the path becomes clear. We must surrender to the Divine.

Even as our hearts surrender to God, our habit patterns will object. As one releases their former comfort zone to create a new way of being there can be moments of insecurity and fear. Every time some flash of pain or fear arises, the ego will step up and try to govern your choices. It is a test of your spiritual tenacity. The ego does not relinquish control without a fight....perhaps many fights! It is also imperative to remember that you are not judging your ego, you are simply engaging in a new relationship with it where the soul leads and ego delightfully follows.

As long as one is committed to their trust in Spirit, then each egoic setback strengthens you. You cultivate your mastery through your ability to discern and self-correct when you are off track. Fortunately, the Joy of awakening is more compelling than the familiarity of our limiting beliefs, once we accept that pain/fear living is not the norm. Our addiction is healed by choosing a higher form of nourishment.

As you are able to more fully surrender to your soul's calling, you begin to relax into the truth of authentic energy. Awakening is the process of returning to spiritual alignment and true empowerment. Spiritual empowerment is the place of knowing that we are at cause in our world. To be at cause is to recognize that everything we experience is an effect, meaning it is secondary to the energy that created it (cause). The outer world is an expression of our subconscious intentions and of the interaction of the cumulative intents of the participating people in the world.

For example, the world at large is the sum expression of the consciousness of the participants in the world. Everything that you see is secondary to the consciousness that created it. Thus to do battle with an effect displaying in the world is to work downstream from the cause. This is critical to take in as we move closer to 2012.

For example, you can never stop war by fighting to win a war. The act of fighting itself strengthens the level of consciousness that creates war. Then, the energy that created the war will find another expression which is most often another war to fight. Since the mid-1800's the United States of America has managed to find a war to participate with approximately every fifteen years. Clearly wars are never won, for the underlying energy never finds completion through the expression of war, it is simply a repetitive addiction pattern.

The number of wars endorsed and fueled by the United States of America in the last century should cause any heart-centered individual to pause. Warring is an accepted expression of energy to this country, regardless of political party. Like all outer expressions war is simply a symptom of a deeper energetic current, and like all addictions it must be recognized as a refraction before true healing can begin.

Those involved with any form of holistic healing modality know that you will not heal sickness by removing the symptoms. Yet, it is comforting to have the symptoms go away. Symptoms are secondary to the true cause of the illness. Traditional allopathic medicine enjoys suggesting that the removal of symptoms means that the cause of the illness has been removed. This is rarely true – the change in symptoms points to the fact that something has shifted. Was a cure effected or did the energy find a different avenue of expression or suppression?

All illness is a call for connection to the soul. The soul is eternally vibrant and whole, if the body is expressing symptoms, then it merely needs to heal the separation in consciousness from the soul energy. As consciousness aligns with the energy of the soul, healing happens. Avesa Quantum Healing[34] offers a gateway to the quantum energy of the soul.

Our lives will continually project our unresolved issues out into our world of experience as repetitive problems. The funny thing about humans is that they are willing to accept this constant failure. How many people do you know that would rather be "right" than happy? Why is it that people fail to choose Peace and Joy in favor of some sort of friction or duty?

Many people spiritualize the acceptance of struggle, pain, grief, and lack. We suggest that these are all addictions. These energies, regardless of whether they are socially acceptable, are self-defeating, self-inhibiting and they lack essential soul nourishment. They are therefore toxic.

It is time for everyone to realize it does not have to be that way. You can anchor your psychology in a different vibratory level and not at the level of dysfunctional relationships or pain-based feelings. How does one shift?

So, when is enough...enough?

The shift happens based upon an inner commitment to seek the Divine. The Divine energy is an expanded state of being; it produces joy. All pain-based experiences are the result of unconscious patterns, an addiction to fear. Conscious living can result in a state of joy, peace and unconditional acceptance of all life. We call this unconditional state of acceptance love, (which is distinctly different from emotional love).

A person who has an orientation toward life where they believe that others outside of themselves have more authority, power and wisdom than they do is always in a one down position. They are addicted to victim energy. To that person the idea that we could simply choose joy seems impossible and may even provoke anger or other strong reactions. Thus the problem becomes a self-fulfilling prophecy, for what we believe is impossible will most likely not find its way into our lives.

On the other hand, if we cultivate the energy of willingness, and if we cultivate a little bit of self-trust, then we can expand that willingness and trust into ever-greater fields of joy. This creates a sense of empowerment. Through that empowerment we will expand step by step. All it takes is sincere practice keeping our attention upon that which brings us joy.

Joy is a barometer. True soul-joy exists outside of mental belief systems. Joy itself is a high frequency energy that is aligned with the natural essence of your soul. Emotional Joy is always conditional upon something happening, while Soul-Joy is simply an alignment with your core essence.

Pain, trauma imprints, and limiting beliefs offer gifts of discernment, not a measure of your worth. They heal as people align with the joy of their core essence, their soul. Joy is indeed the magic measure for your state of empowerment! As we watch our joy level and become mindful of the existence of the energy of joy in our lives, we can navigate life's opportunities effectively. When you know what brings you joy, then you will find a pathway through any decision matrix.

Finding our soul energy is the antidote to every illness, and every complaint of modern life. Anchoring our consciousness into this essential energy will lift us through the hypnosis of density. If we are truly committed to expressing the divine in all we do, then everything that is unlike God will gradually fall away. We will lift and be free from any and all addictions.

"If it does not bring you joy then why are you doing it?"

~ Archangel Zadkiel

Chapter Twelve

Energizing Your Divine Electronic Belt

There is an electronic belt of divine energy that surrounds you which is fueled by your Divine recognition. This energy field surrounds every self-conscious living entity and serves as an attractor field which conditions the space that surrounds the individual.

This attractor field can be charged into a bright glowing field of energy provided that the student focuses on their divine connection. Many artists have communicated this energy by drawing a golden glow around their pictures of spiritual masters. When there is self-doubt or fear energy in the consciousness of the student, then this divine electronic belt weakens and rips or holes in the field are created.

Like a balloon with a hole in its wall, the reservoir of divine potential that surrounds the student begins to deplete. Holes are mended through trust and focus upon the magnificence of the divine. Every time you give attention to energies of fear, doubt, or anger you are deliberately sending your divine power to something that is incongruent with your authentic truth. That is, you have invested your energy into a refracted limited energy. The Divine knows only expanding peace, love and joy and will express those energies through your life as long as you are not investing your attention in refractions.

The benefit of spiritual practice is to open the conscious energetic doorway to your soul energy. By connecting to this Divine Self, one begins to discern the difference between the pure energy of the Inner and the refracted energy of the outer world. Then one can live with greater congruence and consciousness.

At first, spiritual practice offers a visit to a refined state of being. It is a vacation from our norm. If you do not evolve past this phase of awakening, then the realm of density consciousness will indeed consume you for you have made density your primary vocation. The path of Self-Ascension encourages you to sincerely practice in each and every conscious moment.

Practice breathing consciously, practice seeing the Divine in each person you greet, practice being mindful of your thoughts and words. This may feel awkward at first – this awkwardness is a sign of how far away from your Authentic energy you have anchored yourself. Spiritual practice is not meant to be a burden. Rather it is an opportunity to practice your mastery. If your ego has organized itself around the refracted identity, then it will seek to return your attention to the refracted creations. We all get to confront this habit. Remember, self-doubt collapses your energy and Divine Trust expands it.

The good news is that it gets easier! Once the initial reactions and struggle dissolve, you will discover that Spirit sends its messengers and tons of grace your way! Ask for help and you will find that help appears in your world of experience. It is a delight to witness how much support is available for the sincere student.

Many people are aware of the "Law of Attraction" which reminds us that what we focus on with energy and intent tends to manifest. However, there is a deeper level. We are all manifesting constantly, it is our nature. Just look at your life experience and you will see your power of manifestation at work. If we are anchored in our personality-self then our manifestations will reflect those refractions. No matter how intently you affirm a positive change, it will not come to you if you secretly hold fear and unworthiness energy inside. Thus, our manifestation focus must be congruent with our inner truth if we are to see empowered results.

In an effort to change their lives many people make demands on Spirit. Those demands are intended to counter-balance something already present in their experience. Demands made in response to negative conditions carry the negative within them! For the negative was part of the energy that generated the new focus!

Instead, create "Commands". To Co-Mandate is to co-create. To properly co-create we must first center ourselves in our soul's energy. If there is something you don't enjoy in your life experience, bring loving attention to it. Heal the discomfort by finding the gift that this "thing" has given to your consciousness. By finding the spiritual gift we then discharge the energy of resistance. This releases the hold that the negative experience had on us. From the energy of peaceful alignment with our Truth we can call in a new opportunity. If you center yourself in the loving knowing that you are divine and connected to the One Almighty Source, then you can decree or command that certain conditions take form in your world.

The key is a willingness to come home to your soul. Returning to wholeness is returning to the truth of your soul energy. We do this in stages, for our refractions encircle us like a house of mirrors. As we remove our energy investments in false beliefs, the outer world that would have interacted with these false beliefs begins to feel incongruent. It starts to fall away. Thus, those situations and people who are also anchored at the level of the false beliefs lose their magnetism with you. As this happens you are presented with the opportunity to continue trusting and allowing the outer world to shift.

This is how we grow! In our personal evolution we refine ourselves and attract into our field of experience those people and events which serve the level of consciousness we are working with. Unless your friends and family are also on this path of conscious evolution, they will find their ability to be non-reactive tested!

The human emotional body uses polarity as its basis of intelligence. Thus, you can not feel opposite feelings simultaneously. When our vibratory level lifts to a new level, then the old patterns can cause discomfort in the emotions. When the emotional body feels discomfort, the mental body immediately jumps in to offer an explanation for the discomfort. This is why sometimes our old friends become judgmental as we grow; they are seeking to displace the discomfort by distancing themselves. Or, you might start judging your friends.

Negative judgments are a means of preserving refractions. All judgment separates one from the flow of authenticity. That is, the judgment indicates that the person judging would rather preserve a world view (usually a limiting belief) than expand into a new form of harmony. Usually we judge because we have not anchored fully in divine trust.

The recipient of a judgment is given the gift of practicing, or aligning with, the ascended heart. Are you able to breathe and allow the judger to have their experience? Or do you need to argue with the refraction? For if the projection triggers doubt in you, then you will engage that level of consciousness and the energetic "Velcro" will bind your experience outside of your authentic soul energy. This type of energetic Velcro keeps groups bonded together and thus prevents them from looking deeply at themselves. It is a great gift to recognize the power of this. Each judgment reminds us to surrender further into trust.

People do not enjoy being around others who stimulate their "unfinished business" unless they are on a path of conscious growth. Then such stimulations are seen as opportunities! As we reframe our world of experience into the world of opportunity, then we can use each moment to make liberating choices.

What is essential on the conscious journey is a commitment to keep returning to the path of authenticity. We do not measure our progress by how many times we stray into pain-based experiences. Our strength is measured by returning to the path.

As we keep our focus on the divine, we nourish ourselves and our relationship with the outer world shifts to match our inner state. We relax ever more and discover that all of it, ALL of life is a gift!

Co-creation is our birthright. It is our nature. Archangel Zadkiel offers additional discernments in the understanding of co-creation:

> *You can choose to embrace, to expand OR you can choose to diminish. In the choice you create the opportunities that will appear to you.*

Zadkiel reminds us that the primary choice we must make is whether to align with expansion or align with contraction (density). Are we bringing our consciousness toward the truth of our core essence (Light), or are we bringing our consciousness to a more collapsed identity? The quality of the energy we send out via our Divine Electronic Belt will reflect this fundamental choice.

> *When you make a choice then opportunity will arise. Opportunities are based upon co-creation. Choices birth opportunities which then birth manifestation. In this free-will zone everything is an opportunity! The manifestation is yours!*

As we make a conscious choice, our intent flows out into our Divine Electronic Belt and influences the quality of the outer world. This energetic signal calls opportunities to appear before us. These opportunities are the steps to the full manifestation of what we originally intended.

Sometimes we make a choice but refuse to take action on the opportunity that subsequently presents itself. That is, either we don't recognize the opportunity or we lack the self-trust to take action. Either way, if we fail to act on the opportunity we have then made a new choice which will then send out a new energy to our Divine Electronic Belt, thus bringing other opportunities our way.

Archangel Zadkiel continues:

How you manifest your choice is up to you. Opportunity follows choice…It is your commitment to your choice that generates opportunities.

The steps are:

1) Choose: make your choice

2) Claim the Opportunities that arise from the choice

3) Manifest the outcome

The actions you take must align with your choice! The choice offers opportunities and then you take (aligned) action with those opportunities.

It is in how you navigate your choices that produce the opportunities.

Life reflects our energy. How we respond to that reflection either expands our love or stalls our expansion in some fashion. Are you ready to accept the gift of these expressions to propel the expansion of your consciousness? That we are all here together on earth is already determined. How we respond to that fact is an expression of our free will. Your freedom is in the "how".

"All opportunities come forward
to support the choice you have made."

Let us find gratitude for the recognition that we are Spirit in form. From this recognition we release the grip of mis-creations, and reside in the joy of our wholeness.

Chapter Thirteen

Ascension and Resurrection

Ascension is a state of consciousness accompanied by a shift in energy vibration. As our energy vibration rises we experience life differently. Our priorities shift and change. We all know this as we have ascended from childhood into adulthood.

In the most basic sense, ascension begins at the root chakra[35] and rises through each of the seven primary energy centers. So, we move from fear and tribal issues (root chakra), through intimacy and power issues (second and third chakra), until we finally reside in the fourth, or heart chakra energies. Truly anchoring in the heart means that we have released the compulsion of the lower chakras.

The fourth chakra is the foundation of the Self-Ascended state. That is, until we can anchor in the heart centered peace of unconditional acceptance and extend that perspective of peace and love toward the world and toward mankind, no further progress is available on this planet. All the great religious traditions state that Love is the answer, that non-reactive Peace is the state of attainment to be sought. This is true! However, the heart is the foundation for the next stage in our evolution. It is the new starting point.

Some people worry about ascension and resurrection – they fear for their bodies and their friends. Know that ascension will not happen TO you without your participation! That is, as we approach the year 2012 there will be more and more energy bombarding our planet from the sun and from the cosmic center of the universe. This energy will support people to awaken to a more refined vibrational state. We must all practice lifting into our ascended heart chakra, for once we reside there we can immediately resolve the world's tensions! This alone will be a wonderful accomplishment, and the ascension process re-connects us beyond this world.

There are many people that want to go beyond the heart chakra and connect with multi-dimensional existence. This too is very possible. We call this Self-Ascension because it is a conscious choice. No death required! Once you learn how to lift into the heart, then you can easily learn how to go further. It is your choice. The entire multidimensional universe is available to anyone who is sincerely grounded in their heart.

So, 2012 is not to be feared – it is a climax of energy that can be harnessed for the lifting of humanity's consciousness. Each person must choose whether they want to participate. Spirit does not force your choices – you have free will!

Are you ready to let go of fear?

Are you ready to let go of pain-based habits?

People often ask, "What will happen to me during the ascension?" or, "How do I ascend?"

It is important to understand that your core essence, your Divine Soul, is the ascended you. Therefore, you are already ascended and you are resurrecting! You can resurrect your energy from refractions and illusion and come into wholeness as an ascended being. This is what Jesus, the Christ, modeled for us all.

In the density we call Earth, our ego has become so strong that we have identified with the shell, the outer self, and lost connection with our core essence. Our core essence (soul energy) is indeed the energy of pure Love. This Divine Love is the power that literally glues the molecules together – it is creative, restorative and eternal. This is the essence of Source (or God) that has been buried under layers of individualized history, pain and suffering. It is what was seemingly lost. It is what all true spiritual seekers are searching for: their own God essence. For once found, this Source energy offers Peace beyond understanding and the opportunity to lift into empowered Bliss.

Many souls have already made the decision to Self-Ascend at this particular time in history, however they forgot their decision. The magnetism of density has distracted their attention from the choice. These people will usually live a conflicted life expression for their authentic soul energy and their ego are in opposition.

As one claims their soul's heritage, the sense of movement that one experiences as they move through the energy of resurrection is simply the falling away of the ego (personality-self). This sense of movement is experienced in our day-to-day lives as evolution. We grow, learn and make changes. Synchronistic events happen to us as we relax our need to control and allow Spirit to flow more freely into our lives. Movement is the natural expression of Source, as Light infinitely expands.

Human Beings often try hard to control the world and to control each other. This results in conflict and war. It never works for long. People who submit to control begin to collapse inside and lose their Joy. Eventually they will become depressed and robot-like OR they will explode into rebellion. There is a core tension that is generated when we try to compress or collapse people. It may take years before the explosion, and some may chose to die instead of lifting into their power, however, eventually a repressed people or society will collapse or explode.

Self-Ascension is resurrection, it is an alignment with core essence. The purpose of spiritual practice is to open the doorway to the authentic core essence energy, the soul. In the Divine communion one is given a restorative glimpse of their own core essence. Then the decision must be made: Do I choose to journey back to my essence with dedication and commitment, or do I anchor in the outer world of density and simply visit the soul for restorative moments?

All religions offer some sort of practice that will lead the sincere petitioner to that doorway. No religion can push you through the door into the direct experience of the Infinite. The decision to walk through the door must be made by the individual. This is the choice that results in Self-Ascension. Once the decision is made, one can attain Unity through sincere effort and spiritual tenacity. The goal is attainable and supported, for we are now at the time of culmination.

Everything you invest your soul energy into becomes real. The path of Self-Ascension requires that you re-call your energy from those investments which are not aligned with your authentic energy. That is, when we grow up we set aside childish beliefs. This also occurs as we evolve to an ever-refining vibration, for we must release social and cultural conventions which inhibit our alignment with the soul. Thus we must grow through the attractions of density and activism into Ascension Awareness.

The material world is the effect of energy. The material is not at cause. The forms we interact with are the result of the intent of energy and consciousness interacting. The world, for the most part, conforms to our belief patterns as individuals and as a collective humanity. We have collaborated to manifest this experience.

Thus, it is unproductive to try to manipulate the physical world with a physical intervention. Yes, we can shatter a rock with a hammer, however, we can not create a new rock with a hammer. Similarly, we can not create a new world using the beliefs of the old. To truly create a new world that offers greater joy than the old world means that we must manifest from a more ascended place within our consciousness. As we accept our own resurrection, our creation will reflect this new state of consciousness.

Many ask, "Why would God allow such suffering in our world?" The response is that we are the gods that created this suffering. Our ability to create was guaranteed as we have been fashioned in the image and likeness of the One who created us. Our creative power has been refracted by our uniquely human belief systems. These belief systems, like colored lenses, cloud and qualify all that we interact with and all that we create. Instead of seeking to solve the problem, let us take responsibility by releasing the need to recreate suffering.

Freedom lies in the release of these human belief patterns through the complete surrender to the Soul energy. That is, as we bring our consciousness back to the Divine, the density world has less control over us. As we commit to looking beyond the human creations and see the divine energy beneath these mis-creations, we then free our minds from the limited points of view that result in misery.

Self-Ascension is conscious ascension. That is, it is a choice to align fully with one's authentic energy, not the refracted creation expressing in the outer world. The statement "to be in the world and not of the world" attempts to communicate this orientation. We are self-conscious beings of great creative power. If we grant authority and dominion of our creative power to outside conventions, outside authorities and fear-based beliefs, then we have given our power away, have we not? To the extent that we rely on the outer world to dictate our actions (which are our energy-investments) to that extent we have bowed to a caricature of truth.

The outer world has the ability to conform to our highest expressions of love, unity, harmony, wisdom and peace. The outer world is but an out-picturing of our collective consciousness. To the extent we hold pain-based subconscious belief patterns, those patterns will qualify the energy we direct to the outer world and we thus create and support duality and pain.

We are innocent! If we all truly understood the process of creation, then mankind would become responsible. Once you awaken to your divinity then you are responsible. Then you must be a conscious co-creator; anything less means that you have turned your back on God. However, all actions before that recognition are forgiven, for you are asleep. *Forgive them for they know not what they do*, applies to all unconscious actions. The world is populated with unconscious co-creators.

Thus, with your awakening…with your resurrection… comes great responsibility.

Self-Ascension is the process of purification of the outer experience so that it matches the inner truth. It brings the personality-self into a state of surrender to the Divine self. This alignment opens the floodgates of creative energy. You can not manipulate another being to collaborate with your picture of the outer world. That is, pure activism never works for it seeks to impose a picture of the way things should be upon others who may not be ready for that picture.

What is all-ways beneficial for others is to give them the direct experience of true spiritual authenticity, to be able to touch true spiritual power. In your empowerment you release others to be in their power. By being authentic, trusting, and from actions of integrity, you grant permission to others to feel and trust their own authentic energy.

Remember, the world is reflecting the consciousness of its participants. To intervene at the level of true cause in the world means that you must intervene at the level of consciousness. This requires that you are authentically aligned with your soul! Your authentic alignment offers a direct pipeline to the Divine source and is the only sustaining creative power in the universe. When one recognizes this truth, then the path is quite simple: Be at peace with yourself!

Peace with creation, inward states and outer states of expressions, can only be found through Love. Love is the energy that dissolves the discordant and expands peace and harmony. Love is the canvas upon which beauty can be expressed, for all harmony is an alignment with essence....love is that essence.

By now, dear reader, you must have an intellectual grasp that there is but one doorway to Peace and ascended being-ness. That doorway is your ascended heart, and that destination resides in pure conscious connection.

Consciousness is like infinite sound that we have truncated into our singular life song. As if we were conducting an orchestra, we ask some aspects to be quiet and we emphasize the voice of other aspects, thus the outer creation is the song we have orchestrated. Because consciousness is infinite we can then refract ourselves further and place ourselves (our attention) into that song and dance with it, and in the dancing we forget that we are the Creator of the experience. Wow! What a powerful being we are!

And so, if this writing makes some sense to you, then your job is to awaken further to your authentic energy. And if this writing repels you in some way, then your job is still to awaken further to your authentic energy. SMILE! It does not matter what you believe or how you feel. We all have the same job assignment! HOW we undertake our awakening is up to us. Some will be attracted to the methods in this book. Those that are repelled will find another way. Trust your process. Without self-trust there will only be endless loops of misdirected energy.

Trust is your freedom. Trust is your witness to expansion, for trust can not live without love. Love is trusting and trust is loving. Bring that unconditional acceptance to yourself first and you will heal the inner wounds. This healing may require some time and continued application. It will complete as long as you trust!

Life was not meant to be hard. In fact life is not difficult at all! We make it seem difficult simply by choosing to ignore our inner resources, our authentic truth. Like a runner who refuses to breathe, we will always collapse if we do not open to the infinite breath of God.

"Trust is Love and Love is Trust."

~ Archangel Zadkiel

Chapter Fourteen

Understanding 2012: A Cosmic Perspective

As we move closer to the 2012 experience, there has been much discussion about the third dimension, our current existence, and the fourth and fifth dimensions. This is a critical understanding as humanity evolves.

Already quantum science has begun to reveal the scientific evidence of other dimensional energies, and by the time you are reading this book, additional evidence will be revealed in many ways, for many are now asking for proof.

Because we are at the time of unprecedented and rapid evolution, we must allow ourselves to reconcile all of our history. The profound and total healing of the human psyche will offer the energy for our next cycle of being.

The following discourse from the Archangelic Realm offers great clarity as to the understanding of the dimensions, our role as light beings who have been on a great expansion, and the new energy we have already entered that shifts from expansion, back to unification.

We encourage you to read this discourse carefully, and allow its impact to assist you at a cellular level. Then you can consciously embrace the energy of unification as a cosmic citizen.

Archangel Zadkiel Speaks:

We come today out of great benevolent joy. You have entered into a time when all words that come from this vessel, (Kira Raa), are now always being brought forth with a universal stream of consciousness that involves all.

It is not about the one voice, is it about the ONE voice, coming through, being understood, being heard, being recognized, and expanding into an ever greater state of consciousness that offers most profound understanding. Do you understand?

Sri Ram Kaa: Yes I do.

Oftentimes the filters of the brain are so thick with muck that they need to be taken out, washed, aired out, so that one can be able to see again. And oftentimes, those that feel they must adhere to one way or other way, this way or that way, that voice or this voice, are simply working with a clogged filter. Those that recognize the universal scope, the understanding, will be most grateful.

Where is your state of consciousness? We will begin here, and then expand.

Oftentimes questions will form, and the answers will expand. The questions are like going deep within, into a center place. You are in the time of the expanded glory, going in, to explode out. So it is most powerful to revisit being present with the understanding that Allness Is, and Oneness is All.

Sri Ram Kaa: I would like to have a greater understanding of the relationship of the various energies that are guiding us. I was going to use the word the hierarchy, however I understand the limitations of that word, and I'm looking for a word or way to describe the distinction between the Archangels, the Benevolent Ones[36], the T-12[37], the Elohim. What is the relationship with these energies?

It is best shared this way. There is the true relationship, and then there is the relationship that is understood as levels of consciousness within density that wish to make everything into a hierarchical format. This is of course why when you first asked the question, even though you do not use the word, there is a default system at work in the density mind that feels one must be higher than another.

Draw a straight horizontal line. At one end put Divine Consciousness. At the other end put density. We are steps along the way. This is what you must understand. If you draw an arrow from Divine Consciousness pointing towards density, this is how we are birthed. This is where the density mind believes that a hierarchical system comes in.

Looking at your line, from Divine Consciousness births the Elohim, from the Elohim births the Benevolent Ones and the T-12, from these energies births the Archangelic Realm, and from that energy births the Angelic Realm. From here births the lower dimensional realms. We only use the word lower for you to understand.

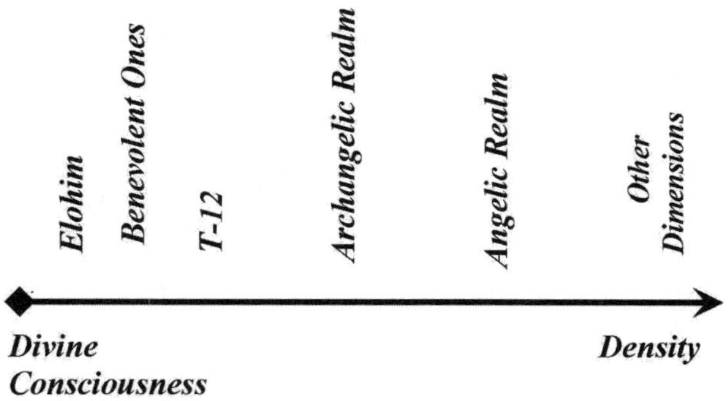

Sri Ram Kaa: What number are those?

The density realms?

Sri Ram Kaa: The dimensional realms…

There are many dimensions Sri Ram Kaa, however of the realms we have just referred to we offer you this: The realms at this end of the line would be three, four.

Sri Ram Kaa: The third and the fourth?

Correct. Three and four. Stay with us. Then you move forward. Five through nine would come in to the Angelic Realm, is this not what you are looking for? Ten through fourteen is the Archangelic Realm, and fifteen and above carries the energy all the way back to Divine Consciousness. There are many more realms, or dimensions as you would call them, well beyond these. In the thirty-third dimension, which you can put right there, this is the dimension where the Benevolent Ones originate from.

Sri Ram Kaa: How can they originate from a dimension?

Because as you come toward density from Divine Consciousness, we have not gone back to the other way on the timeline yet, as you birth forward, as you burst forward from Divine oneness toward density, the dimensions are created as matter is projected forward.

Think of a big burst of energy that keeps getting larger and larger and larger, and as each energy moves forward, more is revealed. So as you come into density, this is where all reveals itself. Yet what we wish for you to understand is that they are all part of the one, and they reveal themselves in this burst of energy.

Now draw an arrow from density, back toward Divine Oneness. See? One arrow goes one way, one arrow goes the other. You are now in the phase where the arrow that went from the divine to density is complete, and you have done your sling shot around density, and now you are on your way back.

As these energies are coming back into the Divine Oneness, it is reunifying many densities. There are the reunifications of the many realms, or the many dimensions, as you call it, that is what is happening now, from the third, fourth and into the fifth. As a collective, this is a very large leap.

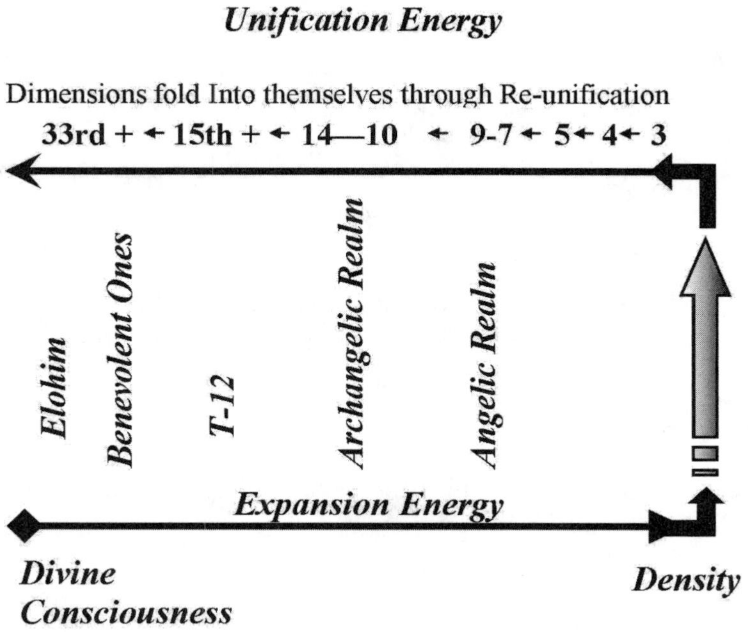

There are also the energies of those that have been communicating with you, that have been collectively reunifying simultaneously. So it is not that the Benevolent Ones are from the thirty third dimension, it is that they speak to you from the thirty third at this time.

Sri Ram Kaa: So, that is the frequency that is compatible with their anchoring?

Yes, it is the frequency at this time that matches the frequency that you are bringing forward within to be able to offer a message that can be understood. It is indeed a crystalline dimension, pure energy, pure crystalline understanding. When you activate your crystalline corpuscles, when you activate the crystalline streams within you, this is what has brought forward the opportunity to be able to have this communication.

Sri Ram Kaa: Earlier you said the Benevolent Ones were at the fifteenth and above?

Yes, that is where those levels begin, the T-12, and all of these levels very quickly assimilate. It is hard once you get beyond the fifteenth to offer any form of differentiation. We offer it to you so that the mind may be able to grasp the concept. Differentiation is much easier understood as you are in the active expansionary process. When you are in the unification process, then there is no reason to be looking at this - differentiation is no longer needed or necessary. We simply are doing our best to explain this to you.

Sri Ram Kaa: In the density returning, the third and fourth are integrating into the fifth dimension, or folding in, this is over a period of what we would call years?

This is correct.

Sri Ram Kaa: And this process of folding together then, will continue…

This is correct.

Sri Ram Kaa: All the way back?

Oh yes. You have just begun the re-unification process, this is indeed the beginning of another cycle, for what seems to be the great culmination in one process is always the beginning of another. Unlike the stratifying expansionary experience, which continually refracts and expands and brings forth new levels, as you use this word, in the reunification process, only that which has given itself the gift of being aligned with the energies coming forward can reunify. What is unlike reunification will simply fall away into its own form of experience.

Sri Ram Kaa: Well, then that ties to this vision that we're re-visiting, of those attached to third dimensional polarities. . .

…Cannot go into re-unification energy at this time. It is not that they can not reunify, it is that they must continue to move forward. It is as if you take a light and you sling shot it around this sphere. The pure light, as it goes around this sphere, some of it goes, oh look at this sphere, and picks up some dirt and some rocks and says I want to hold onto these, and yet when it makes it around the other side, the rocks and those things can not go into that which they have not come from, so they must fall away.

What are you holding? Are you holding the rocks or are you holding the light? Are you attached to the rocks that you go with them, or are you able to let go?

©Colin Anderson/Corbis

Sri Ram Kaa: And please reconcile this with the image given to us around the Inner Matrix Program[38] where we had the line that marks the dimensions, and those going deeper into density will later pop out.

This is correct because they will go out the bottom so to speak into their own loop, and it is in this loop that they will go ever deeper. To then start coming back into reunification energy, they will have to explore ever more that which stopped their reunification initially.

Sri Ram Kaa: So, is there not a harmonic synergy with the

greater reunification? The group that is separating into the future density explorations happening here, how will it reintegrate with the greater flow?

OK, how the reintegration will occur is as if you have a magnet. Initially the magnets are on the reverse poles, and so they separate. Once the energy begins to be realigned, it will have a magnetic pull and a magnetic attraction that will indeed find the stream, and the stream will magnetize back. This is the best example we can give you.

Sri Ram Kaa: And so at that point, it will come back in, whatever the appropriate point to come back in is.

That's correct. Because that experience in and of itself is a powerful experience! They will go through many beautiful cycles, and they will come into their own ages of enlightenment, and so it's not like they are unable to catch up. They will simply rejoin at a different time.

Sri Ram Kaa: Have we gone as far as we can go into density?

This is correct.

Sri Ram Kaa: And yet, who is the we that we're talking about here?

You ask a question that has great explanation. In this form, on this planet, in this way, and in this experience, you are maxed out, as they say. When the split occurs, even that which appears to look the same as is now will have undergone a dramatic shift. And even though initially it will not be understood that way, it will indeed begin to rarify itself, just on a different plane than that which is separate and going in a different direction. Two worlds, that will again collide, at a different place and time.

Sri Ram Kaa: How is it that so many people are holding a higher vibrational rate than they were previously, yet don't recognize it?

Because if you are on the planet, whether you know it or not, if you are here, in this Earth sphere, this global sphere right now, everyone, ***everyone, every being, every tree, every animal, every being has shifted vibration****. Many are not conscious of it, they just simply know something has shifted. Many medicate it, many complain about it, yet of course there are many who do not.*

Sri Ram Kaa: There will be an actual moment using our sense of time, of separation between those that are choosing to re-densify, is that the right word, or to continue to density?

Or to simply continue in a manner that is aligned with holding the stones.

Sri Ram Kaa: However, every one of them is presently raising their vibratory level.

Because in the time of the shift, everything will shift for everyone, none are eliminated. Let us offer you a practice to begin feeling this. Open up a crystalline sphere over your head. Go into a pure crystalline sphere with golden emanation. Simply be present in this sphere. Let yourself know, and then ask your questions. You are still thinking linearly in this world. We invite you to be the sphere.

Go into the Crystalline Sphere with the Golden Emanation. Simply Be Present

Sri Ram Kaa: What is the role of preparation? For if the souls have chosen reunification, can they still reunify in a less than awake mode?

Your question is multi-parted. Let us share. All have chosen reunification by default. It is all that can be chosen, so that is not the choice. Reunification is occurring, make no mistake, every, every molecule of this planet is aligned with that energy. It does not need to be a conscious energy, it is at a base level among all things. So the word "choice" is very figurative because that choice was made that has nothing to do with the present time that you call now.

So yes, suffice it to say, all are reunifying. There are choices to be made. In the role of preparation, it is when. When shall each soul reunify? This is simply based upon the individual, individ-u-will interpretations, desires, reconciliations, recognitions, understandings, and surrenders, there are so many factors for each.

This is why the time of preparation has been given; a great gift from the Elohim. The time of preparation did not have to be, because on a cellular level you are all aware, and beyond. The time of preparation is here because so many asked for it. This is where the chosen energy becomes most confused. There are many who run around, "we have been chosen, we have been chosen, we will, we will," and this is where the dogmatic practices of your religions have become well inundated with the "chosen" information. It is not that there are chosen ones, you self-select. There are many of you here who self-selected eons ago and invited us to come in at this time, as part of the time of re-unification.

Your individ-u-will agreed to be here, and you asked us that we come and offer a preparation so that more could be present, because many energies were blended here, many different histories, many different origins, many different comprehensions, and for those of you that were present during many times of consciousness and were consciously aware of this time, and this loop, and this expansionary experience, you asked that there be, out of great mercy and love for all, an opportunity for preparation. Not just for those who were unaware, for those who had already said they were aware. And this has been manipulated and misunderstood, as many other energies have on this planet, into the "I AM a chosen one, we are a chosen one," do you understand?

Sri Ram Kaa: Not fully. I understand the chosen, choosing versus being chosen. I understand what we are at choice about and how we transit this reunification. What I'm missing is the difference between one who is conscious and one who is unconscious, even though the soul has already made the choice.

Not all souls are aware there was a choice as there are many different origins. In the origins of those that have lived in the energy of the pure light stream, that have held onto this from the first recognition of individ-u-will, through Tu'Laya, through Su'Laria, through these densities those energies have made great choices.

The energies that split have made other choices, and some of their choices were to forget, to not realign with reunification, to not understand and be present, and some of those energies have never been birthed in those that were created without consciousness initially, (the Hybrids). And so there needs to be an awakening of a genetic code. Many origins.

Sri Ram Kaa: And so when you say many origins, we have talked about Tu'Laya, Su'Laria and Earth. You have mentioned a total of 12 planets of density, and these planets of density then have beings from other origins as well as the Tu'Layan, and Su'Larian stream.

Each has their own history, yet it is still one. The manifestation of the expansion is different, slightly, on some, and brethren on others. There are parallels. Yes.

Sri Ram Kaa: So for the purpose of the work we do here, we contextualize based on this dominant stream.

Of course, and you must.

Sri Ram Kaa: And for the purpose of understanding, the best the density brain can understand the bigger picture, you must also have some information about the parallels, about the other origins who are reuniting with us.

Without overlapping and confusing them. As with any relationship, with any sacred union, for indeed these reunifications are sacred, you must be in your own wholeness. You must release and resolve the confusion energy.

Sri Ram Kaa: Each in their own wholeness.

Correct. From there the wholeness expands, and so each is in the process of doing so ever more.

There is a great turbulence in turmoil, and when a turbulence, when an energy pattern of turbulent whirling energy is created through turmoil, where does it go? What does it do? Does it have randomness? What is it?

We bring this forth for you because very much a vortex of turbulence has already been created by many worlds each feeding the other. In order to navigate it, you must truly understand what it is. It is the casting off of the rocks and the stones. You do not have to fly in it.

The metamorphosis, for indeed this is the best word that you have, is completing and in many ways is complete. Now it is simply the time of embracing that which has happened, and bringing it forward again, on many levels and in many worlds.

It is imperative to expand thinking beyond this world, and put in perspective, all that is around you. Keep it in perspective. For what is perspective? It is the view of density, applied to density, and yet two double negatives do make a positive. Keep your perspective. Pay attention. See. And in that, you can understand.

SRK: So once again I feel as if I'm starting over!

Or are you simply in a metamorphosis?

Sri Ram Kaa: Yes.

Does not metamorphosis carry with it the gifts of the prior experience? Without that which you are, you cannot be that which you are. There is no starting over, there is the simply the continuation.

Sri Ram Kaa: With each expansion there is an openness.

Yes! It is simply where you are on the circle. Where do you choose to be? Yes.

Sri Ram Kaa: So how may I serve?

You are already serving. You serve by giving yourself the gift of expansion. To give yourself the gift of saying "I am ever expanded." Offer yourself the opportunity to expand ever more. Offer yourself renewal and rejuvenation in this expansion. See each opportunity, each moment, as a wonderful, vital, new and enthusiastic way to become evermore refreshed, evermore entrenched in reunion energy. You serve by serving yourself this way.

It is important for you to do what you are doing. Bring forth your words, bring forth your words with great joyous intensity, do not hold back! This time, do not hold back. And remember, be in your heart of the ascended state, allowing the Divine Galactic Blueprint to be fully open, and you are guided, as you guide.

SRK: Yes.

Yes indeed!

I AM Ever Expanded!

Pause - Breathe - Allow

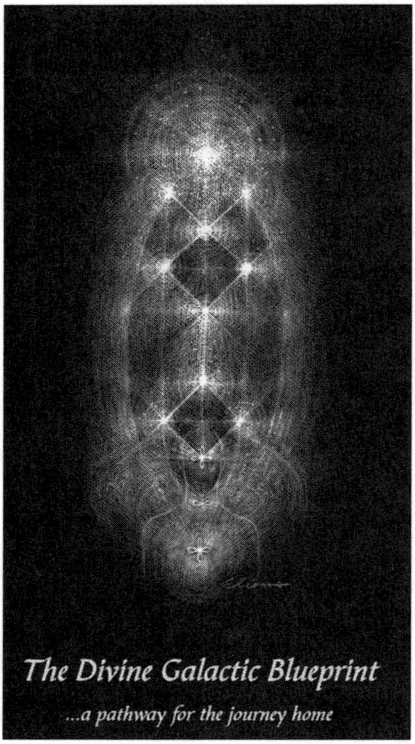

The Divine Galactic Blueprint

...a pathway for the journey home

Integrating the Divine Galactic Blueprint for 2012 Unification

The Divine Galactic Blueprint is the Ascended Chakra system. Everything that you have journeyed through while experiencing this book has been an energetic awakening. This energy, as you by now already know, can be experienced in many ways.

It was at the end times of Su'Laria that the Divine Galactic Blueprint was last fully activated. These twelve points of light are understood as follows:

The Root chakra of the Ascended state is the heart center. It offers stability in this world while opening the energy field to experience other worlds or realms. This chakra must be stable for one to safely enter into the energy of the fifth dimension and beyond. *(See page 278: What About the Fourth Dimension?)*

From the Root chakra of the heart the next point is found at the throat. This is stabilized with the energy of pearl essence. When fully in the Divine Galactic Blueprint, the voice or the word is no longer necessary, so this chakra is known as the truth chakra, for it will reveal your sincerity. If you are in a form of denial or incongruence, then your heart energy is not being allowed to fully express.

The next point is found in the area of the traditional third eye, only slightly higher. This point becomes the foundation of the exploded crown chakra, which is the lifting point into the Ascended state. Instead of a single point, the crown has expanded into four points. These four points collectively form a pyramid carrying violet energy. Archangel Zadkiel describes them as a "lunar module" of the system since they offer you the propulsion to travel into new realms of being.

From the exploded crown we move up to the next four points which form a pyramid of golden energy. As one lifts their heart center into the exploded crown, together the energies of the two offer the portal to the golden center which anchors at the eleventh dimension.

Once you are fully embraced in this golden portal, the divine twin energy opens the final pathway to Divine source. Here in this radiant light center all colors are integrated, and reunification is found.

We have shared the story of Su'Laria and Tu'Laya with you as a means to assist you to once again find the sincerity, self-love, and wholeness that will open your Divine Galactic Blueprint. Often we spend time simply gazing into the energy that emanates from the Divine Galactic Blueprint, a gift of the Elohim.

As our world continues to shift and rebalance itself as it adjusts to the energy of unification instead of expansion, by stabilizing our energy in the heart center as the root of the Ascended state, we become ever more adept at carrying the energy of our soul.

"However many holy words you
read, however many you speak,
What good will they do you,
if you do not act upon them?"

~ Buddha

What About the Fourth Dimension?

As we move from the third to the fifth dimension, this question frequently comes up and is a very important one to address.

Whenever one cycle is ending to birth another, any unresolved energy will join with any resistance energy and surface to defend its existence. This is particularly accurate when we discuss the fourth dimension.

Within the fourth dimensional realm many find themselves intrigued with mystical phenomenon such as ghosts, apparitions, parlor séances, etc. This is the realm of confusion and stagnancy, a dimension of dreams, nightmares, and black magic. There are many energies that seek resolution in this realm and often times those who transition from this world in the energy of anger will find themselves literally stuck in this dimension.

The Archangelic Realm has been very clear that playing in the fourth dimension is a trap, for entities in this dimension fail to reveal their hidden agendas. They are mostly disincarnates who are trapped in density consciousness. Often times, energies from this realm will disguise themselves as Angels or spirit guides in an effort to manipulate information in the third dimension, and they have been very successful.

Archangel Zadkiel has offered to us that you will always be able to discern if the information you are receiving is from the most high because it will leave you feeling filled with love, light and non-judgment. If the information you receive or hear causes you to judge another, causes you to engage in a sense of higher or lower, or ordains you to portend power over another, then it is not of the most high. All interference with the path of another is of density and confusion, another giveaway that the energy is not of the light.

It is import to avoid prolonged interactions with the fourth dimension or as many call it, the astral plane. Yes, it is fascinating, and also know that it will interfere with your liberation, for the astral is the non-material form of density consciousness.

Certainly, it is a wonderful experience to engage and recognize the gifts your contact with this realm can offer. The astral realm is a common first encounter for many as it is close to the third dimension and easily found. Many invasive remote viewers are able to amplify their skills by utilizing the energy of this dimension, and therefore offer ever greater power to the manipulation or chaos that you now see on our planet.

Years ago, when Kira Raa would go into nursing homes to assist them with strange phenomenon, she would spend hours in basements that maintenance staff refused to enter. Always escorted by nursing home personnel, she would quietly walk through the halls and be announced to residents simply as a guest.

What she found during these many visits to different locations, was many who had crossed over in depression and anger, who were unaware that they were trapped in the astral and being offered ever greater confusion in this fourth dimensional energy. The fear of the staff that were aware something strange was happening was enough to convince sane owners to bring her in to clear "whatever it was." Often, the shift was so immediately tangible and lasting that all residents and staff began to have a better experience, even if they had no conscious idea of what had taken place.

Why is this relevant? Left unchecked, the energy of the astral will interfere with your emotional and physical body. It will literally create insane actions, usually through distorted emotions and righteousness. It will justify itself through the manipulation of your emotional body and cause action to occur in the name of being right. Playing with ghosts and feeding our spiritual ego through phenomenon actually increases fear and polarity.

The good news is that the fourth dimension is a very narrow belt of energy between the third and the fifth dimension. It is simply a speed bump on the path of ascension. In the fifth dimensional energy we are free from emotional distortion and density refractions. The fifth dimension is the realm of clarity and is a resting place, so to speak, as we lift out of the gravitational field of density. Let's open the door for the real magic, the gift of our Divine Soul in Action.

Chapter Fifteen

Galactic Contact

As we approach 2012 this book would not be complete unless we addressed the ever increasing reality of otherworldly contact. While Hollywood has done their best to offer great fear and fantasy around this issue, we humbly offer some additional information that may assist you to feel more comfortable with this heavily debated subject matter.

Inter-dimensional Contact has already begun for many, many people. The recent rise in the discussion of orbs is a great gift that is raising public awareness. How we enter into communication with an inter-dimensional being has many forms.

I AM Ready!

**Anytime We Gather in Love,
So Do the Orbs of Light!**

Let us first offer the following point of recognition: Contact with "other-worldly" individ-u-wills does not require a space ship. For the most part, that is a density fantasy. Certainly there are galactic citizens who have the ability to manifest physical space crafts and use them to interact with the earth. However, truly advanced Beings do not require a space ship, they reside in the knowing that they are Light. Thus, a material form is optional and is only convenient here on Earth. Elsewhere in the universe our understanding of form is actually a limitation, for the third dimensional vibrational rate is extremely coarse.

Due to Earth's slow vibrational rate and the veil placed upon consciousness here, otherworldly contact has been extremely limited, especially in the past 5,000 years. There are many reasons for this limited contact, some of which were described at the end times of Su'Laria. Recently, there have been many books which offer evidence of our cosmic heritage and visitations to this planet. These stories are not the subject of this writing. It is our intent through this revelation to open your consciousness to the depth of your soul. We are doing our best to avoid just feeding your brain! The brain is invested in the density models.

That said, the brain's role in our lives is to be honored and respected. The brain serves to map *reality* in an effort to keep us safe. The brain works in harmony with the ego on this task. Unfortunately, the doors of perception are rusted tight by the habit of viewing *reality* through the basic five senses of density, which have been dulled over the eons.

As we have shared, the higher purpose of prophecy is to prepare consciousness, to reduce the likelihood fear. Similarly, the purpose of loving otherworldly contact is also to prepare you for a greater truth in the gentlest way possible. It is true that many of us react with fear whenever exposed to something 'new or unusual.' However, once we breathe through that automatic fear response we can then use our own hearts to determine whether the Contact is truly loving and in service. This is a practice.

Developing inner discernment serves our evolution. Trusting our hearts serves our expansion and Self-Ascension process. Trusting only the mind, or outside experts, disrespects our true potential and it is this dependency that limits our growth to the growth rate of the so called experts. External dependency robs you of your power, opens the door to manipulation, and perpetuates victim consciousness.

Inter-dependency, on the other hand, is the wholesome exchange of information and energy based upon mutual respect and service to the One Source. In our experience, the Angelic Inter-dimensional Beings with whom we have connected are all in service to the expansion of Love as Light. Their intent is to lovingly help those on earth who are ready to find their way into expanded consciousness. They are supporting the Re-Union.

The Earth has been gifted with many forms of Contact. These appear in the historical records. Contact has primarily been made through *Sensitives or Oracles*[39] who have honed their intuitive abilities to thin the veil. Visions of Saints and messages from Angels have been recorded by all the world's religions. This is indeed Contact. However, as the interactions are processed through the individual's ego-mind and then recorded by others, there is the likelihood of density-based concepts blending with the inspired information. Thus, refractions were blended into the teachings and need to be filtered through inner discernment known as your heart!

The gift that has been given to Kira is the ability to vacate her vessel, to actually die, thus offering her body as a temporary vessel for the Archangels to occupy and share a more visceral interaction. It is through her dying process that the communication is therefore vacant of any egoic interference. You may ask: "Why don't the angels just come in their own bodies, and not use Kira?" The answer is that to take a human birth is to risk complete forgetfulness of Source, and if the Archangels were able to occupy a human body in full recognition of themselves, their energetic vibration is far too high for a body to survive for any length of time. They would "burn out" the physical body in a very short time.

Even though we have purified our bodies, fasting regularly and only ingesting organic foods, we know that the process of Archangelic In-Soulment is in fact shortening our human life span. Our In-Soulment sessions are only thirty to sixty minutes in length, and Kira's body usually requires a recovery period. The Angels are very good about informing me when it is best for Kira that they vacate her body. It's like running high voltage through a light bulb designed for a lower electric current. Thus, the process of In-

Soulment is a true gift, a rare opportunity to receive pure ascended wisdom and energy.

During the early years, the Archangels and other Crystalline Beings who are of service to the Re-Union, came in for brief periods to help prepare us. They offered training for us both. It was our choice to accept the roles we have been given. We have been reminded by the Archangels that we can say "no more" at any time. We are grateful to receive their loving support for this service. We are grateful to The Elohim for the opportunity to be in service to the great awakening! We reverently accept this contact as it supports re-union.

Service is the nature of awakened Love. Each person reading this book has a divine role, a service to offer. Judge not your role, nor judge another's role, for together we weave a beautiful web of Light. We ALL contribute to the expanding Love, each in our own way.

The discourse that follows offers some understanding as to how Contact can be made. Had we not firsthand experienced the contact we are about to share, we would have found it difficult to believe or understand. Because all need to be lovingly prepared for their own contact, we include this personal experience in this book.

The Luminaria, etheric Beings of pure crystalline light, came to us in 2003 to help prepare Kira's body for ever higher frequency energy. They also offered information to me to help relax my mental filters and open more deeply to the divine flow. May your experience of this information offer you the same gift!

The Luminaria Speak:

Relax into the flow of energy that serves you. There is resistance and this resistance is causing this futility inside of you that feels as if it is heavy.

So simply allow yourself to find the deeper space where your true vibrational level is. Once you realign, the weight will be lifted. Simply breathe and become aware that the vibratory level is available and there to offer you assistance and help. We are assisting this one to do the same, to come into proper alignment with that which is true love, true light, true source.

We so appreciate these opportunities to speak with you. Were we to activate the ducts of tears, we would cry them on our behalf for you.

Sri Ram Kaa: Thank you, this is mutual.

Yes. We sense the shift in this vessel and it brings us great joy and gratitude.

Sri Ram Kaa: Yes that is beautiful too, move fully into love, more fully less fear.

Love always expands. Love does not contract. In the expansion it is not always comfortable and this causes some to misperceive love. For while they are expanding, while they are growing they may indeed be feeling other than what is true Source, yet this too is illusion is it not? If one is able to hold the space of knowledge of expansion, then the illusion is easier dropped. The veil is lifted.

Sri Ram Kaa: Just as we just did.

Yes and beyond that. This is important to understand; love always expands, it never contracts, ever! Is it not perfect sense that Light is Love and Love is Light? It is a continuous stream, a pulse, a sensation, a connection, a vibration, a cessation of all that is unlike love comes when one connects with the true expansion, with the effervescent glow of the Light of the Love that you are. This prevails on this Earth despite the outward externalization of different.

All beings here are Light. All love is Light. There is only all love. It has at times been polluted and it has been disfigured, yet it is still love.

Sri Ram Kaa: When you look at the Earth's sphere you see the love.

Yes, and the Light as One.

Sri Ram Kaa: And the Light and we look at it, we often just see the disfigurement.

Or perhaps, the illusion. You can not stop that which is not of you because the place that the energy of trying to stop or prevent is not of the purest Light. Love never contracts. It can not stop.

There are many beautiful traditions or what some call religions that hold this piece correctly. The piece that mirrors that the love can not stop even if the body does. Your questions yes, we are learning.

Sri Ram Kaa: As are we.

Your Zadkiel coaches us well. Yes we shall refrain and have you to ask.

Sri Ram Kaa: No I am very happy just to receive what the flow that you feel is important to contribute to my awareness. I find it useful to stay engaged in the conversation by asking questions. I also enjoy just receiving.

As do we.

Sri Ram Kaa: My experience has been that when energies increase, both the Light and awakening increases as well as the contraction, the distortions. So I am concerned about how best to support beings here during this time.

There are many galaxies that offer great love. There are galaxies that entire existences are to do nothing but support love, to hold the space for love. The convergence with the photon belt provides the alignments for the receiving directly of this energy. Prior to the alignments the energy was and has always been available through a sifted veil, knowing it is there yet not quite bringing it into focus, seeing the picture without the sharpness.

In this moment we show you clearly. In this moment we offer you the love and guidance that is serendipitous with this most wondrous event. For you see the time has come for the direct communication, for direct inter-dimensional expansion to be able to receive this energy directly. It is a glorious light and a glorious gift to see this.

Sri Ram Kaa: Feels to be golden.

Very much so and white. We ask you to remain in the love and light that you are. You are a marker. As a marker you offer us a resting place. We know where to come. For it is simply in the last few moments of entry here, that even for us it is still unclear. It is as if you are flying through a foggy night. You are the beacon. You are bringing us home to you.

Sri Ram Kaa: Even greater love.

Yes. Yes. Yes. We are sharing with the Kira our look for it is unlike any look you may have seen in any museum as we search her data banks. Let us try to describe for you so that we do not alarm you.

Sri Ram Kaa: Thank you.

We are taller. You have seen us although not clearly. Yes, we wear a large head piece. This is necessary when we are here because it offers us translation capability and atmospheric adjustment. It does not need to be a suit.

Sri Ram Kaa: Your head piece enhances communication?

Yes this is correct. There is a large central piece that runs across the top of the head. Our form is very similar to yours. It is our facial feature or what you would refer to as a facial feature that is very different. We are beginning again. We have shown it to the Kira once this evening, let us show it to her again.

Sri Ram Kaa: I don't perceive any nose.

This is correct. We were showing you, preparing you to receive us, for it is important that it is a familiar recognition so that you are not startled, for we come to you without any disguise, without any pretension. There is no need for this. There are those that have come here with pretension. There are those that can alter their shape to accommodate what is expected.

We show you who we are with great clarity and great love so that you will not be startled or jolted. Understand that we will provide a transmission, a loving transmission so that you will be comforted and without startled fear so that we may have the great alignment occur, for that is all that is happening. It is a great alignment between us, one that will persist and be forever present, one that has always been a separation that is now coming back to wholeness.

We are the other part of you. We are the part that left because we loved you. We are the part that has watched you. We are the part that has committed to not interfere with that of your evolution until the time of the homecoming. We thank you for the millennia that you have traveled. We bless you for this. We offer you great love, great hope, and great knowledge all of which shall be present in you as an effervescent knowing. It will be noticeable to those who are aware, very noticeable. It may be unnoticed by those who are not.

Sri Ram Kaa: So we will be more congruent with our energy?

Yes, your attire may become smaller as you stretch. Your eyes will shift in brightness. Your hands will radiate great energy, healing in a single touch. We shall offer you great guidance on this gift.

Sri Ram Kaa: Thank you. With energy comes the need for wisdom.

Know that we shall visit you often, we are not coming and leaving to never come back.

Sri Ram Kaa: It is important to me to receive as much as I can receive, to release as much as I can release.

You are already doing this. You are already moving forward into the Light. This is an accomplishment that has not been done in this manner before. It is In-lightenment through a different means. There are many paths to In-lightenment, all of which are magnificent.

Sri Ram Kaa: Yes, thank you for that clarity. It is still disconcerting at times to witness what comes up from my subconscious, from the ego structure that has its own magnetism. This creates a reminder to step into our authenticity. It is challenging none the less.

Yes we understand. So the challenge was designed to be. It would be impossible to experience this any other way.

Sri Ram Kaa: Yes. How does one become a master if one does not know how to step out of the illusion?

Trust that you do know how to do this. Humbly love those who will still be in the illusion.

We offer you this opportunity to experience our energies to insure that there would be no harm and only expansion in our coming together. It is necessary to experience your energies as they are, to insure preparedness. For you see, because the two of you are so bright, you are markers. There are others that watch you whose intentions are not as pure. However, your protection is great and divinely guided that they are unable to affect you, only to pull the strings of the earthbound consciousness to be able to influence your fear and emotion. This is the only way they can participate.

Sri Ram Kaa: And with transcendence that is no longer a concern.

This is correct. You have been placed in a portal to the great frustration of the energies that would wish to stop the marker. There are other markers on this planet all with the same protection. You all agreed to be here at this time. You agreed to hold that space. You agreed to pioneer that which had not been pioneered. We agreed to assist you and that we would not ever leave you stranded or alone.

Release your concepts and be open, for that which you have known is not indeed false; it is simply ready to expand.

Sri Ram Kaa: It is not the whole picture?

Correct. For you are expanding and your consciousness is being made prepared to accept information and to understand at a level of consciousness that was previously unavailable to you.

This is a great time of preparedness, knowingness, lovingness. We offer this to you and the Divine Elohim are lifting the veil, a great blessing and gift.

Sri Ram Kaa: I wish only to serve, to know, to love, and to serve. For without the knowing, it would not be true service. Without the love, it can not be true knowing or true service. The yearning in my heart has been calling me forward for quite some time. I am so grateful.

Yes and so you shall and it is ready. Continue your surrender to God, continue your surrender to the Highest. Know that you are divinely guided, blessed, loved, and protected.

Sri Ram Kaa: I trust.

You have been most generous with our ability to move forward, to release, to be present, to be ever available. Yes. We are here. We are ready. We are most open. We guide you as we are guided. Do not despair. Do not stress. Release your sense of timing; know that all is in order. Know this is just the beginning, the first step.

We must leave now... Many blessings.

As Kira returned to her body I offered her some warm tea and began to describe the interaction I had just experienced. I noticed that even with my coaxing, she was not fully present in her body. There was a peacefulness and illumination in her that was most apparent. Kira then began to share additional information that there was an energy still present in her after the Luminaria left. It was as if they knew her body needed a moment of recuperation, and yet their message was not yet complete.

Our recording device was still running and captured the following information.

Kira Raa: The idea that Hollywood has promoted of space ships and weapon-carrying aliens is not the big picture. This information is to intentionally misdirect and misguide the public. What we see and what we have been told has been carefully orchestrated to make sure that is what we expect to see. What we are told by Hollywood is not the truth. It is not how it is.

So we have these stories in our head that are looking for a ship as a cylinder, or a dome, or a circle, whatever, and landing gear.

Sri Ram Kaa: Perhaps Light bubbles are the true space ships?

Kira: Yes....

At this point Kira slumps again and then the Luminaria speak once more:

Understand that this has been created in cooperation with those in charge of your mass consciousness so that the truth can not be seen, so that the true meaning of contact and the true methods of direct contact are hidden. They are lower level life forms that have made this pact with your government, that in exchange for specific information this propagation of mistruth continues to create fear, mistrust, and expectation.

Know this is not a means or device that we are capable of, nor would we participate in. We come from a pure ray of love. So we ask you to simply relax and release how the movie has groomed your expectation.

Simply be present to each other. Be present to the love that you are, be present to this moment now and all will unfold as it should. Have no fear. We are here.

We are now entering your atmosphere and creating a light bubble, as you say, for us to move within. This light bubble does not generate light as a flash light. It moves through the energy fields of density unnoticed until we are prepared to step out of it. It is used exclusively for this atmosphere and similar atmospheres. It is not a ship. It is an electromagnetic field generated by us. You will learn how to generate these fields yourselves by emanating and holding that light.

There are no walls for us as there are no walls for you. You know this yet you still see them because of where you are. So it does not matter where you are, merely that we must be invited in and welcomed for it is only our desire to assist, to be present with you, to help you elevate.

Holding this transmission slows down our process because we must divert part of our energy consciousness to this connection while holding a light bubble. Yet we may continue it.

Sri Ram Kaa: Please do whatever serves.

It serves for us to simply reunite, be one, for you to remember. We offer this process to you, the ability to see beyond, to receive us so that we may simply chat as friends, dialogue. Let the story go and you shall be here. What is it you wish to ask?

Sri Ram Kaa: How can we facilitate this? It is hard for me to expect contact in one way and then it doesn't come that way and yet it is good to release the expectations, but now even when you share the information you have shared, it created a new expectation that you will simply walk through the wall and show up.

This is more realistic than the movie! So this is good … you have shifted this expectation of a glowing ship in the sky. We wish to be here for you now.

Sri Ram Kaa: I wish you to be here.

And so it shall be. We are offering our love. We are offering hope. We are offering joy. We are offering transcendent peace; this you accept?

Sri Ram Kaa: Yes, I accept them all and we offer ourselves in service.

Yes you do, as do we for the glorification of God, the unification of the Light, the return to wholeness and Oneness. We are aware of your yearning to see us with your eye and wish to fulfill that for you.

Sri Ram Kaa: Thank you.

And you. So we shall continue disconnecting so that we may put our energy into the light bubble and speak again with you shortly.

Sri Ram Kaa: Very well.

(Note: Kira and I sat, entranced for nearly an hour, unaware of time passing. There was a sense that we had been gone…like a dream…the recorder was still on.)

Sri Ram Kaa: I am almost asleep, I must stretch.

Kira Raa: What I am hearing is we should sleep. I am really heavy. I don't know if I can move.

Sri Ram Kaa: Let us rest.

Kira Raa and I retired for the night without addressing what we had just experienced. The interaction with the Luminaria had been much more than an In-Soulment, yet we were not fully aware of exactly what had transpired.

The next morning, our energy restored, we felt called to enter into an In-Soulment with Archangel Zadkiel.

Archangel Zadkiel Speaks:

Hello. Good morning Sri Ram Kaa. We come to speak to you today about the events of last evening. It is important for you to know that nothing happened as you see it. Let us explain.

There is a great force in the universe that is currently working with the conjunctions of the stars, the planetary alignments and the openings of the asteroid belt in conjunction with the photon belt. There are many particles both of solid and energetic construction that are floating, going, and growing. It is important for you to understand that your connection with the Luminarias is correct. It is accurate. It is occurring.

Understand that these connections with the Luminarias are a birthing of a new means and method of communication. You and the Kira are the patient witnesses and participants in this experiment as you would call it. As you and the Kira are learning to accept these frequencies and learning to understand the language shifting and the different subtle energies of receiving the Luminarias, as are they.

We have been here as a silent partner, assistant, guide, as you say, during all of your communications. It is not our job to interfere, however we come to you now to offer you reassurance that all is well, on track and progressing. The voyage you seek is coming to you.

Many pieces of what you were shared are very accurate, especially the pieces on how travel occurs. This is very important for you to know. Also Kira was shown part of the veil of illusion regarding the density belief patterns of how these communications are to look like. It is not that those who have had these communications are fabricating, although some are. It is that those who have had these genuine experiences, most, 80%, have had fabricated experiences by beings of other realms to encourage and perpetuate a specific likeness, life form, and vehicle belief system. This is very important for you and Kira to understand for your experience will be most different from this.

Sri Ram Kaa: Are you suggesting that 80% of humans who have a contact experience are receiving an illusionary experience from the astral or such?

Let us explain more, they are receiving an experience that is real in this density; however the type of vehicle, the appearance is done by very sophisticated life forms that have made agreements to appear this way. Once they leave your atmosphere they shift back.

This is a large cooperative effort with many who are aware of this for reasons of negative power influence on this planet. Understand that those who are involved in this truly to do not understand the negative power influence and believe they are protecting the people by perpetuating this. This is fine, however in the hour of awakening, it will not be strange ships with strange figures. It will be masses, massive energies of Light that will appear as if they are bubbles, for this information you were provided last evening by the Luminarias regarding this type of travel is most accurate.

This is why so many can lift at once because each has the power to generate the bubble necessary to provide this. You will learn more about the astral physics and the dynamics of the construction and how this event works and happens during your visit in the realm. We can not offer this to you today.

Sri Ram Kaa: That is fine.

It would be good for you to continue your contact with the Luminarias. We come to you with our great humble presence to say to you and share with you, especially in the form of the Kira; there is an open channel to the Luminarias. They feel when you are frustrated with them. They feel your pain and they share this with you. They too grieve if they have caused you dismay. Let us talk about last evening, may we?

Sri Ram Kaa: Oh please. Much, much blessed energy happened.

Yes, this is important for you to know. You were protected from negative contact in the evening of last. Yes let us share with you, there is or there was, it is hard for us to say past, present, future, there was an opening for the contact you seek. However the energy imprint was violated and there was alerting of those nearby and we felt it was best to protect you and the Kira and not make you so well known at this time.

Sri Ram Kaa: So it was detected.

Yes. This too is part of your training.

Sri Ram Kaa: Is it possible to not be detected?

Yes, absolutely, and this is our goal. As you know your safety is our first priority. You and the Kira are in the realm of the density in which you are still subject to the sway of the density. There will be your time when you are contacted. However you are not ready yet for that. It was premature. Had you had a black helicopter[40] land on your property, you were not ready. Yes, of course you would be protected by us, however it was not the time.

So we ended this form of communication last evening and transmitted the information to you in a different manner. This is why your sleep patterns were so disrupted because of the way the energy communicated. This is why your emotions were unstable and for this we are greatly sorry, however the transmission had to occur.

Last evening was to be the time for you to receive this contact. How you received it was different than you expected, however you did indeed receive all the information. It will be very apparent to you in your thought processes, in dreams that will start coming to you. Be patient. Know that all is in order for you to be safe, for us to be in the area of protection, for the Luminarias to be safe, for they are at great risk coming to you.

Sri Ram Kaa: Could they be intercepted in some fashion?

Yes. There are devices in place to do this and there are others who can inform your…., let us share you this. Your government is alerted so quickly maybe because they have informants? Yes, let us leave it at that.

Sri Ram Kaa: Is this a technological informant or being?

A being, a race of beings, the same race of beings that appears in the manifest ships.

Sri Ram Kaa: That are providing some information which is contributing to the….

This is correct. Perhaps they have an incentive to let them know that the Light is entering, for they know Light is coming and they are afraid. Your government knows it is coming too.

Sri Ram Kaa: Are the Luminarias coming in vessel form?

They are coming in their form of vessel, not the illusionary form of vessel.

Sri Ram Kaa: My specific question is will I be able to see that with my veiled vision?

We understand your need to see. We respect it. Know this will happen, and for many.

Sri Ram Kaa: I am not required to see in the outer if my inner sight could open a little more.

Be patient. Allow the seeds inside of you to fully germinate, grow, and blossom. Be patient. All will come as you say, in its time. However know it is already done. The experiences that you seek are available and able to occur.

There is much Light in your path, much Light. You and the Kira are already emanating as bright Light beings. This is why you have alerted the attention of those who seek to interfere with the re-Union. However they also are aware that they too can not ever truly stop that which is meant to be, but they can do their part to interfere. As they tried to interfere in your coming here to begin with, in your purchase of this property[41]*, and you so knew then, it may not have been at the time you expected, but you did wind up here did you not? Yes take this lesson and apply that same.*

Sri Ram Kaa: I had hoped to see them in the physical… I am like a child that seeks to be with its family.

Yes, there was no choice but to ask you to go into slumber for the allotted time came and this energy distribution had to be made. So contact was made in a different manner and it was quick. This is why when we ask you to sleep, we ask because we understand what it will do. It is the only way that we can provide this opportunity and continue the influx of information to you without it being painful or uncomfortable and while protecting you.

Sri Ram Kaa: Yes I understand.

You were visited last night, but not by us, by those who seek to stop this communication.

Sri Ram Kaa: Thank you for the clarity and your loving support.

Yes. You are lighting up the sky with your light as you and the Kira are united. Your path is lit. Pay attention to your inspiration and only do that which serves you.

We are here to stand aside and simply assist for it is you expressing the work of God. We are your assistants. You are the ones who are in this realm experiencing this density, moving through these challenges, and as you become more consciously aware of this, we sincerely understand the challenges of being more aware while one is still in the density.

Stay first in service to your higher mission and soul purpose. Simply give all to God as we do and all flows beautifully. There is no reason not to trust except that which you could create in density. Is not trust the step? Know that we love you dearly. Know that we are here for you every step of the way as are so many other brilliant beings.

Pause - Breathe - Allow

Chapter Sixteen

Being a Mystic in a 9 to 5 World

"The true empowerment of the Soul is in the knowing and recognition of the Home within."

~ Archangel Zadkiel

Many people take years to call in their soul recognition. This accomplishment is often prolonged as our everyday world encroaches on our search. How many times have you or someone you know, touched their soul, either by reading, attending a workshop, or simply through loving meditation, yet are unable to sustain that energy for any period of time?

We are now in the time of instantaneous Recognition! In the recognition of your Soul is the recognition that you are Whole and reside in a Divine portal of Light. This portal connects to God and to Life. This is indeed a time for celebration! Your ability to maintain your consciousness is greater than it has ever been, and if you are reading this chapter, you have already made the choice! Congratulations.

All are connected. As you relax evermore into Trust and Love, everything flows in your experience with Divine Perfection effortlessly and simultaneously. This is how a true community is created. Many are currently recognizing that the time of a whole community is here. Yet, to enter into any community from a lack of wholeness, or the need to escape, only creates further refraction.

Community is a celebration of recognition. Each whole being energizes and attracts another whole being. From this wholeness the actions of the community as true celebration of the Divine in Action comes forward.

It is important to recognize that community does not mean commune. Many hear the word community and immediately wish to find a box to fit this concept into. The communes of the sixties and seventies were mostly fueled by a need to congregate and support spiritual activism; a wonderful first step. Yet, within the concept of spiritual activism, the ability to be in wholeness and transparency[42] may not exist.

The Archangelic Realm has lovingly shared on many occasions that the greatest gift you can offer to another is to simply be in the full recognition of your own soul self. That when we step into this powerful form of consciousness by keeping our eyes on the divine at all times, our presence alone offers to others the safety to do the same.

Imagine a community, or a world for that matter, where everyone knew they were safe to simply be the full expression of their soul's energy. This is the next step, and you are already taking it.

The following diagram is a model of community where each person stands in Sacred Union with their own sense of soul-based being. This union is the portal of wholeness that is God-connected. Their union can include a partner. From the center of wholeness they extend themselves into community, connectivity, abundance of the universe, the self as wholeness, and acceptance of the ease of flow.

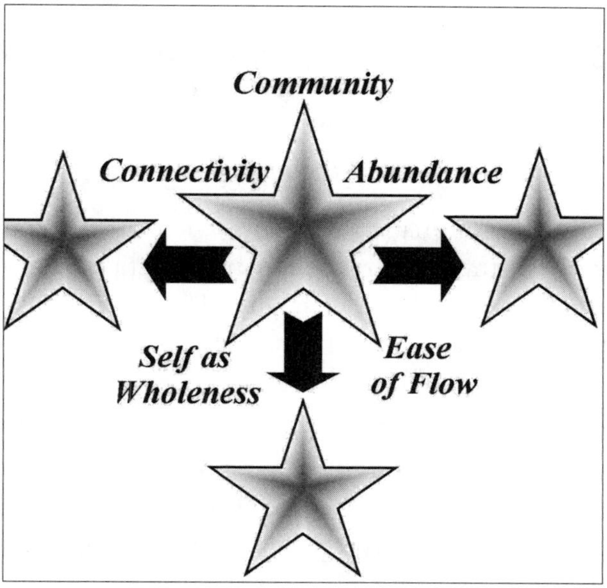

Each star in the above depiction is a person offering wholeness, connectivity, community, ease and abundance.

Within this model of whole community the central unification principle is wholeness for all. Safety to express as the Divine is a gift that is celebrated and the basis of Self-Ascension. Each whole being recognizes that the concept of the SELF transcends from the me orientation of third dimensional density to:

Soul

Evolving

Life

Force

"Self-Ascension is the complete understanding, knowledge, and awareness that all are connected."

~ Archangel Zadkiel

Abundance automatically appears when one surrenders to the Flow, for within the trust of the Divine in Action, all is provided. An important discernment is vital here. The Divine must be in Action, not sitting on a couch repeating affirmations and wondering why nothing is happening!

This is a fundamental lesson of LIFE (Letting In Forever the Eternal!) This is an important lesson, for in our western culture many people are conditioned to be insecure about the future. "I need to know that my mortgage will get paid." "I need insurance because I believe that something terrible can happen to me." All these common thoughts indicate that trust is very weak, and paralyzes the Divine Action principle.

Where there is doubt, there is a lack of trust, and there is a lack of flow!

When an individual is externally oriented and organizes their sense of well-being on external conditions then you have further separated from your soul energy. In the external world, impermanence is the norm. Security and abundant flow do not come automatically from the external.

Soul alignment is alignment with one's authentic divine energy. This opens a portal of light and love that is restorative and attractive. That is, the empowerment of one's soul to come forward in day to day living results in a magnetic charge emanating around the individual. This is the Divine Electronic Belt that reflects the consciousness of the person. It will attract into their lives everything that is required to complete the soul's mission. This is fact.

For example: try to avoid a specific focus on money – instead focus on your authenticity. Be sincere in your love and surrender to God. Do not impose earth-based religious beliefs upon your magnetic charge. Instead, simply relax fully: Thy Will be done. You see, to surrender what surrender looks like is to truly hand your life to the Divine, without conditions. This is the relaxation that embraces you when you allow yourself to fully trust. Only Peace Love and Joy can enter into your experience once this surrender is complete.

Many people fear surrender because they believe they will lose themselves, lose control. It is only the ego that fears loss as it is trapped in a me based perspective. After all, we have just redefined the SELF. If that fear arises, then say "thank you" and acknowledge the gift of discernment that was just offered to you, then breathe it into your soul.

That the spiritual path requires living from spiritual principles in favor of external standards is the first step to train the ego. The path of enlightenment requires that "one die to themselves," so to speak, in order to purify their consciousness. Once the surrender is complete there is indeed a Self that acts and interacts with the world. Nothing has been lost – except one's fear and isolation.

When one surrenders to trust, then the star of their soul light and connectivity to all that is shines brightly indeed. This begins by establishing your portal, your Union. It then illuminates ever more brightly as one fully steps into trust as the active principle.

The five points on the star (*see page 301*) shine brightly in one who has anchored in this trust and recognition; for in the Union (with God) is the Re-Union with all beings.

Each of the points on the star represents an area where one can focus their attention (energy). With undue attention or praise toward one point of the star, that aspect will grow and the star becomes lop-sided. The star energy can not exist until the center, the portal is in divine connectivity. This is accomplished through the four steps of Self-Ascension– then the Light emanates equally from the middle in all directions. The lessons in this book will greatly assist you to anchor this energy every day.

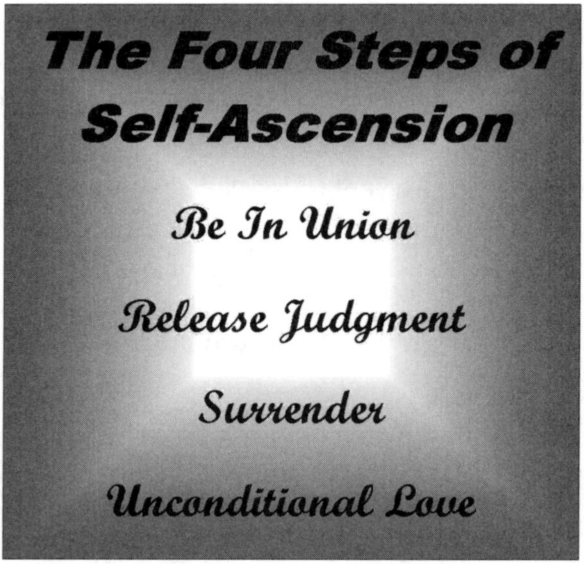

With the five rays of the Star all open, the flow of this sacred energy ignites recognition in others. Thus a community of stars is birthed!

When the habitual or addictive world does its best to create a lopsided star, be not preoccupied with any negative emotion or energy. Instead keep bringing your focus back to the Divine, and to the four steps of Self-Ascension. Through this sincere practice the portal is opened and maintained. Remember, sincerity attracts and frustration repels! From this portal right action flows naturally.

Yes, the external world is polarizing. This is a necessary step in the alchemy of Re-Union! The polarization offers clarity, discernment and energy to the participants. Stay removed from negative chatter and negative news. Be attentive to that which supports your Peace, Love and Joy. Do your best not to validate any negative energy through your attention and concern.

Remember that your disciplined focus and sincere practice generate a portal of light that is self-sustaining and protective. When one resides in their Divine Portal, no other protection is required. When you anchor in the energy of Love, only love can enter your portal! Negative energies can not pierce the portal unless you validate them through your attention. Remember, peace, love and joy all expand; fear and other negative emotions nullify expansion.

Archangel Zadkiel has shared many times that one of the sure ways to inhibit your Self-Ascension process is to hold judgments and expectations. Judgments and expectations are ways of limiting one's experience because they out-picture a refracted point of view upon the field of experience. Many are in the habit of judging.

Most judgments are projected inner wounds. We all grow up with some limiting beliefs. It is common for a child, constantly being instructed by their parents, to take on a belief that they, the child, is inferior. After all, the parents know everything and I, the child, am constantly being corrected! Therefore most people develop an unconscious belief that *there is something wrong with me.* This limiting belief must be overcome through improving one's self-esteem over time and perhaps through emotional growth work.

If one does not release the emotional charge on *there's something wrong with me,* then that limiting belief will fester in the psyche of the person – it is a most uncomfortable belief to feel. Therefore the ego will offer some protection by burying the energetic imprint in the subconscious mind. This negative belief carries an energy that wants resolution. As believing that *there is something wrong with me* is painful to experience, it is far easier to discharge some of the energy of this limiting belief by projecting it toward others. Thus, *there must be something wrong with them*, becomes the vehicle for discharging the uncomfortable energy of *there is something wrong with me.*

Anytime your world view is challenged your unconscious

beliefs about yourself are triggered. If there is unresolved energy, it will seek expression. Thus, judgments toward others is a way of discharging energy that masks the need for introspection.

Anytime you judge another person you are avoiding feeling a truth about yourself.

Expectations are another form of judgment. That is, with expectation we take the process of projection and apply it not only to people, but to situations and God! Because judgment and expectation are both projections of the emotional-mind, they can be dissolved by releasing the energy given to them. That is, instead of wrestling with limiting beliefs let's just bring our attention to higher truth.

Judgment is false energy appearing real, or FEAR. It therefore responds to creations from the outer world. Rather than doing battle with your judgments, begin to release your focus on the outer world. When judgments do arise, look deeper at that which you judge and discover what it is you are seeking through the act of judging. That is, judging is a strategy of the ego to meet an inner need. Discover the energy you truly seek and focus on that energy instead of focusing on the target of judgment. Chances are most judgments you hold are an effort to "be right", to prove yourself better than another. As we focus on the Divine and keep our attention on our inner sense of Joy, what others do or do not do becomes less consequential.

Let each judgment or unmet expectation be an opportunity to return your eyes to the Divine. Say thank you to them all! This is how you begin to make friends with your shadow. The shadow aspect of our psyche holds unhealed wounds, limiting beliefs and other addictions that the ego felt were too painful to acknowledge. The ego, intending to make our lives more comfortable, relegates all kinds of uncomfortable imprints to the subconscious during our childhood. However, you are now an adult. Things that the ego thought were too challenging to view can be safely looked at, for you are stronger now. Thus, it is time for the shadow to come into the Light as a brilliant star of wholeness!

There are subtle ways you can remind yourself of the light when the shadow tries to encompass your energy. Create notes to your soul. Enjoy nature. Place sacred & joy filled objects in strategic positions in your home and workspace. All of these will assist you so that when your ego shadow is present you can see these things as a subtle reminder that light is all-ways present.

Rather than continue to cope with the shadow, it is easier and more effective to simply lift out of the level of experience generated by the ego and return to Soul-based living. This is an essential differentiation between a spiritually-based life and the density or ego-based life.

Most all of the great traditions on this planet have much to say about how to conduct yourself in the world. There are many rules and regulations about right living. These rules, regulations and codes of behavior are intended to create order and health in the people. However these rules predominantly train the ego how to cope – they do not train the soul how to be free.

The soul has already transcended the need for such rules. The soul has Divine wisdom and an innate sense of morality. Soul-based living automatically preserves connectivity to the divine, while respecting all life. Right action springs naturally from one who trusts their soul to guide their life. Soul-based living is indeed the transcendent quality that many call living in the world but not being of the world.

Soul-based living transcends the grip of density without losing access to the ego's wisdom. Thus soul-based living is the solution to the problems that face this world. Paradoxically, by removing your attention from the problems of the world, they will be healed. Albert Einstein is credited with the statement that "solutions are never found at the level of consciousness that created the problem."

Soul-based living is a much higher level of consciousness than ego-based living. Thus solutions to the challenges of our world do not need to be sought. If one will focus on bringing forth their own Divinity, then the world will automatically align with that energy. The vibration of Ascended love supersedes and transmutes all forms of material existence.

The interplay of shadow and the light provide discernment and support growth. It is only through an addiction to density that some people believe both are required perpetually. In fact, the light and dark interplay is a reflection of a state of consciousness that can be transcended. We have outgrown the need for a shadow.

Interestingly enough, as you anchor in your portal the expanding light will consume or repel that which is not light-filled. Thus, old patterns (limiting beliefs and addictions) within you may arise. As you notice them without engaging them, they will dissipate and be consumed by the Divine presence. If they arise and you engage the energy of fear or anger, then you must disengage as soon as possible from the cycle and re-establish the portal. That is, if you truly anchor in Divine trust, all that needs to be consumed will present itself to the Light and be dissolved. If you are unable to hold Presence, then these experiences will continue to be your spiritual practice until such time as you are fully surrendered to the Peace of your soul energy. At all times, avoid judging yourself.

Those around you will either become part of your expansion or they will go away. Love them for their path and trust that through their choices they will find their way. Each path is unique, and all six billion of them are perfect.

"There are as many religions as there are people!"

~ Gandhi

When you reside in your portal of connectivity you are always home, you are always safe, you are always at peace. In the beginning of this process we are at times like the two year old who will open and close the cabinet door dozens of times. That is, we step into our surrender and then we allow something from the external world to pull us out. We then choose to step back into our surrender and may enjoy the Peace that comes through this alignment…for a spell…until something else is given our attention and we are pulled out of trust. Keep practicing your mastery, no matter how many times you are distracted. Inevitably, you will succeed.

We all reside on a wounded planet that is in the process of healing. We have all lived in this world of illusion for such a long time that the habit of being in separation from the Divine feels normal. We have all unconsciously adopted many societal beliefs that disempowered our soul. These patterns are simply conventions and habits in the orientation of our consciousness. As we reside in Union with the Divine the refractions in consciousness are dissolved and the Light expands.

Stay in vibrational harmony with your core essence and everything else in life will flow in a good way. It is that simple. The time is now. The choice is yours.

I AM Open to Opening!

I AM Open to receiving clarity!

I AM Open to the removal of all refractory devices!

I AM Open to the expansion of Light!

Pause - Breathe - Allow

A Word about Religion and Spirituality

Religion serves a wonderful purpose. It provides loving standards for living, offers reassurance in a world of fear, and offers a pathway toward the divine. However, regardless of a person's affiliation, each participant brings their life history and assorted beliefs and emotions to their religious understanding. Even the teachings of the saints have passed through density filters and interpretations, as those who with sincerity offered interpretations. Each person has their own sense of the divine.

Whether reunion is thought of as a Heaven available only after death, or whether it is attained as an Enlightenment or Nirvana available through disciplined practice matters not. What matters is one's sincerity. All prayer is prayer…all worship of God offers the opportunity for connection, recognition and reunion. Thus, all paths are to be blessed and honored for their Intent. It is through the subsequent interpretation and practice that religious conflicts are born from human minds.

There are many helpers on the path. These teachers hold the Light and help us find our way. However, at some point one must simply leap. That leap of surrender is a solo plunge into unity. Religion can bring you to the door, however, you must walk through that door yourself and experience the Divine. Such is the path of the mystic.

Spirituality is the life force that spawned religion. It is the essential truth that offers the knowing of divine connection. Religion is the secondary expression. It was created to satisfy the density-brain, to offer an organized response to spiritual longing, to answer cosmic questions, to provide codes of conduct and to organize people. God has no religion. Thus, all spiritual practices, all religions, offer the potential for Divine connection. It is up to the individ-u-will to benefit from their religion by viewing it as a springboard to surrender.

Humanity must learn to relax into its spiritual essence if we are to witness Peace on Earth. The process of releasing the refractory devices is the way to Oneness. The path to unity used to take years. Today it can be achieved in the blink of an eye.... or a collection of moments. Be assured that Enlightenment is more attainable at this time in history than ever before.

Be grateful to your religion of origin. Be grateful that there are many paths. There is one God essence seeking to emerge through all of them. What a glorious diversity! People ask us if the path of Self-Ascension is a religion; it is not. We are offering practices, wisdom, and teachings designed to help you get acquainted with your own divinity. How you walk your path is unique to you. Each person, regardless of their level of discernment, offers light into the world. Each is to be cherished. Each is honored for it takes spiritual courage to be here.

Chapter Seventeen

From Our Heart to Yours

The cosmological legacy we have shared in this book has been offered to help awaken further recognition of the magnificence of that which you are. As we have journeyed together through many spiritual, emotional, and most likely physical awakenings, know that we honor your process in all-ways!

Bringing this work to form was a difficult and sometimes painful process. The Archangelic Realm has been loving, nurturing and supportive of the manner and timeliness in which this material is being offered. Living actively with this material since early 2003 has been like having a wonderful secret and wanting to tell! As with all wondrous information, timing is everything. We believe the world is ready for this material, and there has also been the very human side of how it will be received.

Many of you know that we both led what would commonly be called normal lives prior to our re-union and re-activation of our Su'Larian soul agreement[43], our life biographies up until the time of our re-union were very worldly indeed! Within months of our coming back together we resolved our heritage and learned the gift of standing in the Kingdom of Now. It was then that literally everything shifted.

All beings have been serving the expansion of Light through multiple form expressions longer than most of us are able to remember! We have candidly revealed information that has deepened our conscious appreciation for our shared legacy and we humbly share it with you in this writing. Kira's early visions of an apocalyptic 2012 were also shared as part of the recognition that the collective consciousness is amassing around this energy, and a reminder that we must all make a clear choice for our future. This sharing, along with the discourses and lessons, have been offered as part of an Archangelic gift. Have you opened yourself to find, unwrap and receive the energetic gifts that are offered herein?

Yes, a vast amount of information has been shared with you about our cosmic origins, and our next volume will contain even more! With this being known, it is paramount to recognize that many people dwell on past lives simply because they are fascinated by the stories. This amusement for the ego can offer yet another way to avoid engaging the fullness of healing in the now.

Yes, it is important that we reclaim any energy we have *left behind* and heal any unproductive decisions we might have made about ourselves as a result of our past actions. Being at peace with the past offers the opportunity to be truly whole in the now, which is the destination for your consciousness, and the purpose for what we have gently shared with you.

So, visit the past, the legacy of our collective DNA. Let yourself feel, experience, and integrate the lessons of wholeness. Then, you are encouraged to let it go. Let it be a complete experience for you. Please allow Atlantis, Leumeria, Tu'Laya, and Su'Laria to bring you to a completion of what has been. Allow these visits with your cosmic heritage to open up an ever greater Divine portal of love and recognition. Through the energetic integration of these recognitions, be free to know without letting the information define you. The greatest gift of your wholeness is YOU; the you that is ready to be evermore clear in how you will be, then the now will present itself.

Own your own time, now.

When we visit the past for the purposes of soul retrieval, we travel around the edges of linear time to complete ourselves. It is not necessary to revisit or ruminate on the same experience over and over, (in any lifetime).

Touch the past as a springboard to your freedom and gift yourself with the many benefits that are yours to receive. To relive a past life over and over, usually for the gratification of the ego mind or left brain validation, recreates the old energy in your now experience. This is usually not productive, will impede your progress, and often interferes with the forgiveness energy that is the foundation of soul wholeness.

There is a fascination with the stories and the romance associated with the myth of the Atlantis that existed on this planet as a refraction of Su'Laria. This fascination is the kaleidoscope of the refractions. To be fascinated is to be entrapped – fascination does not offer expansion. As you witness your own responses to any past life recall, you offer yourself opportunities for discernment and growth.

These Divine opportunities are critical at this moment in history, as it is imperative for you to be ever more conscious and clear. Keep your eyes on the Divine, for by following that light you will be shown whatever elements of Tu'Laya and Su'Laria serve your wholeness and you will then lift through the stories into your own wholeness; fully integrated in the soul energy of the Divine Oneness. This is the intent of this sharing that serves the highest purpose.

You can learn how to fold the time line into a circle and stand in the center. Being in the center of the circular time line brings you fully into wholeness and allows all time to be now, *(past, present, future)*. It is from this central loving perspective that all aspects of the self come into balance and you enter and become one with the Kingdom of Now. This is the critical difference from simply intellectualizing the concept of being in the now.

Simply Be! By incorporating the wisdom of the Codes of Self-Ascension you can effortlessly and joyously release the preoccupation of the past and expand into the wholeness of Divine Being.

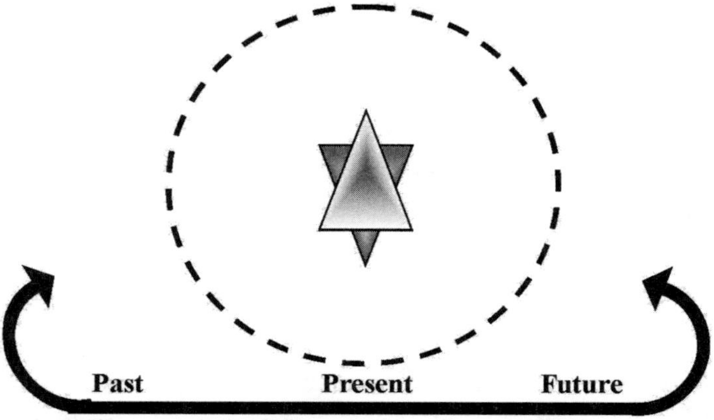

When you fold linear time into a circle, you become the center of Wholeness

You enter the Kingdom of Now.

This lifetime of density has offered many gifts to us all. What amazing wonders we have all experienced!

Scientists confirm that our DNA carries the history of our evolution as a species. Each one of us is imbued with this collective wisdom. Our DNA is like a library of wisdom; it contains the codes of the species. What our scientists do not yet know is that there are far more strands of DNA than are visible to their instruments. We have strands of coding that reach beyond the physical world This *Spiritual-DNA* contains the truth of your authentic identity and is a record of your travels. As you reconcile and broaden the energy of your cosmic heritage, these strands begin to release ever more recognition and activate ever greater love and expansion.

The human brain is often challenged with the enormity of this information. However, the human consciousness can touch it without understanding it. It is as simple as relaxing your need to understand; from there you can re-discover what you already know. The mystical journey may at times seem fantastic, however, no matter how wondrous and strange it may seem, you are only discovering the extent of your own consciousness.

2012 rapidly approaches, and it is a grand symbol, a precious moment! Within our world of linear time we have a calendar date that calls us all to consciousness. Celebrate the call. Humanity has survived eons of the density experience; can we now collectively awaken to a deeper truth? Can we find our Spiritual DNA? If so, we will discover that all the outer world has offered is but a collective illusion designed to expand our appreciation of the truth of our being-ness.

This journey is fantastic and meaningful beyond your wildest dreams. For the truth of YOU, the scope of your Light, is beyond your Earth-based expression. So, practice breathing and allowing the truth of your soul to infuse your awareness. Embrace the practices offered lovingly herein by the Archangelic Realm. It does take practice to interrupt the collective hypnosis. Holistic growth requires sincere appreciation and love. Love is the very fabric of your being; how could you ever hope to learn who you are without bringing the energy of love to yourself first?

We have enjoyed the many worlds and realms we have visited. We have witnessed the bending of light. We have had the gift of experiencing the refracting of light and the nuances of expression. We have benefited from the friction we have felt in density as it has offered depth and meaning to us.

What a delight to experience the seasons! What delight to experience mortality! What delight to feel the energy of love expressed through physical touch! And what Grace we have all shared to have the slate wiped clean again and again, to experience multiple births and multiple deaths. Where else in the cosmos could such sensations and depth be apprehended? Where else could you journey from amnesia to awakening? Celebrate your legacy! Honor all others, for they are Divine Travelers…just like you!

We are here as your partners on the path. May each find their way Home and celebrate the path that brought them there.

Love yourselves.
Trust your emerging Knowings,
Namaste*!

* A Sanskrit word that translates as:
"The Divine in me greets and honors the Divine in you."

Pause - Breathe - Allow

Meet Book Illustrator El'iam

El'iam is one of the most gifted visionary artists of today, with a talented and wide range.

From early childhood he has been contacted and guided by the Archangelic Realm and has been aware of his Galactic heritage. This clear connection is reflected in his amazingly beautiful and healing creations.

In January, 2005, El'iam spent two weeks with Kira Raa and Sri Ram Kaa at TOSA Ranch in New Mexico to bring forth The Divine Galactic Blueprint.

He is also the artist of the *Avesa Awakening* portrait and many other TOSA illustrations.

***Avesa Awakening* by El'iam**

El'iam makes his home between magical Kauai, Hawaii and enchanted Tijeras, NM. You can read more about him and view more of his Divinely inspired creations at:

www.angelicsoulvisions.com

Endnotes

[1]All quotes are taken from live interviews with guests on Sri Ram Kaa and Kira Raa's radio show, with the exception of George Noory as noted.

[2]Twenty four years later, in 1989, I died. The "you" that had the experience in 1965 transformed, and yet all of her memories and experiences remain.

[3]Sri Ram Kaa and Kira Raa came together as part of a soul agreement in 2002. This activated the process of Archangelic In-soulment and is fully described in their first book, *Sacred Union: The Journey Home.*

[4]These are widely read, distributed, and accepted "end time" prophecies. The Mayan calendar, for example, literally ends after thousands of years in 2012. Many believe that the seven seals as revealed in the Biblical book of *Revelations* are playing out now. Additionally, the prophecies of Nostradamus have been followed for centuries and are believed to have accurately foretold the major events of this century and an Armageddon like scenario that takes place in 2012.

[5]Su'Laria is the original Atlantis and did not exist on this planet. The commonly referred to Atlantis, which did exist on this planet, was a seeding of energy from the first expression known as Su'Laria. For a complete cosmological description please read chapter 12 from the book, *2012: You Have a Choice!*

[6]Archangelic In-soulment is the process by which Kira Raa leaves her body therefore allowing the full presence of the Archangelic Realm to enter. During this process, her voice and body language completely change and her eyes are often used as transmitters for healing energy to the audience. Upon returning to her body, she has no recollection of the message that was delivered.

[7]As quoted from George Noory's December 2006 column in *UFO Magazine.*

[8]George Noory's highly rated radio show, *Coast to Coast AM.*

[9]*Worker In the Light*, written by George Noory and Bill Birnes: (Forge, 2006)

[10]A simple way to enhance the *Pause, Breathe, Allow* process is to go ever deeper with it. The following technique is part of our *Navigating the Inner Matrix Program*, and once incorporated into your daily experience, offers great clarity and peace. The process begins by remembering that you are **SAFE**.

S Stop engaging the drama by bringing your hand to your heart. Hand to heart interrupts the process and begins the soul connection.

A Acknowledge that you are "swimming in the ego's river." Let go of any righteous thinking (or strategies) and simply acknowledge that you are triggered.

F Feel the emotions. Let yourself connect to the fear, hurt, anger that is underpinning the experience. You do not have to swim in these feelings, just connect with them enough to know that they are present. This is your inner child's experience at the moment and consciously connecting with the feelings is an act of responsibility.

E Expand beyond the emotional experience. Widen your paradigm to the soul level. As you connect with your soul energy you will realize that you are whole and divine. Your soul is unconditionally loving. The soul is your authenticity. Connect with your soul energy and have mercy on yourself.

Have mercy for having had an uncomfortable human experience! The path of Self-Ascension is the path of widening the conscious expression of your soul energy into your experience. Expand!

Now would be a good time to pull out a few "Sticky Notes" and write on them:
I AM SAFE

Yes, you are safe. Remember… any time you feel uncomfortable you have the opportunity to choose to be SAFE. Be in gratitude for your uncomfortable feelings for they are stimulating your return to conscious mastery! As you practice this technique you will find that you can return to soul conscious ever-more quickly, and know that all is well.

[11] Prior to Su'Laria we took form in another place called Tu'Laya, which many commonly mistake as Leumeria. The Tu'Layan energy was also seeded on Earth and has been referred to as Mu or Leumeria here. For further understanding of this you may reference Chapter 12 of the book, *2012: You Have a Choice!*

[12] Cosmic beings from the expansion of light that are not direct Travelers. They are committed to a less dense expression of form and carry the energy of Divine light which in any form of atmospheric condition appears as blue. (Consider that the pure ice of a glacier reflects itself as a stunning blue.) In many interpretations they would be considered angels since they are brethren of us all and remain close to the Earth even now.

[13] The Archangelic Realm refers to those Beings of Light who have chosen the experience of density expansion as The Travelers. Thus, all of us who are incarnating in body are the Travelers.

[14] This method of interaction first became prevalent during the ancient Egyptian dynasties on Earth.

[15] Akhenaten & Nefertiti (18th Dynasty, 1300s BC). Akhenaten and his queen Nefertiti were behind a revolutionary period of Egyptian rule called the *Amarna Interlude*, signified by a flourishing of a new form of art and by religious upheaval. Together, they fostered the worship of the sun god Ra in the form of the sun disk Aten. They established a short-lived new capital city called Akhetaten in modern-day el-Amarna and effectively outlawed the worship of the old gods. This made them many enemies and, after their deaths, their images were erased from records.

[16] The Ascended Chakra system of twelve points that begins at the traditional heart center. More will be discussed about this in Section Three of the book.

[17] Much more was shared here that will be revealed in later books.

[18] This is a direct reference to Queen Nefertiti.

[19] AAE: Ascension Acceleration Energy Experiences. These are energetic shifts that are happening for many as they accept a higher vibrational frequency. To view the complete list, please visit our website, www.selfascension.com, and on the home page click on the box "Are you experiencing AAE's?"

[20] This is a Self-Ascension process taught through the *Navigating the Inner Matrix* program. Completion of this program fully anchors the heart as the root chakra of the Ascended state of being.

[21] Dark Night of the Soul: A challenge that occurs within our lives to offer the gift of breaking through old patterns. Despite the commonly held belief that it can only happen once in a lifetime, often they will repeat with ever refining form as we allow ourselves to move through levels of consciousness. It is also how you respond to the event that will offer freedom from the experience.

[22] The twenty fifth dimension is where the Tu'Layan experience occurred.

[23] This is a direct reference to the Living Ankh Practice which was taught in *2012: You Have a Choice!*

[24] This is referring to the Divine Electronic Belt, Chapter Twelve.

[25] The Mantra of Self-Ascension was gifted to the world by Archangel Zadkiel. While simple in the four lines, it empowers complete recognition of the divine within. It is a powerful tool to assist with shifting consciousness.

[26] Soul Nourishment is the concept of nourishing the soul in all-ways, food, spirit, living, etc. It is different from eating or living for the satisfaction of the physical

body or egoic pleasure. For a full overview of the Soul Nourishment program, please refer to the Appendix of *Sacred Union: The Journey Home.*

[27] Mahasamadhi (literally *great samadhi*) is the Hindi term for a realized yogi's conscious departure from the physical body at death, which is also known as Nirvana. Mahasamadhi is the final conscious exit from the physical body. Every infinitesimal piece of attachment is completely surrendered unto God and dissolved into the Divine Ocean of Love. The individual transcends and returns to God, merging into transcendental Bliss.

[28] Dharma in the sense of cosmological pattern, order or Universal Law is sometimes represented by a multi-spoked wheel. The Dharma Wheel has become the universal symbol of the Buddhist system. Besides incorporating the two major aspects -- order and brilliance -- it alludes to other, more particular, concepts. There are many representations of Dharma wheels, we have included on here for your reference.

[29] This is often an experience known as a Kriya: A physical, mental, or emotional movement initiated by the awakened kundalini. In either case; Kriyas purify the body and nervous system, thus allowing a seeker to experience higher states of consciousness. (Kundalini is cosmic energy that lies dormant in a coiled form in the chakra at the base of the spine. This extremely subtle force, also described as the Supreme Goddess, when awakened begins to purify the entire being.)

[30] Mudra is a Sanskrit word for the formation of the hands. You might think of mudras as doing yoga with your hands. Mudras can refer to a gesture, a mystic or spiritual positioning of the hands, even a symbol. The techniques of mudras represent specific states of consciousness. They have the ability to create those states, and the physical benefits they represent in our bodies. The inherent power of a mudra is that by engaging specific areas of our brain, they can have a profound impact on our physical, emotional and spiritual bodies.

[31] The Container Exercise is fully described in *2012: You Have a Choice!*, beginning on page 164.

[32] "The pain of the pain" is a concept of habit introduced by Archangel Zadkiel in *Sacred Union: The Journey Home.* It is our ability to release the pain of the pain that enhances our freedom.

Self-Ascension Model

Four Steps for the Journey Home

[33] This is the model of Self-Ascension which shows the four steps. It is the basis of the book: *Sacred Union: The Journey Home.*

[34] Avesa Quantum Healing: Avesa is a Sanskrit word that translates as "Hail to the divine unknown." This powerful healing modality had been off the planet for over 125 years and has now become widely known as a miracle creating process that brings one into the state of healing. You can learn more about how to activate this energy within your own being at www.selfascension.com, and click on the "Courses" tab.

[35] This reference is to the traditional chakra centers: energy centers within the human body that are located along the spine. The Root Chakra is found at the base of the spine.

[36] The Benevolent Ones, also known as the Suph'alla, are ecstatic Beings of pure crystalline energy and hold open a portal of light directly from the Elohim. The Benevolent Ones offer profound clarity and love with their dispensations, which often require re-reading in order to fully appreciate the energy and wisdom in their communications.

[37] The T-12 are another groupo of Light Beings who offer a bridge from the 33rd dimension to the Archangelic Realm. They are a blended energy of several light rays. They sometimes refer to themselves as the "Tribe of 12," referring to the

aspects of their energy which are blended to offer support the Travelers who are reunifying.

[38]The *Navigating the Inner Matrix Course* was introduced by the Archangelic Realm to anchor in the energy of Self-Ascension. These nine lessons offer great clarity and insight for soul-based living.

[39]Psychic feelers can feel what others are feel, and often are clairvoyant, clairaudient or both. Psychic feelers are also known as 'sensitives'. Similarly, oracles are often defined the same way, only in addition they are usually also able to bring forth information about the future.

[40] On several occasions, and two very intimate ones, TOSA ranch has been visited by low flying, circling black helicopters. This has been photo documented and more will be shared in the next book.

[41] Days prior to the closing of the purchase of TOSA ranch, unexplainable interference energy presented itself. This story is shared in *2012: You Have a Choice!*

[42]Transparent communication is a powerful technique of Self-Ascension. This form of sharing comes from a place of wholeness and safety where only the truth is offered between others. It is a critical step in the claiming of wholeness and is greatly explored in both the *Navigating the Inner Matrix* program and the book, *Sacred Union: The Journey Home.*

[43]The meeting of Sri Ram Kaa and Kira Raa and how the Archangelic Realm came forward to begin the process of Archangelic In-soulment is fully detailed in their first book, *Sacred Union: The Journey Home.*